A CULTURAL HISTORY OF THE EMOTIONS

VOLUME 2

A Cultural History of the Emotions
General Editors: Susan Broomhall, Jane W. Davidson, and Andrew Lynch

Volume 1
A Cultural History of the Emotions in Antiquity
Edited by Douglas Cairns

Volume 2
A Cultural History of the Emotions in the Medieval Age
Edited by Juanita Feros Ruys and Clare Monagle

Volume 3
A Cultural History of the Emotions in the Late Medieval, Reformation, and Renaissance Age
Edited by Andrew Lynch and Susan Broomhall

Volume 4
A Cultural History of the Emotions in the Baroque and Enlightenment Age
Edited by Claire Walker, Katie Barclay, and David Lemmings

Volume 5
A Cultural History of the Emotions in the Age of Romanticism, Revolution, and Empire
Edited by Susan J. Matt

Volume 6
A Cultural History of the Emotions in the Modern and Post-Modern Age
Edited by Jane W. Davidson and Joy Damousi

A CULTURAL HISTORY OF THE EMOTIONS

IN THE MEDIEVAL AGE

Edited by Juanita Feros Ruys and Clare Monagle

BLOOMSBURY ACADEMIC
LONDON • NEW YORK • OXFORD • NEW DELHI • SYDNEY

BLOOMSBURY ACADEMIC
Bloomsbury Publishing Plc
50 Bedford Square, London, WC1B 3DP, UK
1385 Broadway, New York, NY 10018, USA
29 Earlsfort Terrace, Dublin 2, Ireland

BLOOMSBURY and the Diana logo are trademarks of Bloomsbury Publishing Plc

First published in Great Britain 2019
This edition published in Great Britain, 2022

Copyright © Bloomsbury Publishing, 2019

Juanita Ruys and Clare Monagle have asserted their right under the Copyright, Designs and Patents Act, 1988, to be identified as Editor of this work.

Cover image: Engagement ceremony (Photo by: Leemage/UIG via Getty Images)

All rights reserved. No part of this publication may be reproduced or transmitted in any form or by any means, electronic or mechanical, including photocopying, recording, or any information storage or retrieval system, without prior permission in writing from the publishers.

A catalogue record for this book is available from the British Library.

A catalog record for this book is available from the Library of Congress.

ISBN: HB: 978-1-4725-3577-1
PB: 978-1-3503-4498-3
Set: 978-1-3503-4769-4

Series: The Cultural Histories Series

Typeset by RefineCatch Limited, Bungay, Suffolk
Printed and bound in Great Britain

To find out more about our authors and books visit www.bloomsbury.com and sign up for our newsletters.

CONTENTS

LIST OF ILLUSTRATIONS — vi
GENERAL EDITORS' PREFACE — ix

Introduction: Medieval Emotions Near and Far — 1
Clare Monagle

1 Medical and Scientific Understandings — 17
   Nicole Archambeau

2 Religion and Spirituality — 31
   Daniel Anlezark

3 Music and Dance — 49
   Constant J. Mews and Carol J. Williams

4 Drama — 65
   Sarah Brazil

5 The Visual Arts — 83
   Katherine M. Boivin

6 Literature — 101
   Juanita Feros Ruys

7 In Private: The Individual and the Domestic Community — 119
   Lisa Perfetti

8 In Public: Collectivities and Polities — 133
   Jehangir Yezdi Malegam

NOTES ON CONTRIBUTORS — 151
NOTES — 155
REFERENCES — 159
INDEX — 177

ILLUSTRATIONS

INTRODUCTION

0.1	Church of Saint-Ouen de Rouen (interior).	2
0.2	*The Descent from the Cross* (detail), by Rogier van der Weyden, *c.*1435.	3
0.3	The Douce Apocalypse.	5
0.4	*Augustine*, by Simone Martini, *c.*1320–1325.	10
0.5	Exorcism of the Demons at Arezzo, fresco (detail), Saint Francis cycle by Giotto (*c.*1267–1337).	13

CHAPTER 1

1.1	Saffron in the *Circa Instans*, *c.*1280–*c.*1310.	21
1.2	The Three Spirits.	25
1.3	Veins in the Body, *c.*1420–30.	26
1.4	Ventricles of the Brain, *c.*1347.	27

CHAPTER 2

2.1	*Temptation of St. Anthony*, by Master of Bonnat (active *c.*1475–1530).	34
2.2	*St. Jerome in His Study*, by Albrecht Dürer, 1514.	36
2.3	St. Wiborada in her anchorite cell, St. Gallen, 1451–60.	41

CHAPTER 3

3.1	The responsory *Fulgebat in venerando*, thirteenth century.	54
3.2	Statue of Guido of Arezzo, outside the Uffizi Gallery, Florence, Italy, sculpted by Lorenzo Nencini, *c.*1837.	56
3.3	Detail of Love's Dance (*La karole d'amours*) from the *Roman de la Rose*, depicting ten figures dancing to drum and bagpipes.	59

CHAPTER 4

4.1	Lid of a box, fragment, ivory. Thalia, Muse of Comedy with lyre, masks, and sword, fifth century.	67

4.2	The Three Marys at the Tomb, Benedictional of Aethelwold.	72
4.3	Battle of Patience and Anger (*Pacienciam ira percutit gladio*), Prudentius, *Psychomachia*.	75
4.4	Ambrogio Lorenzetti, *Miracle of the Poor Youth, Scenes of the Life of Saint Nicholas*, c.1332.	79
4.5	God confronts Adam and Eve, mosaic, Cathedral of the Assumption, Monreale, Sicily, twelfth–thirteenth century.	80

CHAPTER 5

5.1	Slaughter of the Innocents, Codex Egberti, tenth century.	87
5.2	Adam and Eve after the Fall, Vienna Genesis, sixth century.	91
5.3	Expulsion from Eden, stained glass, Cathedral of Soissons, c.1200–1225.	92
5.4	Last Judgment Tympanum of the Fürstenportal, Cathedral of Bamberg, c.1230.	92
5.5	Lintel frieze from the Last Judgment Portal, Cathedral of St-Lazare, Autun, c.1130.	93
5.6	Throne of Wisdom/Enthroned Virgin and Child, c.1150–1200.	96
5.7	Röttgen Pietà, c.1325.	97
5.8	Giotto di Bondone, Lamentation (The Mourning of Christ), 1304–1306.	98
5.9	Penitence, Devotion, and Contemplation, MS Yates Thompson 11, c.1290.	98

CHAPTER 6

6.1	Chastity pierces Lust with her sword (*Pudicicia transfigit libidinem gladio*), Prudentius, *Psychomachia*.	104
6.2	Boethius, Philosophy, and the Muses. Miniature from Boethius, *De consolatione philosophiae* (*Consolation of Philosophy*).	106
6.3	Hildegard of Bingen receives a vision from God and dictates it to her scribe and secretary. Illumination from Hildegard of Bingen, *Liber Scivias*, Rupertsberg Codex, c.1175.	112
6.4	Tristan and Isolde, c.1250–75.	116
6.5	"The Lover enjoys the Rose," Guillaume de Lorris / Jean de Meun, *Roman de la Rose*.	117

CHAPTER 7

7.1	Mother instructing her daughter, *Die Winsbeckin*, c.1300–1340.	122
7.2	Mother buried cradling a child, excavated in 1985 at Butler's Field, Lechlade, Gloucestershire.	130

CHAPTER 8

8.1 Peter looking remorseful. Carved alabaster column from the tabernacle of the high altar, St. Mark's Basilica, Venice. — 138

8.2 Suicide of Judas. Carved alabaster column from the tabernacle of the high altar, St Mark's Basilica, Venice. — 139

8.3 Penance on a tailless horse, *Romance of Lancelot du Lac*, c.1320–30. — 143

8.4 Gestures and emotions in council, Bayeux Tapestry, eleventh century. — 146

8.5 An extravagant female mourner. Polyptych with scenes from the life of Christ, the life of the Virgin, and saints, workshop of Ferrer Bassa, Spain, c.1345–50. — 149

GENERAL EDITORS' PREFACE

The General Editors, volume editors and individual authors of this series have many organizations to thank for helping to bring it into existence. They gratefully acknowledge assistance from the Arts and Humanities Research Council (UK); the European Research Council Project, The Social and Cultural Construction of Emotions, University of Oxford, and its Director, Professor Angelos Chaniotis; and the Leverhulme Trust. Above all, the series has depended on support from the Australian Research Council Centre of Excellence for the History of Emotions (CE110001011). The project was conceived as a key part of the Centre's collaborative research work and has benefited greatly from the generous help of its academic and administrative staff.

The General Editors also express their deep gratitude to the volume editors and authors for their time, expertise and gracious willingness to revise essays in the light of readers' comments. Many other people helped in reading, tracing images and advising in various ways. Our thanks go to Merridee Bailey; Jacquie Bennett; Sophie Boyd-Hurrell; Frederic Kiernan; Mark Neuendorf; Fiona Sim; and Stephanie Thomson; and to the patient staff at Bloomsbury: Dan Hutchins; Claire Lipscomb; Beatriz Lopez; and Rhodri Mogford. We especially acknowledge Ciara Rawnsley, who as Editorial Assistant for the entire series has tirelessly helped authors and done indispensable and meticulous work on all aspects of the volumes' preparation.

This series is dedicated to the memory of Philippa Maddern (1952–2014) who was an original General Editor, and an inspiring friend, mentor and colleague to many of the contributors.

Introduction

Medieval Emotions Near and Far

CLARE MONAGLE

EMOTIONS HISTORY AND THE MIDDLE AGES

At first glance, the world of the European Middle Ages seems very far removed from our own twenty-first-century experience. We are separated by time, yes, but also by technology, language, economy, religion, and myriad other aspects of being. Even after many years of studying the Middle Ages, I am often struck by what feels like the foreign formality of the period expressed within its cultural artifacts. Standing in a Gothic cathedral (see Figure 0.1), or reading medieval theology, or gazing at a manuscript, I feel that I am inside a world of codes and rules that I can respect, but which remain distant. We know that medieval people loved, fought, birthed, and died. They lamented, fumed, sulked, smiled, and sobbed. We feel like we know that because they were human like us, and we think we know because extant medieval sources give us glimpses of the way their feeling bodies expressed themselves in language and gesture. But given the distance between them and us, can we ever properly encounter the emotions of the Middle Ages?

This volume is devoted to that question, as it is to the possibility of a recovery of emotions in the Middle Ages via the cultural products of that past. To answer this question, to which our contributors offer very different responses, it is necessary to engage with a range of methodological and interpretative questions. What type of cultural products mediated emotions, or ideas about emotions, in the Middle Ages? What were the generic conventions that governed the production of these texts and objects? What unspoken ideological assumptions framed artistic and intellectual production in the Middle Ages? What impact did theological notions of self and God have upon theories and experience of emotions? Does our set of emotion words have any correlation with the various languages of medieval Europe?

Of course these questions would obtain for any scholar attempting to get to the heart of emotional practices and representations in any period. One of the tasks of the historian is to pay attention to practices of mediation, to understand the practices of representation in the period under study. That is, every cultural product is made, it is never in identity with a feeling or a person, it is always a representation of something outside itself. Studying emotions in culture, then, forces us to take into account the situated rules of representation, whatever the period. Studying the Middle Ages, however, adds another level of difficulty to that of mapping mediation. This period is characterized by the cultural dominance of elites. There are almost no sources from the European Middle Ages authored by what we might call "ordinary people" until the later stages of our period. Talking generally about medieval people, or medieval experiences, is empirically fraught. Our cultural artifacts emerge from such a slim section of the

FIGURE 0.1: Church of Saint-Ouen de Rouen (Interior). Image courtesy of Wikimedia Commons.

population, that of elite clerical populations, that we need to be wary of extrapolating too much from them.

So given these many caveats, why proceed to a study of emotions in the European Middle Ages? What does "emotions" as a category of analysis do for us? What does it help us to know? How does it help us to think? The answer, perhaps, is that it is a category that forces us to think about the possibilities and limits of what we can know about the past. Thinking emotions asks us to do everything we can to engage with the affective and embodied lives of historical subjects. It forces us to take their humanity seriously and to consider how they experienced the world through feelings, and what they understood those feelings to mean within the cultural frameworks in which they lived. In short, the history of emotions as a practice depends upon historical empathy. The field insists that we try to engage meaningfully with the complicated subjectivities of past people. The history of emotions as a practice, however, must also take seriously historical distance. For all the reasons articulated above, we cannot assume unmediated access to historical subjects. When we read an account, for example, of the tears of holy woman in the Middle Ages, we cannot assume that we know how those tears felt, or indeed what those tears meant, because we ourselves have cried. Instead, an account of weeping compels us to try to reconstruct what work weeping did in the Middle Ages (see Figure 0.2). The history of emotions insists that emotional displays or registers deserve a contextualization as thorough and multi-faceted as any other historical phenomenon. We may never be able to apprehend the actual feelings of the past, but we can reconstruct the world in which they worked and we can explore the ways individual people expressed their subjectivity in relation to their feelings.

FIGURE 0.2: *The Descent from the Cross* (detail), by Rogier van der Weyden, c.1435. Image courtesy of Wikimedia Commons.

Medievalists have long negotiated this tension between respecting historical distance while making a case for our capacity to engage deeply with the past. In fact, this tension has been productive for Medieval Studies. In order to take medieval people seriously, to render their choices and the world they created in a respectful way, it has been necessary to undertake the work of detailed contextualization. Medievalists learn many technical skills in order to be able to dwell in the past. They study paleography to apprehend manuscripts (see Figure 0.3); they learn Latin and a range of medieval vernacular languages to read and translate these texts. They study diplomatics (the study of documents), codicology (the study of manuscripts), numismatics (the study of coins), and iconography (the study of symbols), to name but a few auxiliary disciplines, to reconstruct the world within which medieval people lived. Medievalists need these skills because so many of the texts and objects that bring the medieval to us arrive in formats and genres with which we are unfamiliar. A medieval papal letter, for example, does not resemble forms of correspondence with which a twenty-first-century person would have experience. The language is flowery and obsequious and often flooded with biblical allusions that are woven into the text without citation. These documents were crucial agents of authority and power, were disseminated throughout Western Europe, and were a key technology of communication in that period. We know that they were very important. But to get to their meaning, the contemporary medievalist has to learn to unpack these documents technically, in order to ascertain how they were able to do the work they did. And I could say the same for any medieval text or object: the interpreter needs a complicated set of tools to make sense of it.

Medievalists, then, are well aware of historical distance, and of the rigorous work that is required to broach it. They aim to respect their historical subjects by making sense of the logic in which their culture operated. We work in a field for which popular representations of the Middle Ages seek to "other" medieval people. They are depicted as exotic others, superstitious and religious, trapped in a world dominated by popes and kings. In short, the Middle Ages is all too often seen as an irrational "other" against which a rational modernity is constructed. Medievalists have long been used to debunking this idea of their period, suggesting that medieval culture contains its own coherent logic within which its systems and beliefs make sense. We might disapprove of medieval society and its attitudes in relation to modern ethical measures. We might not agree with the foundational ideas that underscore Western medieval culture, particularly those regarding the utter primacy of Christian revelation. But, as medievalists, we think it is too simple to posit a story of backwardness or ignorance. Instead, we work to reconstitute the culture within its own terms.

Perhaps then, given the methodological necessities of Medieval Studies, it is not surprising that medievalists have been leaders in the field of the study of the history of emotions. They have the tool kit to disaggregate emotions from genre, style, and form. And they are also used to defending the putatively nonrational as the subject of historical analysis. Medievalists have long argued, often against the prejudices of their modernist colleagues, for the importance and necessity of their field. And, appositely, innovations in the studies of medieval emotions were initially prompted by a foundational account of emotions history that derided and profoundly misunderstood medieval culture. In Norbert Elias's *The Civilizing Process*, first published in 1939, Elias had argued that medieval expressions of emotion were irrational, explosive and impulsive (Elias 2000). He suggested that one of the processes that characterized modernity was the rationalization of emotional processes. During the Middle Ages, he theorized, emotions followed a hydraulic model: they burst out when the pressure grew too great. Modernity, however, developed forms of etiquette that conditioned emotional responses into socially

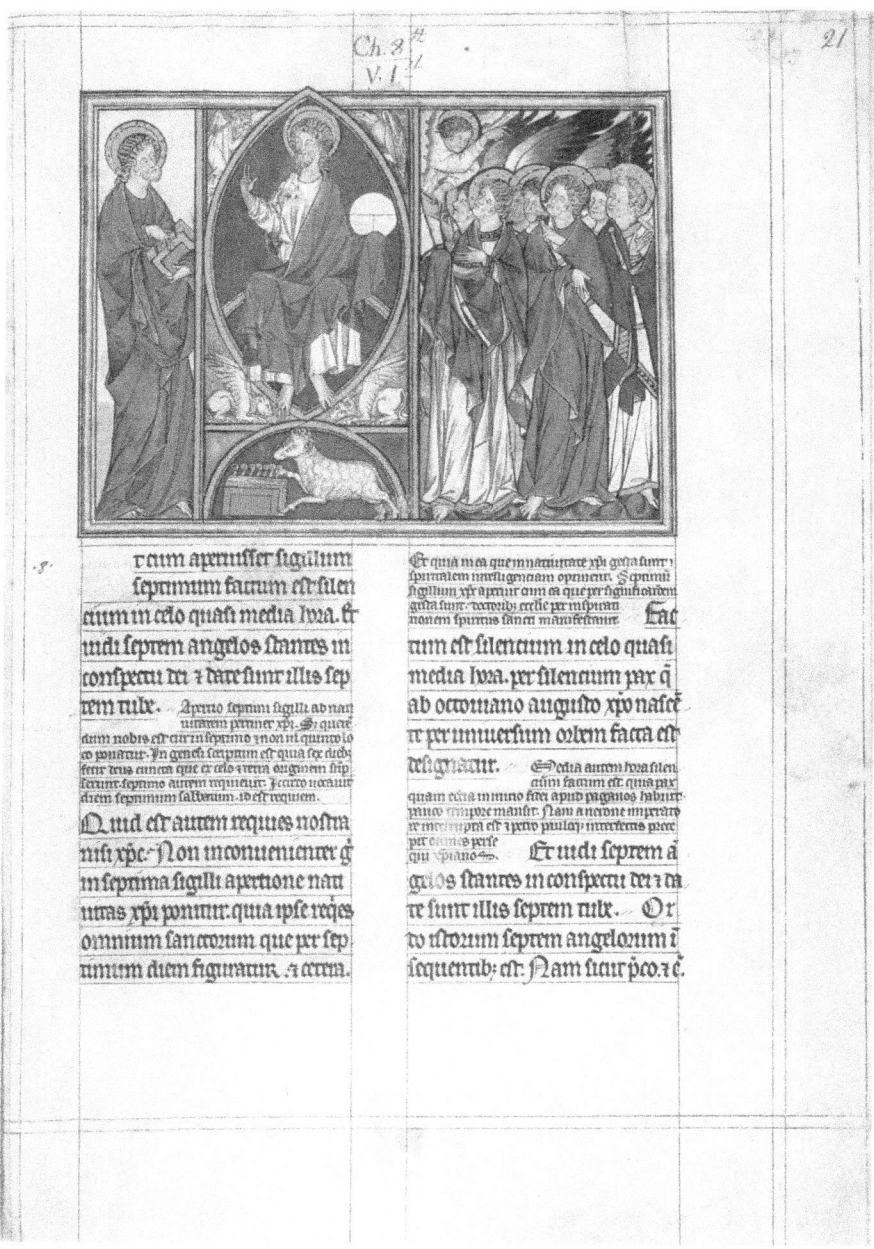

FIGURE 0.3: The Douce Apocalypse; Oxford, Bodleian Library, MS Douce 180, fol. 21ʳ. Image courtesy of Wikimedia Commons.

appropriate modes. Elias's work was immensely influential, and this paradigm of juvenile and hydraulic medieval emotionality would become enormously influential. Writing in the *American Historical Review* in 2002, the medieval historian Barbara Rosenwein took aim at this vision of emotions in the Middle Ages. As a historian who had long worked on the relationship between sociality and power in the early Middle Ages, she was convinced of the strategic and complicated expressions of emotions that she read in and into her documents. Her intervention would be crucial in the field, and lead to the widespread application of her concept of "emotional communities" (Rosenwein 2002)

In a 2010 interview with Jan Plamper, Barbara Rosenwein wrote in relation to her critique of Elias that

> I should ordinarily not want to refute a thesis that was produced in the 1930s. Rather I would prefer to appreciate it for its contribution at the time of its writing. Unfortunately, Elias's theory underlies most studies of the history of emotions done even today. For modernists, it presents a convenient tabula rasa—a sort of historical "state of nature"—from which modernity, with all its complexity, can arise.
>
> —Plamper 2010: 252

Rosenwein's Middle Ages was no *tabula rasa*, it was not a site of primordial essence out of which the modern subject could emerge. The Middle Ages was not an unformed infant, requiring development into maturity. Instead, Rosenwein insisted that close studies of medieval communities revealed the complicated linguistic and gestural registers in which people expressed emotions. A king might express righteous anger in order to inspire his knights, or he might weep to show his human frailty in imitation of Christ. A mother might groan in grief at the loss of a child, in line with normative depictions of Mary's lamentation at the loss of her son. Yet other sources from the period depict deathbed scenes as places of stoic contemplation, characterized less by unrestrained grief than by measured serenity. In short, medieval emotionality seems to have been as acculturated as in any other period. Emotions were expressed in a variety of ways and often in relationship to clear cultural norms. Rosenwein refuted the idea that medieval people were fundamentally different emotional creatures than those from later periods, showing instead that their emotions were as complicated and diverse as our own, and that their emotions did not just erupt in unbidden ways, but were constituted in what she called "emotional communities."

Rosenwein defined "emotional communities" as

> precisely the same as social communities—families, neighborhoods, parliaments, guilds, monasteries, parish church memberships—but the researcher looking at them seeks above all to uncover systems of feeling: what these communities (and the individuals within them) define and assess as valuable and harmful to them; the evaluations that they make about others' emotions; the nature of the affective bonds between people that they recognize; and the modes of emotional expression that they expect, encourage, tolerate, and deplore.
>
> —Rosenwein 2002: 842

In suggesting that scholars work with the conceptual frame of "emotional communities," Rosenwein was implicitly arguing that emotions never exist in a vacuum and can never be reified into a pure thing such as "anger" or "melancholy." Rather, her paradigm suggests that emotions can only be understood and analyzed in relation to the social location in which they are produced. Rosenwein thus argues for a situated emotions history that reads the operations of emotions within the terms of the community of their making and expression. In part, Rosenwein was in conversation with the historian William M. Reddy who had suggested that we should think about emotional practices under the rubric of "emotional regimes" (Reddy 2001). Reddy's regimes situated emotional practices and expressions within power relationships and understood emotions to be disciplined within structures of authority. For Rosenwein, the concept of a "regime" was not adequate to nonmodern societies, as it assumed a centralized and normative power source against which orthodoxy could be judged. The term "emotional communities," on the other hand, suggests that individuals live within a number of communities each of which pulls the person in a different direction, is constituted by different norms, and the importance of which will change over time. In short, Rosenwein deploys "community" against "regime" to resist the idea of hegemonic authority.

Whether or not one agrees with the aptness of Rosenwein's designation, what is important here is the insistence on a model that can obtain for a variety of periods, locations, and modes of social organization. The risk of thinking through "emotional regimes" is that it reifies top-down power of the sort that we see in modern states as a norm. Emotional communities, Rosenwein argues, offers a more flexible and capacious frame, one that enables us to map subjectivities as the result of various and asymmetrical forms of identification and social formations. Even more crucially, working with the concept of communities also enables the refusal of the Elias model that posited a naïve and childish medieval emotionality, as opposed to the rhetorical, mannered, and circumspect emotional ranges that characterize the modern era. Rather, where there are discernible differences between medieval and modern emotions, this is the result of the particularities of social logics that obtain at that given time, and in that given place, and for those sets of people.

I have focused at length on Rosenwein's theory because it deals precisely with the tension that I have argued characterizes the study of emotions in the Middle Ages—the space between historical distance and imaginative empathy. The idea of community proffers a basic insistence on relationality and organization as the site for the making and expression of emotions. The idea of community suggests that identities are produced within a number of relational frames that intersect in complex and particular ways. The idea of community insists that the object of the history of emotions is not to isolate and essentialize particular emotions, but to make sense of the work they do within the world of their making. At the same time, the idea of community means that emotional expressions are never merely rhetorical or discursive, but are the result of the feeling that we know occurs between people and which we assume to be a condition of the human. This is the empathic part of the equation, the conviction that we must respect the humanity of our historical subjects and resist the urge to take away their agency or their complicated subjectivities, even if they seem to come from a place far distant.

The answer to the question that I posed earlier—why we study emotions in the Middle Ages in spite of the tyranny of chronological distance that prevails—is that it takes us right to the heart of the ethical project of historical inquiry. Emotion Studies is based on taking the leap of faith that historical subjects felt feelings that resemble our own and that those feelings did cultural and political work. It forces us also, however, to confront the limitations of our apprehension of the past, particularly of the subjectivity of our historical subjects. While we cannot elide these limitations, studying emotions in history does take us to their edge and encourages creative and empathic engagement with the past.

THIS VOLUME AND ITS TIMEFRAME

The period covered by our volume, 350–1300 CE, is a long one. In Western Europe, this timeframe covers periods we normatively call Late Antiquity, the early Middle Ages, and the high Middle Ages. Taken together, our period can be described loosely as "medieval," although this designation runs the risk of conflating all manner of distinct historical phenomena. In the next section of this Introduction, I will aim to provide a historical survey, in the full knowledge that compression risks flattening out. In the first instance, however, I want to ask what it means to describe our period as "medieval," as I have above. What are the defining characteristics of this millennium in European history? What permits us to yoke these years into an epoch? The answer is the religious dominance of the Catholic Church. Between the fourth and fourteenth centuries, the Church gradually took responsibility for the spiritual life of the vast bulk of inhabitants of the continent. As such, the Church wielded extraordinary ideological power. To perform this role effectively, across this period the Church developed religious institutions to enable the administration of sacraments, produced doctrine, and educated priests. While there are, of course, myriad historical shifts that take the place in the timespan of this volume, it is also fair to say that it is defined by the central role played by the self-styled "One Holy Catholic Apostolic Church" in Western Europe.

Loosely, Late Antiquity refers to 250–750 CE, the period in which Roman imperial forms of governance were replaced with more local forms of authority, both religious and secular. It should be noted, however, that this process was not mirrored in the East. Contrary to the cliché of the "Fall of Rome," the Eastern Roman Empire endured until the fifteenth century. Western Europe, however, experienced waves of migration and invasion that disabled residual forms central governance, resulting in the emergence of new forms of social organization and polities. Concomitantly, the Catholic Church consolidated itself into a coherent ecclesiastical structure and refined its doctrines via conciliar processes. When scholars use the term Late Antiquity, they deploy it to describe a world in transition, in a state of disruption. As Peter Brown wrote in his groundbreaking *The World of Late Antiquity*, "looking at the late Antique world we are caught between the regretful contemplation of ancient ruins and the excited acclamation of new growth" (Brown 1971: 7). The designation of Late Antiquity implicitly refers to the historical process through which this dissonance was managed, the mapping of Christian and barbarian culture upon the residual Roman world.

The early Middle Ages, as a term, corresponds to the new world that emerged as a result of this historical process around 500–1000 of the Common Era. I am loath to speak of dates in this way, as their imposition is somewhat arbitrary, and as there is overlap. These are the names that historians have overlaid upon this time in the past to enable us to make sense of what transpired then. They would have made little sense to people at the time. In fact, writers in the twelfth century referred to themselves as *moderni*, as "moderns." They certainly did not experience their period as a "middle age." With that caveat in place, the period we call the early Middle Ages is one in which ruralization, decentralization, and population decline emerge as patterns across Western Europe. Rome's withdrawal from its colonial outposts enabled waves of population movement across the continent, as peoples sought safety and land. At the same time, this instability disabled trading practices and reduced birth rates.

Local forms of authority, namely local kings and monastic foundations, emerged as sources of security and stability. During the early Middle Ages, the inhabitants of Western

Europe looked to local leaders for protection, rather than to a distant emperor or pope. Individuals pledged themselves to these leaders via oath and these were the bonds that held societies of people together in this period. Charlemagne's rule over most of Western Europe at the turn of the ninth century offers an exception to this narrative, but his empire could not be sustained after his death. Human beings were not ordered into citizenries the way they are within contemporary Western liberal democracies. Rather, they pledged themselves to whomever could best offer them food, shelter, and safety. The period of the early Middle Ages, which has been pejoratively known as the "Dark Ages," was an incubator of new forms of social organization based on kinship and oath. Current historians resist calling this period "dark" because where some might see only decline and ignorance, they see novel survival strategies at play. The most important literary remainder from that period, the epic poem *Beowulf*, testifies to the period's creative possibilities.

The final period of our volume, the so-called high Middle Ages, takes place between around 1000–1350 CE. We use this name to describe the period of demographic growth and institution-building that took place after the early Middle Ages. By around 1000, it seems that the waves of invasions as well as the migration of peoples that had taken place earlier had ceased, resulting in more stable populations. This relative security in turn enabled the reemergence of trade and an increase in the birthrate. At the same time, kings, queens, and popes begin to consolidate their structures of governance in order to manage and tax these larger populations. All these changes facilitated the return of urban life, as locations were needed for the operations of trade and nascent bureaucracies. These changes also fueled the need for literate communications in order to record information and negotiate long distances. The increasing complexity of the society of the high Middle Ages drove demand for the written word as a technology of governance as well as a vehicle of education and entertainment. Official communications took place in Latin throughout the period covered by this volume, though by the end of our timespan, the vernacular languages were gaining traction, particularly within literary genres. And the rise of the vernacular enabled greater participation by women in literary production. Women had not often had access to training in Latin, a few prominent exceptions notwithstanding. By the close of our period, however, we can glimpse the emergence of powerful holy women who wielded spiritual and political authority.

And so, given the enormous shifts that occur between 350 and 1300, the contributors to this volume have been set a tough task. The chronological sketch above is necessarily brisk and admittedly limited, but I present it in order to convey the profound historical shifts that they must cover in their remit. They have been asked to map the cultural history of emotions over this millennium. They must begin with a set of historical actors who understood themselves within the context of Rome's glory, even if they were devoted to the radical critique of earthly things made within Christianity. It was not self-evident to them how the Christian could make sense of the things of the world and the desires those things produced. Augustine of Hippo is the obvious exemplum of this subjectivity, an intellectual framed with the discourses of Rome, and yet called to the message of Christ (see Figure 0.4). As we shall see, Augustine's experience of this cognitive dissonance between his two worlds, and his manner of making sense of it in body and soul, would be tremendously influential upon theories of emotions in the Middle Ages. By 1300, however, we find ourselves in a world that calls itself "Christendom," in which holy wars are being fought under the sign of the Cross and in which the pope lives like a prince. To tell the story of the emotional transitions that occur throughout this period is a large ask, and it is impossible to be exhaustive in a volume of this size. Our contributors have,

FIGURE 0.4: *Augustine*, by Simone Martini, *c.*1320–1325. Image courtesy of Wikimedia Commons.

however, surveyed the field as well as providing close readings that enable a detailed relief of the history of emotions in the Middle Ages.

LATE ANTIQUITY: CONVERSION AND RENUNCIATION

When we think of emotions in Late Antiquity, it is tempting to contrast clichés of pleasure-seeking Romans with the ascetic renunciations of early Christians. Romans were in the world and concerned with its glories such as status, family, beauty, and sensation. The early Christians, however, sought radical otherworldliness, eschewing the pleasures of the flesh. One would think, with that account, that Romans were emotionally expressive and that the Christians were muted in contrast. The work of our authors reveals, however, a much more complex set of emotional codes in operation than this simple binary would suggest. Classical accounts of emotional management privileged Stoic formulations that encouraged the individual to practice detachment from his or her feelings. The early Christians, on the other hand, declared their emotional ambitions to live a life infused with the sweetest joy of Christ's love. They were not emotionless, but rather desired very particular emotional experiences that were of a different order to those desired within classical culture.

In the chapters that follow we shall see many examples of writers and artists reckoning with this emotional shift. Constant J. Mews and Carol J. Williams, in their chapter on music, describe the ambivalence with which theologians and ecclesiastical luminaries dealt with the emotional impact of music. On the one hand, it had the potential to offer a spiritual feast for the senses, leading the listener closer to God. On the other, such excess of pleasure made the feeling subject vulnerable to desire and temptation. We can see an analogous concern about the emotional risk of drama in Sarah Brazil's chapter on drama. She explores Augustine of Hippo's famous condemnation of stage plays, in which he cautions against viewing drama as it leads to excessive compassion for the characters in the play. Since these characters are fictional, Augustine worries that this compassionate identification will take the viewer into him- or herself, rather than using this emotional state to become closer to God. In the case of both music and drama, Christian writers of Late Antiquity feared emotional responses that could not be funneled into a desire for God. According to this world view, the human person had great capacity for spiritual exaltation, but was also very vulnerable to the addling distractions of emotions.

As Jehangir Yezdi Malegam writes in his chapter, "In Augustine's writings, cognitive and cosmological change are co-extensive." Christian revelation brought not only a new view of time, but also demanded that believers feel that temporality in their bodies. That is, they should attempt to discipline and refine their perceptions of things in the world in order to apprehend the truth of Christ's sacrifice. Late Antiquity was a culture in the throes of conversion, and a conversion was considered to be true when it was felt in the heart, a pure desire for God. At the same time, humans were surrounded by the temptations of carnality, their burden since the Fall, and had to be on guard against deceptive feelings that would take them away from God. For Augustine, then, feelings were everything, and yet also a site of potential undoing. Membership in Christian community proffered the ultimate liberation, that of the love that leads to eternal life. But it also required constant vigilance, since erroneous feelings could take a person away from that ultimate love object, the divine.

Christian writers in Late Antiquity, in spite of their self-professed sense of being newly born, did not come to their understanding of emotions entirely through Christian revelation. Instead they inherited the Stoic tradition, which gave them conceptual tools for thinking about emotions. As Juanita Feros Ruys discusses in her chapter on literature, writers such as Prudentius and Boethius produced allegories that dramatized the suffering produced by emotions, and suggested steadfastness and equanimity as the best way to endure life in the world. These authors combined a stoic insistence of the necessity that emotions be overcome with a Christian sense of the urgent spiritual threat posed by overwhelming feeling. Elite writings on emotions that survive from Late Antiquity, then, tend toward this hybrid position. Emotions are a serious risk to the individual because they threaten the person's focus on, and desire for, union with God. Emotions can be derailing, within this formulation. They can best be managed through awareness and detachment, the Stoic way, which is not emotion-denying, but rather emotion-objectifying. The Stoic position attempts to render emotions as discernible objects that can be separated from the subject.

The emotion language of Late Antiquity, at least within elite discourse, belonged to a world dominated by the imperative of conversion, of making a turn. Christian conversion had the ritual of baptism as its public manifestation, but the theologians were clear that ritual itself could not effect the change. Christian conversion required a pure heart and the infusion of grace to be effective. In marked and self-conscious distinction to Jews and pagans, the Christians insisted on the necessity of internal psychic reform for participation in the community of believers. Emotions were the battlefield of this project. The believer, or would-be believer, had to wrestle with desire, second-guess feeling, and repudiate alienation in order to join the community of the holy. Only then could they experience bliss. The path to bliss was the refusal of pleasure. The emotional terrain of Late Antiquity, then, as explored by the writers in this book, was this conundrum that the emotions were not to be trusted, and yet they were also the mode to the purer self who could be redeemed.

THE EARLY MIDDLE AGES

Conversion, as we have seen, required a dramatic revolution of the heart. It was an emotional process that, conversely, created a suspicion of emotions. As we move from Late Antiquity into the early Middle Ages, we also move into new emotional landscapes and communities. The writers, artists, and thinkers of the early Middle Ages were not so much caught up in the drama of radical transformation as they were in world-building. During this period, people clustered in communities defined through kinship networks, as well as through monastic affiliation. In the absence of either systematic top-down governance or mass culture as we understand it, these communities had to negotiate the rules of engagement. People had to work out how to live together and depend upon each other in straitened and volatile times. As the essays that follow reveal, the development of emotional norms was a crucial part of how communities produced their social order. Drawing upon biblical exempla, the oral tradition of storytelling and emerging theological apparatus, early medieval communities produced cultural products that encoded emotions in a way that suited these new worlds.

Cultural artifacts from this period privilege stories of heroic, saintly or demonic figures, in spite of Augustine's earlier warning against the psychic perils of narrative. Monasteries produced hagiographical accounts of the lives of their founders, invariably imbuing them with thaumaturgical qualities. For example, this is the period that gives rise to the cults of SS Patrick and Martin, two saints from Late Antiquity who functioned as intermediaries between the old and new orders. These Christian heroes, and many others who followed in their wake, were miracle-workers in the world, engaging with the local strife and struggle. And their enemy was the Devil, who also appears regularly in early medieval storytelling (see Figure 0.5). The Devil lurks and is an active adversary against those who seek to live good Christian lives. The Devil is of such importance that skills in exorcism were understood to be a crucial part of the skill set for an early medieval pope or bishop. This was a world where the issues of good and evil were urgent and not a matter for philosophy. The saint could not retreat to a world of contemplation, he also needed to be a warrior against the Devil. These same themes were mirrored in non-

FIGURE 0.5: *Exorcism of the Demons at Arezzo*, fresco (detail), Saint Francis cycle by Giotto (*c*.1267–1337), Upper Basilica of St Francis. Photo by De Agostini/Archivio J. Lange via Getty Images.

religious literature that survives. Although poems such as *Beowulf* were not explicitly religious in content, they dramatized the same stark world of real and terrifying threat that was only ameliorated by the safety of the hearth, that is, the embrace of community.

Daniel Anlezark's analysis of the Anglo-Saxon poem *The Dream of the Rood* explores this fusion of Christian ideas overlaid with values of the warrior culture from which it emerged. In this poem, Christ's sacrifice was revered as an act of stoic heroism by a suffering penitent who was meditating upon it. This poem emphasized Christ's human suffering during the Passion and incorporated it into his nobility as God. Suffering then, in this schema, could be folded into concepts of divinity. Katherine M. Boivin, in her chapter on the visual arts, has noted also that early medieval visual representations tend to the depiction of calm assurance as the most aspirational emotional state. She argues that these depictions do not reveal an absence of emotions, but rather a higher spiritual state in which petty emotions have been transcended. She contrasts this with images of Adam and Eve after the Fall who are highly expressive in both body language and facial expressions. They are living in the fallen world and are mired in earthly emotions of despair and shame. Early medieval literature and visual arts depend upon a binary between an emotionally controlled and regulated world of the virtuous, defined against an excessively emotional world of the fallen. In the volatile world of early medieval Europe, emotional control was understood as a way to endure the slings and arrows of a tumultuous world.

It is within this context that we can best apprehend accounts of grief and loss in this period, which may trouble our normative expectations. Lisa Perfetti describes accounts of early medieval parents steeling themselves to celebrate the deaths of their children in the understanding that they were moving on to a better place with God. It is not that these parents did not feel pain, but rather that, heroically, they wanted to overcome these earthly feelings in order to celebrate greater truth, as they understood it. Parents owed it to their children to overcome their own covetous feelings of love in order to inculcate the virtue within them that would take them to eternity. Regulating emotions, then, was a crucial part of household and self-management in the early Middle Ages. In complete contradiction to our mainstream psychological idea that emotions needed to be processed, our extant early medieval sources suggest that people at that time felt that they needed to protect themselves against emotions and emotionality. Hence, as Nicole Archambeau reveals in her chapter on medical and scientific approaches to emotion, a number of texts suggested medical remedies for emotional states. These texts suggest that emotions were not thought to be necessary or helpful maps to the self, but rather unhealthy conditions to be fixed.

The evidence suggests that early medieval culture aspired to the transcendence of emotions. They embraced texts that starred heroic impassive figures, dignified and purposeful, who were able to win battles and overcome evil. Even the most sensitive of loves, that between parents and children, they considered to be earthly and corrupt in comparison to the love that one should feel for God. And they sought to medicate emotions, not as symptoms of deeper problems, but as irritants that must be obliterated. Our contributors suggest, however, that this resistance to emotion should not be read as emotionally lacking or unsophisticated. Rather, they read this resistance as a measure of the very fraught and complicated situations within which medieval communities found themselves. Is it surprising that in a very unstable world, one riven with violence and change, groups should seek to regulate feeling and its expression?

THE HIGH MIDDLE AGES

This period witnesses the proliferation of new forms of social organization and cultural representation. Many readers will be familiar with the commonplace depiction of medieval society as a pyramid, divided into three sections. The top section, and therefore the least populous, represents those who pray, the middle section those who fight and the section below those who work. This schema differentiates medieval society into the clergy, the nobility, and the peasantry. If this pyramid, however, could be said to represent the society of early medieval Europe, at least to some degree, it cannot be said to correspond to the growing complexity and diversity of roles within this later stage of the Middle Ages. The revitalization of trade and towns, with a concomitant diversity of tasks related to their operation, produced new sites of communal engagement, forms of worship, and artistic patronage. Consequently, we see a flourishing of art forms that respond to and in turn are constitutive of this transforming society. The emotions are no longer broadly construed as something to be transcended and overcome, but are rather encountered and explored as part of an increased interest in the make-up of the Christian subject.

At a scholarly level, new interest in the emotions is fueled within the institutions of higher learning that emerge in the towns, as well as by the new monastic orders that are founded within the period. These cathedral schools (later to be the universities) and orders such as the Cistercians and the Carthusians developed new theological frameworks for understanding the relationship between the emotions and spiritual practice. A number of the essays in this book refer to the Cistercian Aelred of Rievaulx's work on friendship in which he discusses the necessity of loving human relationships as part of an orientation toward God. In this book, written between 1164 and 1167, Aelred described how shared discipleship of Christ between fellow believers could enhance devotion, fortify resolve, and model higher spiritual love. The famous twelfth-century correspondence between Abelard and Heloise, discussed in this volume by Juanita Feros Ruys, also dealt at length with different types of human love and their relationship to the divine. These texts do not propose pure Stoic equanimity as a response to the loves of the world, but rather attempt to come to grips with human love in its complexity as a way into the ultimate love that one should feel for Christ.

The visual and dramatic arts reveal this same dynamic. Katherine M. Boivin explores this development by contrasting images of Mary from the early Middle Ages with those appearing later. In the early Middle Ages, Mary was most often shown enthroned next to her son, impassive and regal. By the thirteenth century, however, many artists depicted her in the form of the Pietà, as a mourning mother cradling the body of her son. These images were designed to elicit empathy and identification on the part of the viewer in order to enable meditation and compassion. The performative arts, as well, deploy emotionality in many registers to produce identification with both the fallen and the risen Christ. Christ's Passion was elaborated on the stage through sound and image, an eternal human drama into which the believer could enter and immerse oneself. Those who theorized performance in this period were emphatic that these were not the idolatrous and distracting performances of Late Antiquity against which Augustine had railed. Instead, performance in the high Middle Ages was conceived in didactic and pastoral terms as offering a space of mediation between the world and God.

These representational shifts can best be understood under the term "affective piety" which is used within Medieval Studies to describe the rise in embodied and emotional devotional practices during the high Middle Ages. There seems to have been an efflorescence of new spiritual practices, particularly emerging out of growing urban centers. Women and men, such as Francis and Clare of Assisi for example, repudiated normative forms of social organization in order to live in non-cloistered religious communities. We also see a number of lay women, after having lived lives of marriage and children, developing public mystical practices and reputations as holy women. Within the frame of affective piety, emotions were not to be transcended, but were in fact crucial elements of the journey to God. To be creaturely, and therefore emotional, was not something that needed to be disciplined and overcome. Rather, this creatureliness was in itself holy, as Christ himself had suffered in the fullness of humanity. This is not to say that this was a new insight. As Daniel Anlezark's discussion of *The Dream of the Rood* attests, meditation on Christ's embodied suffering was not a new thing. The core difference between the periods was, however, that by the high Middle Ages, performative devotion had become much more mainstream. As the essays in this volume attest, the development of affective piety after the year 1000 demonstrates a profound movement away from the emotional norms of the early medieval period which are replaced with a newfound belief in the utter necessity of emotions for human development.

This reevaluation of the utility of emotions was mirrored by a similarly profound shift in scholarly understandings of the work performed by emotions. Until the thirteenth century, mainstream theological speculation upon the "passions of the soul," as the emotions were called, had stayed close to the Augustinian framework articulated above. Throughout the late twelfth and early thirteenth centuries, however, scholars in the Latin West gained access to a much greater number of texts by Aristotle that had sought to describe and taxonomize the things of the world with precision. Thomas Aquinas was the foremost interpreter and exponent of these new intellectual frameworks and he deployed them to recast emotions within a radical new psychosomatic frame. Through Aristotle, but also combined with his Christian framework, Aquinas tried to understand the *telos* of created things, that is, the ultimate end of their existence. If everything in the world had a *telos*, a reason to be and an implied end, this meant that nothing in the world was pointless or without value. The emotions then, as a part of human functioning, could not be negated. Rather, it was the task of people to understand the role of emotions within human functioning. They were a crucial means to an end. And that end, within a Christian framework, was love of God. The emotions themselves, in this understanding, were a crucial part of the relationship between the body and the soul—they navigated between the two. Emotions were now considered an utterly crucial part of human identity, and it was the task of scholars to investigate how they functioned. This meant that they needed to be part of the study of the natural sciences as well. Emotions could not be abstracted from the body and so needed to be understood from a biomedical, as well as a theological, point of view.

CONCLUSION

This volume draws on a variety of historical sources to explore, explain, and illustrate the historical processes that generate depictions of emotions in the Middle Ages. They look at art, music, textbooks, poetry, letters, speeches, sermons, and a great many other things. Taken together, our various chapters deploy these sources to tell a story of a profound shift in the understanding of emotions between 350 and 1300 CE. What we see in 350 is a world grappling with political and social fragmentation, which is at the same time gripped by the fervor of new revelation. In this historical moment, human emotions were often considered as distractions from the main psychic game, that of the attainment of spiritual bliss. By 1300, however, the emotions were theorized and performed very differently. The chapters in this volume reveal the myriad ways that emotionality was considered a crucial part of the spiritual journey of the pilgrim. As Christ had suffered and feared and desired, so too did humans. Emotions were understood to be complicated psychosomatic experiences, constitutive of the human condition. To love Christ properly, then, the Christian had to feel in the fullness of their body and soul.

It is a commonplace to read the Middle Ages monolithically, as a millennium of superstition and irrationality. This is partly due to the sense that this period was entirely bounded by the authority of the Church. And, as mentioned above, the hegemony of the Church is indeed one of the ways in which we define the coherence of this historical period. What this volume reveals, however, is that there was great change in the period in matters of belief, political structures and social formation. From what we can tell, here in the twenty-first century, feeling felt very different at different stages in this medieval millennium.

CHAPTER ONE

Medical and Scientific Understandings

NICOLE ARCHAMBEAU

By 350 CE, the highly decentralized late antique West experienced the slow emergence of Christianity as a dominant religion in a divided Roman Empire. By 1300 CE, there was a far more centralized Christian religion in the West and a well-developed Scholastic mode of learning in a growing university system. The many changes taking place, especially the Carolingian Renaissance and the emergence of universities, had a significant impact on medical and scientific (or natural philosophical) views of emotion.[1]

We have only hints of the medical view of emotion in Late Antiquity and the early medieval West. Those hints show that there was no single or even primary medical approach to emotion. Examples from an array of late antique and early medieval medical texts reveal this diversity. By the high Middle Ages, however, during what is often called "the translation movement" in the eleventh to the thirteenth centuries, the Galenic system of medicine became the dominant one in the West. Two terms for what we now call emotions—the passions and the *accidens anima* (the accidents of the soul)—appeared in high and later medieval medical and philosophical texts, revealing the fluid concepts about internal states.

EMOTIONS IN THE MEDICAL TEXTS OF LATE ANTIQUITY (350–700) AND THE EARLY MIDDLE AGES (700–1000)

There is no single way that emotions appear in medical texts from Late Antiquity or the early Middle Ages. Some of these texts, like herbals, lapidaries, and bestiaries, clearly reflect a broader Hellenistic, Mediterranean medical culture. Others, however, may look more like magic or superstition to the modern audience. It is important to keep in mind, however, that the boundaries between medicine and magic that modern audiences perceive did not exist at that time (Kieckhefer 1994). In the Western medieval worldview, God (sometimes through the distant influence of celestial bodies) had imbued stones, plants, animals, and words with secret power—the lodestone being the most obvious example. Humans might not be able to see the cause or fully understand those powers, but they could still use them (Kieckhefer 1989: 129–31).

Many argue that medical learning in the West disappeared after Galen of Pergamum, perhaps the most famous historian of Roman medicine, died in the early third century.

However, Vivian Nutton, a historian of medicine, rightly warns of the "distorting effect of Galen and the Galenic Corpus" on medicine in the third through sixth centuries. Galen wrote and argued extensively for a specific view of medicine based on both philosophical learning as well as experience. Seeing Galen as the norm of Roman medicine "creates the impression of a catastrophic decline" after his death (Nutton 2013: 301). But in many ways, Galen was an outlier, not a representative of his time. To focus too much on Galen is to miss the long continuity and the slow change of less prolific authors and local practitioners who combined Hippocratic medicine and local remedies with charms, amulets, and prayers over the centuries.

That said, Galen's writings, as well as writings attributed to him, Hippocrates, and other ancient physicians, did profoundly shape medicine in the later Roman Empire. The impact differed in the East and West, however. In the fourth through sixth centuries, Hippocratic texts and Galen's prolific sprawling writings were collected, redacted, and compiled into different forms. Nutton points out that even when authors appeared to be creating similar kinds of medical compilations in the East and West, there were significant differences. For example, in the East, doctors were relatively more available in cities and towns. That was not true in the West outside coastal Mediterranean cities. Western authors, like Marcellus of Bordeaux, emphasized that while the sick should call on doctors if possible, they must themselves "be *empirici*, not as followers of the Greek Empiricist sect, but as experts in what worked" (Nutton 2013: 307). In other words, doctors were few and one should know how to take care of oneself.

Many historians of medical texts in Western Late Antiquity used the metaphor of islands of learned texts in a sea of local, often oral, culture. The most famous island of learned texts was the monastery of Vivarium in the southern Italian peninsula. The monastery was founded by Cassiodorus, a statesman who lived in the sixth century in both Rome and Constantinople and gathered books from around the Mediterranean. The list of Cassiodorus's medical texts in Vivarium upholds the importance of Galen and the Hippocratic tradition he built on. But further analysis of those texts shows significant local changes in that textual tradition.

Cassiodorus's list included texts such as Gargilius Martialis's third-century *Medicines from Fruits and Vegetables* and Caelius Aurelianus's fifth-century translation/adaptation of Soranus's *On Acute and Chronic Disease*. A text such as *On Herbs and Cures*, attributed to Hippocrates, was more likely not a separate treatise but extracts from Hippocrates' *Diet*. Other texts that would have been available in Latin in centers of monastic learning, like Vivarium, included Hippocrates' *Aphorisms*, *Prognostic*, and *Airs, Waters, Places* (Nutton 2013: 307). The limited number of texts and their limited spread in the West did not mean that people had no medicine. Instead, it emphasizes Nutton's point that medicine in Late Antiquity was a field typified by diverse local practice.

Emotions appeared in diverse ways in many learned texts. For example, Caelius Aurelianus's *On Acute and Chronic Disease*, discussed emotions in a way that reflected Methodic medicine, rather than Galenic. The Methodic tradition, one of three main medical traditions in the Roman Empire, emphasized observation of the illness and treatment, with less emphasis on the individuality of the sufferer (Gourevitch 1998: 112–15). In Aurelianus's text, emotion appears most clearly in several illnesses thought to exist in the head: incubus (nightmare), epilepsy, mania, and melancholy. Emotion appeared in descriptions of symptoms and therapies for these illnesses. For example, the text states that "those who have suffered from the affliction [of nightmare] for a long time are pale and thin, for because of their fear they do not get sleep." Along with poultices, cupping, and fasting to treat nightmare, the text also recommends "having the patient lie in a moderately light and warm room. His mind and body should be at rest." The person offering treatment should also try to keep the sufferer from fearing the nightmares by telling gentle and strengthening stories (Caelius Aurelianus 1950: 476–7).

Emotions such as anger and levity appear in Aurelianus's descriptions of symptoms of and therapies for mania. In his therapies, he suggests calming an overabundance of one emotion (like levity) with its opposite (seriousness), through methods like conversation and having the sufferer read aloud to an audience. In particular, he contradicted practitioners who believed that love could heal forms of insanity because it distracted the sufferer and therefore purified the problematic thoughts. Aurelianus argued instead that sufferers of mania could not appreciate beauty and therefore could not love. Instead, he considered love a cause of insanity rather than a cure and sex as a potentially dangerous activity that could weaken the body (Caelius Aurelianus 1950: 558–9; Wack 1990: 11–13).

Music was another therapeutic approach to distressed emotions that appeared in some medical texts. Music was considered to be a mathematical discipline searching for order, including hearing the harmony of the celestial spheres (Stahl 1962: 193–202). The sixth-century Roman philosopher and politician Boethius wrote the *Fundamentals of Music* based on Pythagorean and Neoplatonic thought. According to Boethius, music was also associated with morality. Lascivious music, for example, could corrupt the chaste, causing them to feel and act lasciviously (Boethius 1989: 3). As a therapy for extreme and potentially unhealthy emotional states, Boethius wrote: "It is common knowledge that song has many times calmed rages, and that it has often worked great wonders on the affections of bodies or minds" (Boethius 1989: 5).[2]

But it is important not to overgeneralize about emotions and medicine at this time from the work of Boethius and Caelius Aurelianus. While they give us glimpses, there was not one system of medicine in the late antique West. Instead, Roman, Hellenistic, and Germanic ideas were gradually melding in local and oral cultures and possibly in written texts that no longer survive (Duffin 2005: 50). Medical texts, as they were copied and adapted across the West, were changing too. For example, while Aurelianus's work was available in certain places in the late antique West, by later centuries most of his work appeared only in excerpts and much of the information on emotion was lost (Wack 1990: 11–13). Boethius too, with his strong ties to Plato and Pythagoras, was eclipsed in later centuries by Aristotelian ideas about nature (Horden 2000: 103–8).

The local nature of Western medicine continued into the early Middle Ages. As Peregrine Horden notes, over 160 medical texts survive from the period 700–1000. But the manuscripts, mostly in Latin and Old English, remain difficult to contextualize or generalize as a group. The manuscripts are highly individual and, when taken out of context (or, as is more common, remain difficult to contextualize at all), often appear quite strange to the modern reader (Horden 2011).

If medicine in Late Antiquity looked like islands of learned text-based medicine in seas of local practice, in the early Middle Ages, those islands grew even farther apart. While some local practice may have had links to a broader Mediterranean culture of medicine—Gregory of Tours' description of local doctors suggests a learned culture of healing—we have little surviving evidence of their practice or any theories of emotion they might have had (Gregory of Tours 1974: 263–4, 570–1; Amundsen 1971). The survival of medical texts in Anglo-Saxon, including the 500-folio Bald's *Leechbook*, a medical recipe book, gives us a northern island of medical texts to look at, but again, no medical theory of emotion (Cameron 1993: 30–1).

That does not mean, however, that emotions were not part of late antique and early medieval medicine. Anglo-Saxon medicine has the potential to reveal some interesting local melding as Roman and Christian ideas mingled with knowledge particular to England. And while references to emotion were not placed in a theoretical framework, we get glimpses of how they were considered. One dramatic example appears in *Lacnunga* (*Remedies*), a commonplace book perhaps compiled by several monastic authors in the early Middle Ages (Grattan and Singer 1971). This text, with influences from Hellenistic medicine, Roman magic, and Christian liturgy, addresses emotions (broadly defined) particularly through moral ideas of temptation and lack of control. For example, the book includes a quasi-Christian ritual against "elfin enchantment and for all temptations of the Fiend." The remedy suggests ritual phrases, herbs, psalms, and prayers that would protect against negative emotions/moral states (Grattan and Singer 1971: 109–10; Kieckhefer 1989: 64–8).

The moral overtones of emotion in medicine also appear in early ideas on regimen. Isidore of Seville, the archbishop of Seville in the early seventh century, wrote the influential *Etymologies*, an encyclopedia that gathered and summarized much classical knowledge. Isidore described medical treatment as having three parts: regimen, pharmacy, and surgery, to be tried in that order by practitioners (Isidore of Seville 2006: 115). In the West, texts on regimen (also referred to as hygiene or diet) were few, short, and frequently in the form of letters from a famous physician to an important person. But they did exist, and Isidore's inclusion of regimen as a necessary part of medicine suggests their importance (Gil Sotres 1998: 296).

For someone like Isidore and other scholars writing in Late Antiquity, regimen would have had many parallels with the emerging monastic rules like that of Benedict of Nursia, living in the early to mid-sixth century. For Benedict, an ordered moral state was part of a healthy regimen. The Rule of St. Benedict discussed how monks should govern their food and drink, activities, sleeping, prayer, and internal selves. Governing their internal selves included developing a multistage humility and not giving in to anger, lust, sloth, jealousy, pride, or hate (Benedict of Nursia 1975: 52–4). This list is familiar as the seven deadly sins, but can also be seen as a list of emotion-like states that could ultimately damage one's physical and mental health (Wenzel 1960: 3–46). It also has strong parallels with ancient philosophical writings, including Galen's *Passions and Errors of the Soul*, in which humility was crucial to control emotions dangerous to health.[3]

Emotion appeared in other late antique medical texts like herbals, lapidaries, and bestiaries. These texts gathered information on what we now call pharmacy or *materia medica*. Herbs, stones, and animals had medicinal virtue. Some had an impact on specific kinds of emotional distress or produced desired emotional states. Copies of Pedanius Dioscorides' popular first-century herbal were produced and circulated in Late Antiquity and the early Middle Ages in Latin. A pseudo-Dioscoridean text called *On Feminine Herbs* was copied frequently as well (Collins 2000: 148–91; Nutton 2013: 307). Dioscorides' sense of divine power in *materia medica* dovetailed with Christian understandings of God imbuing herbs, stones, and animals with healing powers (Touwaide 1998: 265–6).

While there was no overarching system of emotion apparent in these texts, Dioscorides mentions several herbs, like bugloss, that could cause happiness when mixed with water or wine, but also several, like henbane, that could cause negative mental states (Dioscorides 2005: 298, 276–7). Certain portions of the skink, a lizard that Dioscorides said could be found in many places in the eastern Mediterranean and the Indian Ocean, were considered an aphrodisiac (Dioscorides 2005: 109).

MEDICAL AND SCIENTIFIC UNDERSTANDINGS

In most herbals, lapidaries, and bestiaries, the brief entries do not explain why the plant, stone, or animal has a particular effect on people, but are more concerned with describing them and their preparation. Dioscorides' entry on saffron provides a useful example. In the entry, Dioscorides describes the best saffron for medical purposes, where it grows, and how dishonest sellers would adulterate it. He also includes a long list of

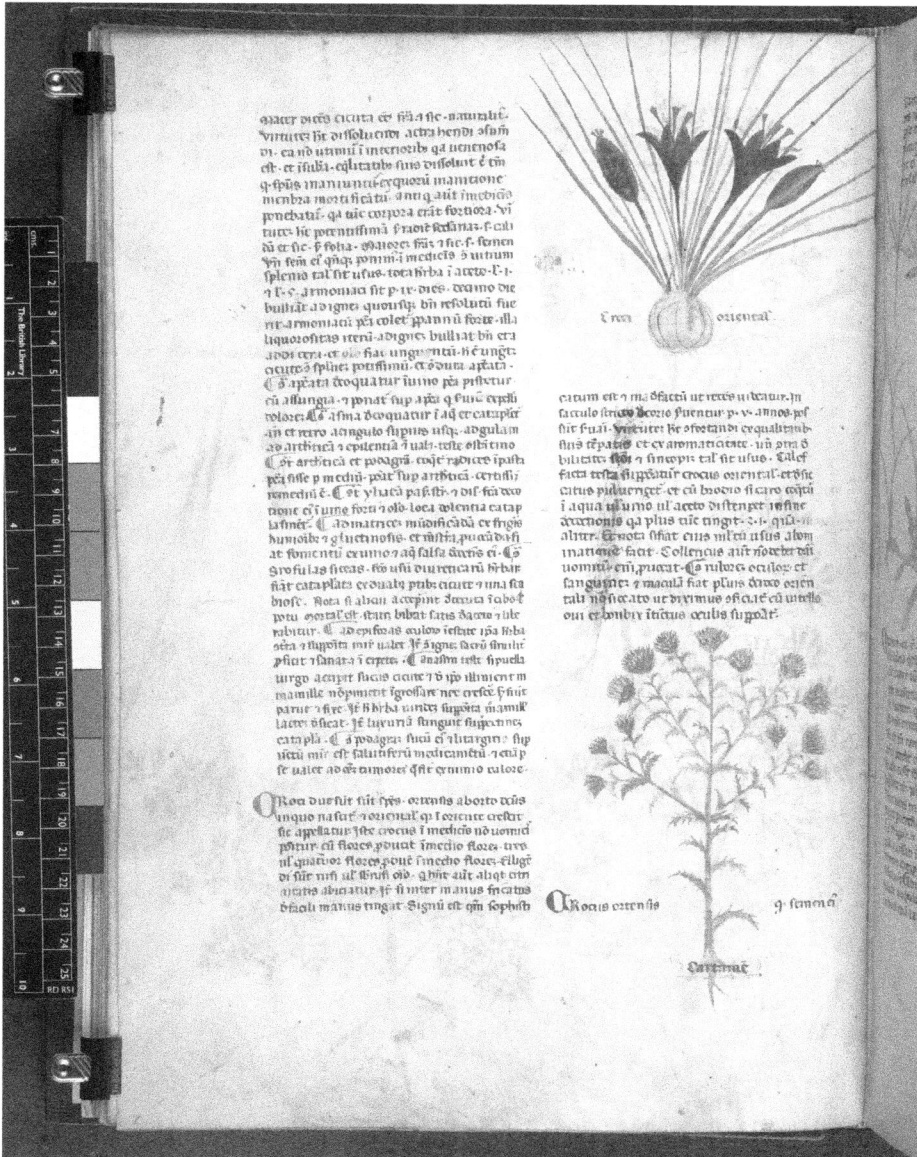

FIGURE 1.1: Saffron in the *Circa Instans*. Miniature of a croci orientalis, or saffron crocus plant; miniature of a crocus ortensis, or safflower plant. British Library, MS Egerton 747, fol. 24ᵛ, *c*.1280–*c*.1310. © The British Library Board.

uses. The text states: "It is mixed advantageously with draughts for internal afflictions and with pessaries and poultices for the uterus and anus. It is an aphrodisiac, it soothes inflammations caused by erysipelas when anointed, and it is useful for inflammations of the ears" (Dioscorides 2005: 23–4).[4] From this entry, we see that problematic emotion (in this case lack of desire) was included with many other kinds illnesses. While the information may appear jumbled to a modern reader, for the medical expert of Late Antiquity, this text included all the necessary information.

Dioscorides' texts and those attributed to him were not the only texts on *materia medica*. An Anglo-Saxon herbal attributed to Apuleius, which included 185 plants, survives in multiple copies (Voigts 1979). While some have argued that these texts were not in practical use in the West in Late Antiquity and the early Middle Ages, because many of the materials could only be found in the eastern Mediterranean, scholars like Linda Voigts point to the active trade among monastic houses during this time to suggest that these materials could have been obtained (Voigts 1979: 259–60; McCormick 2001).

Isidore of Seville's overview of medicine gives a glimpse of learned medicine in Late Antiquity and the early Middle Ages. His presentation of regimen, medicine, and surgery reflects a centuries-old approach following Greek and Roman ideas. But texts like the *Lacnunga* also reveal complex, local medical practice that wove emotion into ritual practice. The rarity of these texts does not allow us to argue for a systematic approach to medicine.

MEDICAL APPROACHES TO EMOTION IN HIGH AND LATE MEDIEVAL WESTERN MEDICINE, 1000–1300

In conjunction with the spread of monasteries, cathedral schools, and, eventually, universities, the Hippocratic/Galenic tradition of medicine that had flourished and expanded in Alexandria, Constantinople, Baghdad, and other Greek- and Arabic-speaking areas of the Mediterranean spread in the West (Lindberg 1992: 215–24). In comparison with Late Antiquity and the early Middle Ages, people in the high and late Middle Ages had greater access to a far more systematic view of medicine.

The eleventh and twelfth centuries saw an active translation movement in the West. Through the translation efforts of scholars like Constantine the African, living in Monte Cassino in the eleventh century, and Gerard of Cremona in Toledo in the twelfth century, Arabic medical encyclopedias, like Haly Abbas's *Pantegni*, became available in Latin for the first time.[5] In addition, at the earliest medical school in Salerno, several influential translations were gathered together to create the *Articella*: a group of Galenic and Hippocratic medical texts and influential Arabic commentaries that formed a kind of medical textbook (Siraisi 1990: 58).[6] The *Pantegni*, the *Articella*, and commentaries on these texts, formed the basis of medical education in West for centuries (Temkin 1973: 95–110). There continued to be conflicting interpretations of emotion in the core medical texts, especially around certain contradictions inherent in Galenic medicine, and in conflicting views of the body articulated by Galen and Aristotle.

The Latin translation of the *Isagoge* (a text of the *Articella*) and the *Pantegni* shaped Western medicine in several ways (Horden 2007).[7] The first way was structural. Both the *Isagoge* and the *Pantegni* had a two-part structure—ten theoretical chapters paired with ten practical chapters organized by illnesses from head to toe (Demaitre 2013: 77).[8] Encyclopedic texts written by Western authors in later centuries imitated this structure.

The second way was through its availability. Although Avicenna's *Canon of Medicine* eventually replaced these texts as the most respected medical text, the *Isagoge* and *Pantegni* were more readily available and therefore more influential from the eleventh century until the end of the thirteenth.⁹

The main influence of the *Isagoge* and *Pantegni* was the framework they provided for medical knowledge. These two texts presented medical knowledge around three main categories: natural, nonnatural, and contra-natural. In this system, which merged several separate Galenic ideas, natural things were the parts of the body and how those parts functioned, nonnatural things were processes that influenced how the parts of the body functioned, and contra-natural things were those things that caused damaging humoral imbalance, like illness, bad habits, weapons, and poison (Demaitre 2013: 13–23). It is worth exploring the three categories in order to understand the sometimes contradictory ideas about emotion in the medical system in the West.

Table 1.1 indicates 'natural things' in the schema established in the *Isagoge* and *Pantegni* and later clarified in Avicenna's *Canon*.

These natural things were both visible parts of the body and invisible functions and materials (Demaitre 2013: 15–21; Harvey 1975: 13–21; Siraisi 1990: 101). They combined with a person's date of birth, geographical location, and temperament to form something called the *complexio* (Ottosson 1984: 129–54). Each person had a unique *complexio* that reflected all the natural things of his/her body and birth.

Balance of the *complexio* formed a person's continuum of health and illness. Based on all of the *complexio*'s factors, a person would have a balance uniquely their own that would determine when during the year they were more likely to become ill, what illnesses they were more likely to get, and the best ways to bring them back into balance. Fundamental to the physiological features of a person's *complexio* were the characteristics of the four elements: dryness, moistness, coldness, and warmth (Harvey 1975: 13–15). Physicians understood that it was not only people that had a *complexio*: food, drink, and medicines did as well. Accordingly, physicians could use these to balance a person's

TABLE 1.1 The Natural Things of the Body

Elements	These included earth, fire, water, and air and their qualities dryness, heat, moistness, and cold.
Humors	These were blood, phlegm, yellow bile, and melancholy (also known as black bile).
Members	The members were the producers and distributors of the humors. These were primarily the brain, heart, and liver, which were each at the center of a system in the body—the nerves, arteries, and veins respectively.
Virtues or Spirits	The virtues were also produced in the members. These were the nutritive, vital, and animal, linked to the liver, heart, and brain respectively.
Faculties	These were specific abilities necessary to the organs, including appetitive and eliminative abilities that allowed organs to draw nutrients from the blood and expel superfluities. Faculties differed by organ. For example, only the brain had the imaginative, cogitative, and memory faculties.
Operations	These were the functions of the primary members. For example, the liver turned digested food into nutritive blood.

complexio (McVaugh 1966). For example, a physician might prescribe smelling violets (considered cold and moist) to someone who had been dried out by a southern wind.

The second category introduced in the *Isagoge* and *Pantegni*, nonnatural things, included activities and bodily states necessary to the body, but not of it (Rather 1968; Jarcho 1970; Bylebyl 1971). The list includes air and breathing, motion and rest, sleep and waking, eating and drinking, excretion and repletion, and the *accidens anima* (accidents of the soul). These things, depending on their intensity, could influence the body's *complexio*. Breathing corrupted air could corrupt the body, for example, while too much excretion of semen in sexual intercourse could weaken the body. The term "six things nonnatural" first entered Western medicine through Constantine the African's translation/adaptation of the *Pantegni* (Niebyl 1971). Manipulating the nonnaturals through regimen was the primary way that high and late medieval physicians attempted to maintain or restore a person's health.

The nonnaturals are particularly important to Western ideas of emotion because of the *accidens anima*, or the accidents of the soul. Due to its name, physicians linked *accidens anima* to the brain (the seat of the *anima* and animal spirit) and expressions of emotion (the *accidens*, or changeable features, of the *anima*). Physicians discussed a range of *accidens anima*, but used a few in particular to highlight their main effects on the body (Cohen-Hanegbi 2017: 18–66). These emotions were *tristicia* (sadness), *leticia* (happiness), *gaudium* (joy), *ira* (anger), *timor* (fear), and *pudor* (shame) (Gil Sotres 1994: 185).

The historian Pedro Gil Sotres has shown that standard medical texts like the *Isagoge* and the *Pantegni* contain no clear definition of what the *accidens anima* were or how they functioned in the body and mind (Gil Sotres 1994). In many ways this reflects Galen's own flexible presentation of emotion and the many philosophical views that shaped his thought (Staden 2000). The unclear usage also reveals, however, the difficulty of incorporating Greek and Roman ideas about the soul into a monotheistic worldview. This appears in medical texts especially, as texts like the *Pantegni* used the term *accidens anima*, but described a different concept: the passions. The passions (from the Latin verb *patior*, to suffer) also included a list of emotions similar to that of *accidens anima*: hope, courage, anger, fear, and discouragement. The term was familiar in theology and natural philosophy and well-studied in university texts. Defining the two terms—*accidens anima* and the passions—will help us understand the complexity of the concept of emotion for Arabic, Jewish, and Christian scholars, all of whom had monotheistic belief systems (Thijssen 2000).

For medieval scholars, *accidens* is a term from the study of natural philosophy and reveals the increasing influence of Aristotelian thought. A medieval teaching example of *accidens* (or accidents) is still quite useful. When explaining Aristotle's ideas to his students, Peter Abelard used Browny the donkey as an example. Browny is made from matter in the form of a donkey. That is Browny's substance—what Browny is—and that is not going to change. Browny will not wake up one morning as a duck or a shovel. *Accidens*, however, do not come directly from matter or form, but are a subset of Browny's substance, so they can change. Things like Browny's height, his eye color, and his hair color are *accidens*. These things can change with age, for example, or physical injury.

From this definition, we see that medieval physicians understood what we call emotions (the *accidens anima*) as the changeable parts of the *anima*'s substance. Changes in *accidens* (from joy to sorrow, for example) would not change the *anima* itself—nothing would—but the *accidens* of the *anima* could be influenced by factors such as age, season, geographical location, and injury. Above all, stimuli entering through the senses affected the *accidens anima* because those stimuli entered the brain, the seat of the *anima*. These changes in the *accidens anima* could affect the balance of the *complexio*, like any of the nonnaturals.

Like *accidens*, the term *anima* also requires scrutiny (Rocca 2012). For Arabic and Western thinkers, *anima* usually meant "soul," that one undying thing in a human being which linked the earthly human to the celestial realm. Because the soul was celestial and undying, however, it had to be incorporeal. The more corporeal something was, the more corruptible it was. Nothing corruptible could be celestial or undying (Burnett 1994: 104–6). But this posed a problem. The idea of a single, undying, incorporeal soul was not compatible with those ancient Hellenistic understandings of the *anima* that most deeply shaped Western medicine. Philosophers like Aristotle, Galen, and the Stoics—not limited by an Islamic or Christian theology—posited theories of multiple *animae* within the body that were corporeal enough to move the body to act and, especially for the Stoics, to die with the body (Staden 2000: 96–105).

Building on these ideas led Islamic and Christian physicians to some difficult questions. They observed that the soul did interact with the body, but if the soul were incorporeal, how did it move the corporeal body? If the soul were unified and resided in one part of the body, how did it move the different parts of the body? Without a corporeal component, the soul would have no ability to interact with—to move—the body (Burnett 1994). In response, Islamic scholars and later Christian scholars transformed the ancient theory of the three souls into three spirits (or virtues) in the human body—the natural, vital, and animal—that acted as intermediaries between the soul and the body (Wolfson 1935). The spirits were formed from the humors and elements and refined in different organs of the body until they were so pure that they were as close to incorporeal and celestial as a corporeal thing could be. These highly refined spirits could then be influenced by the soul and transmit the soul's influence to the body. In the *Pantegni*, the three spirits were distinguished as in Figure 1.2.

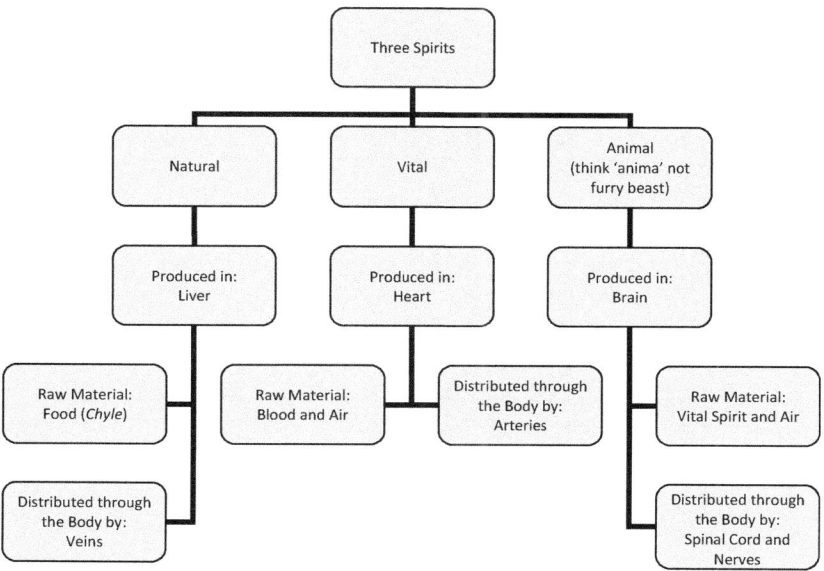

FIGURE 1.2: The Three Spirits © Nicole Archambeau.

As we can see in this diagram, the three spirits worked in conjunction with one another. Broadly speaking, the process worked this way: food, broken down by the stomach into *chyle*—its most refined form—moved to the liver and there became natural spirit. The liver sent this natural spirit, along with other nutrients, to the body through blood in the veins. Blood from the veins then entered the right ventricle of the heart and passed through a porous membrane into the left ventricle where it mingled with a rarified type of air drawn in from the lungs (Siraisi 1981: 186–95). This mingling formed the vital spirit. The process of mingling heated the blood, now filled with the vital spirit, and sent it out through the arteries to the body helped along by the body's pulses. Blood filled with the vital spirit traveled to the brain and joined there with air drawn in by the nostrils to form the animal spirit.[10] The animal spirit then traveled through the body by means of fluid in the spinal cord and the nerves, carrying directions for the body.[11]

The *accidens anima*, linked so closely to the animal spirit in the body, would have been part of the functioning of the brain.[12] Figure 1.4 maps out a general picture of the brain's ventricles and what happened in each one.

The first ventricle of the brain gathers and preserves the information collected by the external senses. This means that as you see, hear, or smell something, air enters through the eyes, ears, or nose and eventually collects in the first ventricle.[13] That information is then sent to the middle ventricle where the sights, sounds, tastes, and smells are grouped together in meaningful ways by the *cogitatio*.[14] This process can produce fanciful images,

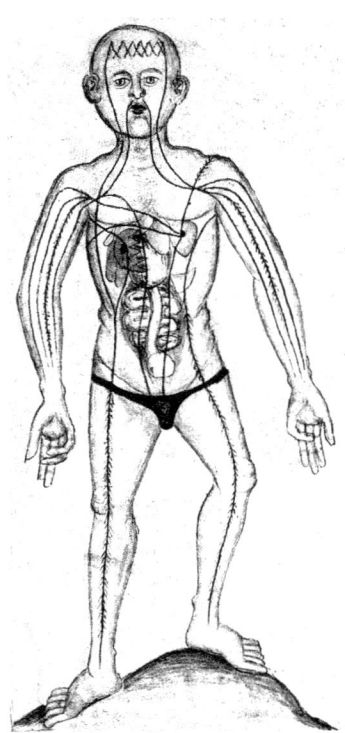

FIGURE 1.3: Veins in the Body. Modified image adapted from Wellcome Library, London, MS 49, Apocalypse, fol. 35ᵛ, *c*.1420–30.

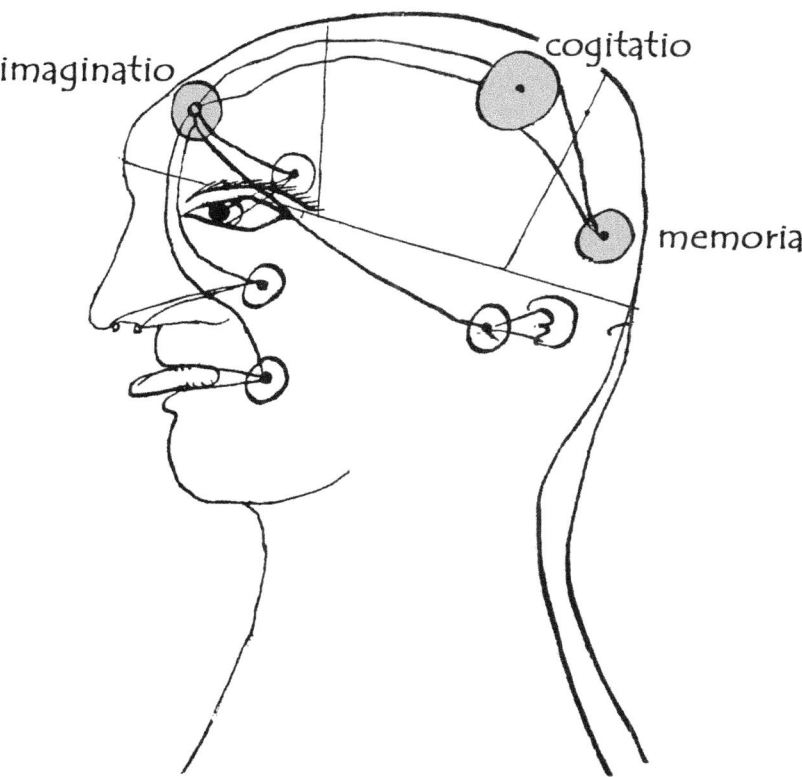

FIGURE 1.4: Ventricles of the Brain. Modified image adapted from Wellcome Library, London, image L0010724. [Taken from Walther Sudhoff, "Die Lehre von den Hirnventrikeln in textlicher und graphischer Tradition des Altertums und Mittelalters," Archiv für Geschichte der Medizin, 7:3 (1913), 149–205, p. 190.] Original image *c.*1347.

like dragons and unicorns, by mixing and matching sights that did not appear together. It can also produce logical thought when reason is applied to the sense information. Once information has been processed, it moves to the last ventricle where it is stored. At this point the body can send animal spirit out through the spinal column and nerves, causing the body to react to sense information.

A separation emerged here between physicians and natural philosophers. Although these two groups of scholars studied at the same universities and attended many of the same lectures, they had different goals in their scholarship. Physicians were ideally supposed to care for the health of the body, while theologians and natural philosophers worked to understand why things happened in the world created by God. In some cases they also trained those people, like priests and bishops, who would provide pastoral care (Garcia-Ballester 1988). The *accidens anima* and passions would have been important to both groups, since they related both to the functioning of the body and in many ways to moral behavior (Harvey 1975: 30–61).

One of the essential debates between physicians and natural philosophers concerned the primary member of the body. Galenic medicine considered the brain primary and argued that emotions emerged primarily in the brain. Aristotle considered the heart to be the primary member and described emotions as the sensations of blood filling with vital spirit and moving to and from the heart. The famous thirteenth-century Italian physician, Taddeo Alderotti, and his students give us one example of how physicians and natural philosophers resolved the heart/brain discrepancy. Alderotti and his students argued that although the brain is the seat of reason and the animal spirit moves the body, the heart contains the vital spirit. The vital spirit is that thing that differentiates the living from the dead. The body dies much more quickly if the vital spirit is cut off than if either the animal or natural spirit is cut off. So the vital spirit is more important and in a sense rules the body.[15]

Here we see the impact of the unclear presentation of nonnaturals in foundational texts like the *Pantegni*. Alderotti and his students had to make their own sense of the brain/heart debate because of confusion between the *accidens anima* (brain) and the passions (heart) that they encountered in their texts. Even though the *Pantegni* included a discussion of the passions, the creation and experience of emotion was still not clear (Harvey 1975: 19). According to the *Pantegni*, the vital spirit was linked to the passions. The passions were external factors, which caused movement of the vital spirit either toward or away from the heart, creating the sensations of emotion (17). It is not clear how these external factors influenced the vital spirit without going through the brain and animal spirit first, but it seems they caused an instant reaction in the vital spirit. According to the *Pantegni*, however, after the instant reaction, the animal spirit in the brain could influence these sensations, if a person moderated the sensations using reason (or *cogitatio*).

A familiar medieval example might help clarify the awkward meeting of these two understandings of emotion. If someone hears thunder and instantly becomes frightened, vital spirit (transported by blood) would rush from the extremities toward the heart, seen by the skin turning pale and cool. While this was considered a type of suffering (or *passio*), it was not considered an illness. Ideally the person would use reason to determine if the fear was justified or not, and that would change the emotional response to the stimulus, thereby returning the person's blood and vital spirit to its healthy flow. If someone could not use their reason appropriately and stayed frightened for a long time, however, this continuing rush of vital spirit to the heart could cause damaging loss of vital spirit to important parts of the body like the brain.

While the overlapping systems of *accidens anima* and passions might not be clearly defined and delineated in medieval medicine and philosophy, they do reveal a base of Hippocratic/Galenic medicine that had spread throughout Europe by the middle of the thirteenth century. For learned physicians, emotions fitted in a framework of the nonnaturals that influenced the balance of the body's *complexio*. There was significant diversity in understanding the process, but the organs, senses, and spirits were all involved in producing emotional response and controlling it when it became disordered.

TREATING DISORDERED EMOTIONS IN THE HIGH AND LATE MIDDLE AGES

Natural philosophy in the high Middle Ages did not have a directly practical side, but medicine did. Although it is difficult to determine medieval medical practice from surviving texts, some allow a glimpse into the disordered emotions medieval physicians encountered and how they tried to treat them. The most common type of text was the *practica*, which were encyclopedic texts that organized illnesses from head to toe including causes, symptoms, prognosis, and treatments. These were sometimes included together with theoretical chapters, like the structure of the *Pantegni*. Less formal texts survive as well, including recipe collections and *consilia*, which were collections of physicians' brief descriptions of particular patients, their symptoms and treatment (Archambeau 2011).

In *practica*, learned physicians categorized disordered emotions as malfunctions of the brain. These impairments could be temporary, as during drunkenness, or chronic, like melancholy. Melancholy is a particularly useful illness with which to consider the many treatments for disordered emotions. Thought to reside in the head, melancholy represented a group of imbalanced states in which an overabundance of black bile caused a mist to rise to the brain and obscure rational thought. Behavior could also show which ventricle of the brain had been affected, since those with an impaired memory would act differently from those suffering problems with the imaginative faculty (Demaitre 2013: 129–140; Siraisi 1981: 226–34).

Physicians primarily manipulated the senses and the six nonnaturals to treat melancholy. Treatments included spending time in pleasantly colored rooms with sunlight and beautiful companions. Friendly conversation (no gossip or complaining) could also help. Treatment could move from regimen to medicine through scent therapy and warm baths to more extreme measures such as placing animal parts on the sufferer's head to draw out the damaging mist of black bile. Surgery and cautery were rarely considered (Demaitre 2013: 134).

Consilia for the treatment of melancholy survive, especially in Mediterranean Europe (Giralt 2002; Siraisi 1981: 281). These *consilia* show an awareness of emotions like worry and the behaviors that accompany worry, including sleeplessness and mental exertion. Regimen was again important for treatment and could be specifically tailored for people with different occupations. *Consilia* also show that physicians believed the emotions causing melancholy could cause other health problems as well. These physicians targeted the disordered emotions as part of treatment (Siraisi 1981: 287).

One of the earliest medical texts translated in the West, Constantine the African's *Viaticum*, discussed the fixation on one love interest as a particular form of melancholy. The *Viaticum* was a translation/abridgment of *Provisions for the Traveler and the Nourishment of the Settled*, written by Abu Ja'far Ahmad ibn Ibrahim ibn Abi Khalid al-Jazzar (d. 979). Constantine conceived of the text as a summary of medicine for those who found the *Pantegni* too difficult. He significantly abridged the section on obsessive love, however, limiting the broad Arabic term *'Ishk*, which could include overwhelming desire for a diverse array of things, to a fixation on one person (Wack 1990: 34–40). This type of love, called *eros* (or in later texts "heroic"), was a diseased kind of pleasure that was an "affliction of the thoughts" (38). As the sufferer spent more time separated from the object of desire, he/she experienced the symptoms of melancholy and required treatment.

Love, lust, and coitus had always been part of medical ideas of emotion, whether as a potential source of madness, unhealthy temptation, a healthy purgative, or a dangerously weakening activity. Like Caelius Aurelianus in the early Middle Ages, the Arabic tradition of lovesickness also suggested that love could cause melancholy. But since these texts followed a Galenic model rather than a Methodic one, they suggested different kinds of treatment than Aurelianus had. The simplest treatment was uniting the sufferer with the object of desire. If that were not possible, texts suggested variations on the treatment of general melancholy, including recreational sex, though in limited doses.

CONCLUSION: NONNATURALS IN LATER REGIMENS OF HEALTH

While manipulating the regimen had been an important part of medicine for a long time (as we saw in Isidore of Seville), in the later Middle Ages in the West, regimens of health gained new importance (Rawcliffe 2010). Unlike the short letters from famous physicians to kings seen in the earlier centuries, these were more elaborate texts that focused on preventive medicine by teaching the reader how to regulate the nonnaturals, like food, sleep, and exercise for a balanced *complexio*. Although regimens were supposed to be tailored for one person and his/her unique *complexio*, by the fourteenth century some regimens, like that for the King of Aragon, became popular for people living in the same Mediterranean environment (Garcia-Ballester 1992).

Two types of regimen serve as a useful conclusion for this overview and a foundation for emotion in medieval medicine after 1300. The first was the *Tacuinum Sanitatis*, a group of tables (*taqwim*, in Arabic) for maintaining health written by Abu'l Hasan ibn Butlan (d. *c*.1070) and translated into Latin at the latest by the mid-thirteenth century (Arano 1976: 10–12). In the fourteenth century, this became a popular and often beautifully illuminated handbook available to the wealthy for understanding the impact of seasons, foods, and exercise on health. The second type of regimen was the plague treatise. These started to appear in 1348 in response to the first wave of plague. As civic leaders and nobles prepared their communities for the epidemic, a specialized genre of the health regimen emerged that attempted to help people avoid the illness. These texts were written for an urban community and the authors expected them to be copied and read out loud to help as many people as possible.

The passions/*accidens anima* were important in both these types of regimens. The *Tacuinum Sanitatis* and other pre-plague health regimens specified foods and behaviors that could regulate emotions, especially stress and worry. In many cases this looked like preemptive treatments for melancholy, emphasizing the importance of pleasant air, light, food, company, and bathing. Plague regimens emphasized the importance of emotional state for avoiding epidemic illness. A famous example is Jacme d'Agramont's plague regimen written in 1348 for the city of Lerida. For d'Agramont, internal state was as important as any food or exercise. As he stated, "among other influences that must be avoided in such times are especially those of fear and imagination. For from imagination alone can come any malady. So one will find that some people get into a consumptive state solely by imagination" (Duran-Reynals and Winslow 1949: 84). He even suggested that churches not ring their bells for the dead, since the excessive ringing could drive some to despair.

This sampling of medieval medical regimens reveals that both the passions and *accidens anima* held a crucial place in preventive and restorative medicine in the high and late medieval West. And while it is important to remember that the passions/*accidens anima* are not identical to modern ideas about emotion, they are an important corollary. They appeared in everything from hospital guidelines to commonplace books as an important part of maintaining and improving health, and they give modern audiences a glimpse into medieval ideas about the individual's interior life.

CHAPTER TWO

Religion and Spirituality

DANIEL ANLEZARK

The Middle Ages begin where classical Antiquity ends, but of course there was no single moment when this transition took place. Christianity was a major religion within the Roman Empire by the fourth century, and especially during the decades either side of the year 400 CE, Christian thinkers and writers engaged with the classical philosophical inheritance and its treatment of human psychology. The classical world and its philosophical schools were alive and well at the time, and many of the assumptions made about the human person, psychology, and emotion were shared by Christian authors and pagan philosophers alike. Often these assumptions must have been unconscious as large numbers of people converted to the new religion. Among the more educated and more rigid followers of the Christian religion, however, many of the old pagan ideas were reassessed and changed to conform them to a Christian understanding of the world, the flesh, and the devil. Many of the leading thinkers were practitioners of a strict asceticism which first emerged in the Egyptian deserts in the wake of founders like Antony of Egypt and Paul the Hermit (White 1998), who inspired tens of thousands to follow them into the wastelands to wrestle with their desires and demons, thus laying the groundwork for more than a millennium of Christian thought and practice in the pursuit of holiness (Russell 1981; Ward 1984).

At the heart of this endeavor was the problem of human emotion. Devotional and spiritual writers of the early Middle Ages worked within this dual inheritance, informed by a theology of Christ the God-man. Christian spirituality was about relationship with this human deity, and the belief in his full humanity gave emotion an important place in Christian devotion. This chapter will look at the origins of some Christian ideas about emotion in spirituality, and their application and development in two key texts from early medieval England, the devotional poem *The Dream of the Rood* and the instruction work for female hermits, the *Ancrene Wisse*.

One of the more important studies of emotions in the early medieval period is Barbara Rosenwein's *Emotional Communities in the Early Middle Ages*, which traces the emergence of a medieval way of thinking about emotion from the antique past and offers a number of case studies of the ways early medieval communities expressed themselves emotionally. She writes: "I use as my starting point the Early Middle Ages because the Middle Ages remains, despite caveats, a direct ancestor of modern Western civilization, and the Early Middle Ages is its link to the ancient world and thus to the Greek and Roman legacy of ideas and words having to do with the emotions" (Rosenwein 2006: 2).

Rosenwein takes issue with the relegation of the Middle Ages by two important commentators on the history of emotions, historian William M. Reddy and philosopher Martha Nussbaum (Reddy 1997; Nussbaum 2001). Nussbaum, she notes, passes over the

Middle Ages in her search for a love that looks beyond the self and becomes altruism—in this quest the Middle Ages are considered wanting. Reddy is not interested in the medieval period in itself, but "because he proposes a theory of social transformation based on the nature of emotions" (Rosenwein 2006: 16), his ideas suggest a way in which the Middle Ages might be integrated into a new history of the emotions.

Nussbaum cannot find a love in the Middle Ages "that appreciates individuality, is respectful of human agency, and leads to compassion for the hungry, the grieving, and the persecuted" (Rosenwein 2006: 17; see also Nussbaum 2001: 563–4, 580–90). The notable exceptions are the ideal of courtly love and Thomas Aquinas's neo-Aristotelian philosophy. The main culprit for Nussbaum is Augustine, because unlike the Stoics whom he mocked, there remained for him a deep distrust of fallen human feeling for any object except God. Nussbaum aligns herself with a long historical tradition when she sees in Dante a liberator of love and finds in the Italian Renaissance the stirring of a new sentiment in Western culture. Rosenwein argues that Reddy's analysis of "emotional regimes," such as in eighteenth-century France, cannot simply be applied to the Middle Ages, but this does not mean the period was without its own emotional "styles," often represented by an elite faction or royal court, however transitory its moment might have been (Rosenwein 2006: 23; Reddy 2001). She argues that "there were (and are) various 'emotional communities' at any given time . . . An emotional community is a group in which people have a common stake, interests, values, and goals. Thus it is often a social community. But it is also possibly a 'textual community,' created and reinforced by ideologies, teachings, and common presuppositions" (Rosenwein 2006: 23–5; citing Stock 1983).

THE ANTIQUE INHERITANCE

The ancient world had varying ideas about and attitudes toward emotions comparable with those found today, and passed these on in modifying ways to the medieval Christian world. The most important distinction can be summarized briefly: Aristotle thought that emotions could be useful, but the Stoics tried to root them out and eradicate them (Rosenwein 2006: 32). A few recent significant studies have sought to examine the ways in which this classical legacy was transformed into a system of Christian thought that was to dominate Christian religion and devotion for a thousand years (Colish 1990b; Sorabji 2000; Knuuttila 2004). In the practice of Christian asceticism, the Stoic view became influential in shaping Christian thought about and response to emotion, including the emergence of the concept of "vices." Most important in this development were the Desert Fathers of Egypt and those who studied them. These Fathers completely shunned society, and passed their days in extreme asceticism, with prayer, fasting, and penitential practices. The movement was enormously popular around the year 400 CE, and attracted practitioners and admiring observers from across the Graeco-Roman world. In the corpus of Patristic writings, the Desert Fathers occupy a place disproportionately small compared with their great influence. The works of the Fathers reveal an ambivalent attitude to emotions, welcoming them at times, but often aligning them with sin. This complex inheritance was passed on to their medieval followers.

Plato and Aristotle had presented two quite different theories of the emotions. Plato's *pathos* roughly equates with the modern English "emotion" (Rosenwein 2006: 33). His *Timaeus* tells a creation story in which the children of God recklessly "gave 'dread and inevitable' emotions (*pathēmata*) to mortals" (Rosenwein 2006: 34; Plato 1888: *Timaeus* 69c–71b). In this text, which was known even in the early medieval West along with the commentary of Calcidius (Calcidius 2011), Plato aligns emotions with the idea of vice, a lead that would be followed in earnest by the Christian writers Evagrius Ponticus and John Cassian, with the Stoics as intermediaries. Plato presents emotions as removed from the immortal soul, below the neck; the better of these, manliness (*andreia*) and anger (*thumos*), are found in the heart, the more base lower down in the liver (Rosenwein 2006: 35; for the medical literature on which Plato drew see Galen 1980: 361; Vegetti 1995: xiii). The appetites of the emotions resisted control and had to be moderated by reason through the use of anger. Aristotle's theory was fundamentally different. In his view, the *pathē* were rational. The emotions were cognitive and depended on a person's convictions and derived from judgments about *phantasia*, those things which are either remembered or hoped for (Rosenwein 2006: 35; Viano 2003). Aristotle agreed with Plato that emotions presented an admixture of pleasure and pain, but generally emphasized their painful aspect, found in emotions such as pity and envy, though not anger which was full of pleasure in the hope of revenge (Rosenwein 2006: 36; Konstan 2006).

The school of Stoic philosophy was at its height at the time of Chrysippus (d. *c*.206 BCE). The Stoics drew on the legacies of both Plato and Aristotle, agreeing with Aristotle that the emotions were rational judgments (which they characterized as bad judgments), and with Plato that emotions were the enemy of the virtuous life. Stoic thinkers diverge, but it is possible to characterize Stoic thought on emotion in general—emotions consist of two judgments: appraising whether something is good or bad, and assessing the way to react (Rosenwein 2006: 38; Colish 1990a; Sorabji 2000; Knuuttila 2004). The Stoics reduced all emotions into four categories, two relating to the present and two to the future. The present emotions were pleasure and pain, the emotions pertaining to the future were desire and fear. One of the great exponents of Stoic thought in the West was Cicero who translated many of its concepts from Greek into Latin. Within this grid of four emotions fell all kinds other emotions and Cicero provides a great list of *perturbationes* ("disturbances"; his rendering of *pathē*) in his *Tusculan Disputations* (Rosenwein 2006: 39–40; Cicero 1945: 4.7.16, 344; Cicero 2002: xii–xv).

The wise person, according to the Stoics, was undistracted by these passions. The process of emoting began with a pre-emotion, or "first movement," which indicated that an emotion was coming. This distinction between first movements and actual emotions (which required assent) would be of great significance to Christian thinkers from the late fourth century onward. First movements might look like emotions, but were not: they simply signaled that something happening might be perceived as good or bad. The Stoic sage used his or her judgment to discover that appearances were deceiving, and so avoid the emotion, refusing assent both to the interior feeling and any bodily reaction that might accompany it. A century after Cicero, Seneca, another philosopher politician, developed the theory of first movements. In a further significant step in the history of thought on emotions, he introduced the idea of the will (*voluntas*) into the process, so that it became the part of the reason that assented to the movement and allowed it to become an emotion. In another development that would greatly impact later Christian thought, he called anger not simply an emotion, but a *vitium* (vice) (Rosenwein 2006: 39; Sorabji 2000: 69–70; Inwood 1993).

Between the time of the death of Jesus and the later fourth century, Christianity underwent profound developments, both institutionally and doctrinally. What started out as a minor Jewish sect gradually became a minority religion independent of its Jewish roots and spread across the Roman world, occasionally reaching beyond it. Most early Christians were Greek-speaking and centered in the eastern Empire, but gradually the movement also consolidated in Roman North Africa, Spain, Gaul, and on the Italian peninsula. The two main languages of Christianity were Greek and Latin, and it was in these two languages that Christians expressed emotion and ideas about emotion. These languages were shared with non-Christian neighbors and philosophical forebears, and it was only over time that new Christian meanings cohered around the ancient vocabulary of feeling. Once this transformation had taken place, however, it left a legacy that would endure many centuries. The major intellectual centers of the Christian Church by the late fourth century were Alexandria and Antioch, which were often locked in bitter disputes about the nature and person of Christ, especially the way in which his humanity could dwell in the same person with his divinity. As we shall see, these disputes had implications for the way in which humanness itself, and emotion within it, came to be understood. One important movement within Christianity was focused on the hinterland of Alexandria in the Egyptian desert. This movement itself produced very few writers, but is nevertheless of the greatest importance in the history of the emotions because of the highly influential spiritual writers who took these extreme ascetics as their models.

FIGURE 2.1: *Temptation of St. Anthony*, by Master of Bonnat (active *c*.1475–1530). Photo by DEA / G. DAGLI ORTI via Getty Images.

One of the most famous Latin Fathers of the Church, Jerome (d. *c*.420), was also closely associated with the desert ascetic movement in Palestine. Jerome is best known for providing a translation of the Hebrew and Greek texts of the Old and New Testaments into Latin, which came to be known as the Vulgate Bible. Working from two languages, and describing a range of experiences and emotions expressed in biblical books themselves written many centuries apart, Jerome had to use a vocabulary familiar to Latin speakers. As Rosenwein points out, Jerome never intended to provide an inventory of emotion words (Rosenwein 2006: 43), but because of his work's widespread popularity, he incidentally provided not only a vocabulary of emotion for the Bible, but for those who came to know the Latin language through the close study of the scriptures, he provided a repertoire of emotion words that would in turn influence other linguistic communities. Of the sixty emotion words identified by Cicero, Jerome used only forty-six in his translation, but he also added to this list. We can see that these new words are emotion words because they are paired with others that are identifiable terms of affect. Rosenwein provides a number of examples from Jerome, based around certain emotions. The example of love is informative (Rosenwein 2006: 45).

Love words were an especially problematic category for the Christian translator because the character of the emotion is dependent on who is loving, what is being loved, and how. The highest Christian sentiment is love—God loves, is love, and wants to be loved, as neighbors must be loved—but carnal love can represent the worst form of vice. So when Jerome came to translate Eccl. 9.5–6, "For the living know that they shall die, but the dead know nothing more, neither have they a reward any more: for the memory of them is forgotten. Their love also, and their hatred, and their envy are all perished," the Latin term he used for this earthly love was *amor*. His choice is quite different when translating the lofty sentiments of 1 Jn. 4.8 and 4.16, so that "God is love" is "*Deus caritas est*," with *caritas* translating the Greek *agapē*. The connection between *amor* and *caritas* could be quite complicated, as Augustine of Hippo tried to explain: "For if it is someone's purpose to love [*amare*] God and to love [*amare*] his neighbour as himself, not according to man but according to God . . . this is usually called *caritas* in holy scripture. But it is also termed *amor* in those same holy writings" (Augustine 1955: 14.7, 421; Rosenwein 2006: 45). *Caritas* might also then be the equivalent feeling to *amor*, in relation to God. But does this mean that *caritas* and *amor* were the same? In the works of the Church Fathers the lines are indistinct (Pétré 1948). As we shall see, this left space in which later writers could develop their own thought.

In places, Jerome's Vulgate also implies a theory of emotions influenced by Stoicism (Rosenwein 2006: 46). When Christ explains his parable on how the things that come out of man defile him, he comments: "For from within, out of the heart of men, proceed evil thoughts [*cogitationes malae*], adulteries [*adulteria*], fornications [*fornicationes*], murders [*homicidia*], thefts [*furta*], covetousness [*avaritiae*], wickedness [*nequitiae*], deceit [*dolus*], lasciviousness [*impudicitia*], an evil eye [*oculus malus*], blasphemy [*blasphemia*], pride [*superbia*], foolishness [*stultitia*]. All these evil things come from within, and defile a man" (Mk. 7.15, 21–23). One of these words, *avaritia*, had already been classified as a sin by the Christian writer Lactantius around a century earlier. Even in Jerome's day, the concept of *cogitationes malae* was being aligned with Stoic first movements with results that had important implications for the history of Christian asceticism and theories about the relationship between emotion and sin. The idea that evil thoughts were inseparable from emotions emerged from the thought and experience of the Desert Fathers of Egypt (Rosenwein 2006: 46). Their ascetic life led to a rejection of most, though not all, emotions.

FIGURE 2.2: *St. Jerome in His Study*, by Albrecht Dürer (1514). Image courtesy of Wikimedia Commons.

An important and influential writer on the topic is Evagrius Ponticus (d. 399), a cleric who fled personal scandal in Constantinople to become a hermit for the last decade of his life in the desert of Nitria in Egypt. His eremitic life did not preclude him from teaching a number of followers, and he left a body of written work, often influenced by Origen of Alexandria (d. *c.*254) (Casiday 2013). Origen had integrated both Platonism and Stoicism into his Christian thought, and was the first to make the connection between "bad thoughts" and pre-emotions (Rosenwein 2006: 46; Sorabji 2000: 346). In his *Practical Treatise*, Evagrius speaks of "eight thoughts": gluttony (*gastrimargia*), lust (*porneia*), avarice (*philaguria*), distress (*lupē*), anger (*orgē*), acedia, vanity (*kenodoxia*), and pride (*huperphania*) (Rosenwein 2006: 46; Evagrius Ponticus 1971: 2.506–9). These are not considered emotions, like the Stoics' first movements, but from the point of view of Evagrius, these first prickings were caused by demons, an idea he borrowed from Origen (Sorabji 2000: 359). Sin came if thought assented to them and allowed them to stay, so stirring up real emotions. Consenting to the "pleasure of the thought" is the sin (Sorabji 2000: 360).

Evagrius's thought concerning emotions was transmitted to the Latin West by one of his disciples, the monk John Cassian. Originally from a region coinciding with modern-day Romania, after some time in Egypt Cassian established a pair of monasteries in Marseille. His widely and enduringly popular *Collations* collected the wisdom of the Desert Fathers in Latin and includes a Latinized and reordered list of "thoughts" which are also called *passiones* by the author, equating them with emotions (Rosenwein 2006: 47; Cassian 1886: 5.5, 124; 5.7.1, 127). They have various names: gluttony (*gastrimargia*; *ventris ingluvies*), lust (*fornicatio*), avarice (*filargyria, avaratia, amor pecuniae*), anger (*ira*), sadness (*tristitia*), anxiety (*acedia, anxietas, taedium cordis*), ostentation (*cenodoxia, iactantia, vana gloria*), and pride (*superbia*). A major difference between Cassian and Evagrius however, is that Cassian treats these as sins in themselves, not simply prior to them—they constitute the chief vices (*principalia vitia*). Cassian is not entirely consistent, however, especially when it comes to the problem of the human nature of Jesus, who was tempted by *fornicatio*, but not contaminated by the passion (Rosenwein 2006: 47; Cassian 1886: 5.2, 121).

Evagrius and Cassian can be seen in the wider tradition as hardening the views of the Stoics and Plato concerning emotions, even to sharing the goal of a Christian form of *apatheia* (though not all Christian writers would agree with this) which could be reached by eliminating the experience of emotion from the soul. From this tradition, Pope Gregory the Great (d. 604) would create the most famous list of the seven deadly sins, removing pride (*superbia*) in order to make it the root of all the others which included vanity (*inanis gloria*), envy (*invidia*), anger (*ira*), sadness (*tristitia*), avarice (*avaritia*), gluttony (*ventris ingluvies*), and lust (*luxuria*) (Rosenwein 2006: 47; Gregory the Great 1985: 31.45.87, 1610). Cassian, unlike Evagrius, did not aim for *apatheia* or see all emotions as sins—indeed compunction was a desirable aspect of the monk's emotional life, and manifested itself in shouts (*clamores*), groans (*gemitus*) and tears (Rosenwein 2006: 49; Cassian 1886: 9.27, 274). A contemporary of Evagrius and Cassian, Augustine of Hippo (d. 430) completed the Christian revolution in attitudes to the emotions. Augustine's admiration for the Desert Fathers included the influence on his own Christian conversion of reading the Life of St. Antony of Egypt. Augustine's contribution to the Christian attitude toward the emotions was crucial throughout the Middle Ages and beyond. For Augustine, with some notable exceptions, emotions might be considered morally neutral—good if directed rightly, bad if wrongly (Rosenwein 2006: 50; Sorabji 2000: 400–17). And more significantly still, Augustine conjoined "first movements" with emotions, and considered all such "motions" as subject to the will. In this way, in the tradition of Seneca, will itself was an emotion. The connection between will, emotion, and the individual Christian's way of approaching God are all drawn together by the Anglo-Saxon poet of one of the earliest devotional poems focused on the crucified Jesus: *The Dream of the Rood*.

EMOTION AND HUMANITY IN
THE DREAM OF THE ROOD

The life of the ascetic was lived in imitation of the crucified Christ, with a desire for communion with God. In this way, a select group lived to the extreme the ideal that was sought by all Christians, and it is important to note that the spread of Christianity in Western Europe in the Middle Ages was accompanied by the spread of the monastic life. The tension between heresy and orthodoxy in relation to understanding the person of Jesus fell upon the fault line between his humanity and divinity, a problem first dealt with at the Council of Nicaea in 325 CE, but which took many centuries to resolve (Davis 1983: 33–80). The problem of the degree of Christ's humanity is crucial to the ascetic life—a fully human Christ would have experienced human emotion.

The heresies about Christ's natures and person dating from the fourth and fifth centuries lingered with their implications into seventh. An ecumenical council was called at Chalcedon in 449 in an attempt to resolve the ongoing dispute. The council offered a new definition of Christ's person, composing its own *Definitio Fidei*, which was deeply indebted to Greek philosophy in its description of how two natures, human and divine, could be united in one person (Davis 1983: 170–206). The crisis over Christ's person revived in the Monothelete crisis in the seventh century, and was finally resolved at the Third Council of Constantinople (680–1), the sixth of the seven great ecumenical councils (Davis 1983: 258–89). There the heresy that Christ had only one will, rather than a human and a divine will, was anathematized. This last Christological heresy touched directly on Christ's capacity to share in human emotion, and its outcome had profound implications for the emotional strategies of asceticism and Christian devotion for centuries to come.

It is important to understand the social context in which this early theology was undertaken and doctrine developed. In the first centuries of the Christian Church, we are not dealing with professional philosopher-theologians in universities, as will be the case later in the Middle Ages: philosophy might be taught in schools, but theology was learned in the desert. In this early period, practitioners of theology tended to be monks, and the Christological dispute was inseparable from its implications for a life of asceticism. The superficially simple structure of *The Dream of the Rood* is set around a midnight vision of the Cross, led aloft, and vividly described; this leads into this cross's account of its experience of the Crucifixion, followed by an exhortation to the dreamer. The dreamer then explains to the reader his life since the vision, before an anticipation of the triumphant joys of heaven. This straightforward narrative frame, and its disarmingly simple use of sophisticated rhetorical devices, support a great complex of ideas. The poem draws together finely honed doctrinal concepts concerning the person of Christ, the way in which the God-man experienced death on the Cross, Anglo-Saxon cultural values concerning a good death (especially the ideal of warrior loyalty on the battlefield) and the history of liturgy and popular devotion to the Cross (Ó Carragáin 2005). As we shall see, it also shows an intimate concern with the emotions of the believer. Some of the poem's text is inscribed on the Ruthwell Cross (*c*.720–50), a stone monument also carved with panels illustrating episodes from the Gospels and early Egyptian monastic history (Burlin 1968: 25–6).

Rosemary Woolf has explored the relationship between the poem's representation of Christ and the Cross, and the theological concepts and disputes current in the late seventh century. She suggests that the poet is using the figures of the cross and the young hero crucified on it to represent the two natures of Christ, the human and the divine. Woolf's thesis on *The Dream* is simple: "The stress that will be laid on the Crucifixion as a scene of triumph or a scene of suffering depends upon the stress that is laid on Christ as God or Christ as man" (Woolf 1986: 30). Woolf argues that "The most remarkable achievement of the poem is its balance between the effects of triumph and suffering" (29)—the power of this opposition operates at the emotional level.

It is crucial in understanding the link between doctrine and emotion in *The Dream* to appreciate how inseparable its ascetic and devotional frame is from the theology of Christ it develops (Fleming 1966; Grasso 1991). *The Dream* is not simply about Christ's death on the Cross, but rather how encountering this event transforms the dreamer emotionally. At the heart of the ascetic struggle in early monastic spirituality is the moment when the soul, receptive and reaching out to God, finds things difficult because of the emotional burden of its weakness, and this is where we find the dreamer at the beginning of this poem:

> Listen! I wish to tell the choicest of dreams,
> which came to me at midnight,
> while speech-bearers lay occupying their beds.
>
> —1–3[1]

Whether this opening is designed to evoke the prelude to the midnight monastic office of vigils, slothfulness in sleep, or both, the opening of the poem places us in the heart of the ascetic struggle. The dreamer sees the wondrous cross with his eyes, but is more preoccupied with his own interior weakness and emotional state:

> Wondrous was that victory-beam, and I stained with sins,
> badly wounded by woe.
>
> —13–14

This self-preoccupation with sin, the human subject with its own weakness, is starkly portrayed in the dreamer's prone inaction:

> However, I, lying there a long while,
> beheld, anxious in spirit, the Healer's tree,
> until I heard that it spoke.
>
> —24–6

The dreamer's anxious soul is trapped in sloth: he is irresolute, listless, and desiring nothing; his contemplation is inward toward his own self and sin. It is at this moment that the dreamer encounters the speaking cross, a metaphor of Christ as Logos. Christ speaks through his human self (that is, the talking Cross), explaining the experience of his obedient suffering in the Crucifixion. The ascetic struggle is echoed in the gesture of the young hero, before he mounts the cross:

> The young hero stripped himself—that was God Almighty—
> strong and resolute. He climbed the high gallows,
> bold in the sight of many, when he would free humankind.
> I trembled what that man embraced me. However, I dared not bow to earth,
> fall to earth's plains, but I had to stand fast.
>
> —39–43

The hero's stripping of himself presents multiple allusions, one of the most striking of which is the wrestler about to engage in a match, a common metaphor for the ascetic struggle (Aldhelm of Malmesbury 2001: 2.11–18, 33–7). The tree is united to him in an embrace that is highly emotive and borders on the erotic, while the cross's obedience emphasizes its metaphoric role as Christ's human will, united with his divine intention to die.

The titles used for Christ are fundamental to how the poem works in Old English, and how it often fails to work in modern translation. The key term is *Hælend*, often translated as "Savior" (the Cross is *hælendes treow*, the healer's tree, 25), but much closer in meaning to Latin *Salvator*, "the one who preserves, heals, makes safe." Also important is the stated purpose of Christ on the Cross: he wishes to "mancyn lysan," often translated "redeem mankind," but more accurately rendered as "free humankind"—an act that enables the human will, rather than having it enter passively into a transaction, as is implied by "redeem." This theologically careful treatment of Christ is integral to the ascetic process and emotional transformation experienced by the dreamer. The poem's treatment of the two wills of Christ in the context of the ascetic struggle of the dreamer trapped in sloth—his will unfocused, his energy sapped, his desires disordered—evokes the struggle involved.

The transformation we find in the dreamer in *The Dream of the Rood* is the result of this self-absorbed sinner's encounter with the healing, liberating Christ, so that he emerges from a state like *apatheia*, rather than moving toward it:

> I prayed then to that beam with *happy mind*,
> with great courage, where I was alone
> with a small troop. My *heart* was
> *thrust on the way forward*; much have I endured
> of *longing*. Now is my *life's hope*
> that I can seek that victory-beam
> alone more often than all others,
> honor it well. My *yearning* for that
> is great in mind, and my protection
> rests in the cross . . .
>   And for myself I *hope*
> each day for the time when the Lord's cross—
> which I saw here on earth before—
> will fetch me from this borrowed life
> and then bring me to where there is *great bliss*.
>
> —122–31, 135–9; emphasis added

Christological doctrine and dispute, the ascetic life and the experience of emotion, are inseparable in the early Middle Ages because at the heart of Christian belief is the God-man who shows us how to live the perfect human life, and who made such perfection possible for those who choose to follow him. Christian orthodoxy came to accept the fullness of Christ's humanity, and with it the authenticity of his emotional life. This in turn validated a range of human emotions as not only free of sin, but as Christ-like, imitable, and ultimately liberating. In *The Dream of the Rood* we find a lethargic dreamer drawn from his listlessness and preoccupation with his sin to joy and love by an emotional encounter with the God-man, tree-Christ, and by the experience of catharsis that the Crucifixion narrative represents—a narrative that has been told with emotion by the tree that represents Christ's humanity itself.

FEELING FOR GOD: *ANCRENE WISSE*

The *Ancrene Wisse* (*Guide for Anchoresses*) is a rule for female hermits, originally written for a small group of English anchoresses (in the first place three sisters) in the second quarter of the thirteenth century.[2] The author of the text may have been a Dominican friar, and his wide reading and education are evident throughout. The early Middle English literary dialect used by the writer places him in the north of Herefordshire or

FIGURE 2.3: St. Wiborada in her anchorite cell, St. Gallen, Stiftsbibliothek, Cod. Sang. 602, p. 315 (1451–60).

southern Shropshire in the west of England, not far from the Welsh border. If the author was a Dominican, as most suspect, then this rule is unlikely to have been written before 1221, when the young order first arrived in England. The author may also have written a number of other surviving Middle English religious works, including three saints' lives (of Katherine, Margaret, and Juliana), a treatise on virginity, and another on the custody of the soul.

The text of the *Ancrene Wisse* is bilingual in Latin and English (though mostly in English), and the author often renders, rather than translates, his Latin material. The sources quoted by the author, apparently often from memory, are wide and varied, and point to extensive reading in spiritual literature. The most extensively quoted source is the Bible, and in particular the Book of Psalms, one of the most emotionally expressive biblical books. By the thirteenth century, the biblical texts quoted in the guide had accrued much interpretative glossing, which the author often draws on, though he also develops his own ways of interpreting the sacred text. He repeatedly makes use of the most significant Fathers of the Latin Church—Augustine, Jerome, and especially Gregory the Great—as well as the sayings and lives of the Desert Fathers. He is well read in medieval authors, including the *Prayers and Meditations* of Anselm, Archbishop of Canterbury (d. 1109), and two of the great Cistercian writers of the twelfth century, Bernard of Clairvaux and the English monk Aelred of Rievaulx (H. White 1993: xix–xx). In Bernard's treatise *On the Love of God*, the *Ancrene Wisse* author found an emphasis on the idea that we should love God because God first loved us (Shepherd 1959: xlviii; Bernard of Clairvaux 1959).

The rule's style is very familiar and full of storytelling, often accompanied by allegorical interpretation. The focus on emotions throughout the text, particularly the importance of love in relating to God, is striking, and lies at the heart of meaning for the solitary existence led by the women for whom the work was written (Georgianna 1981). In the psychology of the thirteenth century, love was considered one the four dispositions (*affectus*) of the mind, beside fear, joy, and sadness (Knuuttila 2004: 228; Shepherd 1959: lii). The influence of the Stoics is obvious, and *affectus* does not have exactly the same meaning as modern English "emotion." In the twelfth century, the Augustinian idea that love of God and love of one's neighbor (Mt. 22. 37–9) represented the fusion of one ideal of love was influenced by the rereading of Cicero's moral treatises, leading to a more naturalistic idea of love which sprang from the one *affectus* (Shepherd 1959: liv–lv). Bernard of Clairvaux developed this idea into a progressive understanding of love, namely that love of the good things of this world could lead to God, an idea that is crucial to the emotional strategy of the *Ancrene Wisse*.

One of the pervasive influences running through the guide, especially in its discourse on love, is the Old Testament Song of Songs, originally an erotic poem about the love between a man and women, but allegorized in the Middle Ages as an account of the love of Christ for the Church, or the soul.[3] The Preface of the *Ancrene Wisse* opens with a direct reference to this biblical book: "In the name of the Father and of the Son and of the Holy Ghost, here begins the Anchoresses' Guide. *Recti diligunt te* (*in Canticis sponsa ad sponsum*), etc.— 'Lord,' says God's bride to her precious bridegroom, 'the right love you.' " (1).[4]

The kind of nuptial imagery that the author develops throughout also represents the influence of the thought of the Victorines, Augustinian canons of the abbey of St. Victor in the twelfth century, though the impact of other spiritual writers on the rule is more direct (Shepherd 1959: l–li). Through all its colorful explorations of the ascetic life and discussions of sin and how to avoid it, the focus of the *Ancrene Wisse* is on the emotion of love and a personal attachment to Christ. Later in the Preface the author draws further attention to this focus of his work when describing the different kinds of rule that might be written and lived by:

> The one rules the heart and makes it even and smooth without the lumps and pits of a conscience crooked and accusing . . . this rule is the charity of a pure heart and clean conscience and true faith . . . The second rule is all outside and rules the body and bodily deeds. It teaches everything about how one must conduct oneself on the outside, how to eat, drink, dress, sing, sleep, wake . . . And this rule is only for serving the other; the other is like a lady, this like her handmaiden. For all of the second, outside, all that is ever done is only done to rule the heart within.
>
> —1–2

His anchoresses are to keep the inner rule day and night, and the outer "for her sake." Significantly, the hierarchical relationship between the two rules is to be understood in terms of their emotional importance, their effect on the heart. The inner rule is not a human invention, but God's commandments "for these rule the heart":

> The things that I write here about the outer rule—you keep them all, my dear sisters, Our Lord be thanked, and shall do so, through his grace, better and better the longer you go on. And yet I do not wish that you should vow to keep them as obligations, for after that, whenever you broke any of them, it would hurt your heart too much and make you so afraid that you might soon—which God prevent from happening to you—fall into despair, that is, into a lack of hope and a lack of trust in being saved.
>
> —4

Part One of the *Ancrene Wisse* prescribes the women's outward prayers and devotions. These external practices have an inward emotive meaning. The prayers to be said (some in Latin) during Mass emphasize the affective bond between the anchoress and Christ, especially present in the Eucharist:

> *Quis michi dabit ut uenias in cor meum et inebries illud et unum bonum meum amplectar te?* (Who will grant me that thou come into my heart and make it drunk and that I embrace thee, my good one?) . . . After the mass-kiss, when the priest consecrates, there forget all the world, there be entirely out of body, there in gleaming love embrace your beloved, who has alighted into the bower of your breast from heaven, and hold him tight until he has granted you all that you ever ask. This prayer before the great cross is of great strength.
>
> —17–18

The language of erotic love used to describe the emotional bond between the anchoress and Christ is used elsewhere in the rule (always recalling the Song of Songs), but nowhere else does the author suggest the intensity of mystical experience that he allows for here, in the context of receiving communion and praying before the cross. Paradoxically, at this out-of-body moment, the incarnational aspect of Christ's love for the soul is brought to the fore, both by the iconography of the bleeding figure of Christ on the great cross being prayed to in the church, and by the presence of Christ bodily in the sacrament (which takes on a new emphasis in thirteenth-century theology and devotion). As we shall see, the author returns to the practice of praying before the crucifix of the church, and develops its meaning further in terms of erotic love.

The heart as the locus of feeling, especially love, is at the center of the work's ascetic theology, and the second part of the guide concerns protecting the heart through the senses: "The heart's guardians are the five senses . . . The heart is a most wild beast and makes many a light leap, as Saint Gregory says: *Nichil corde fugatius* (Nothing is more fugitive than the heart)" (27). The human heart is unreliable and for this reason ascetic practice is required. This practice of control is discussed in relation to the guarding of the five senses. Again, however, the author surprises in the inflection he gives to the ascetic tradition: "Always the more the recluse gazes outwards, the less light she has from Our Lord inwardly, and likewise with the other senses" (47).

This Augustinian turn, which looks to the God who is within by turning from the world outside, presents a focus on the heart of the anchoress as the locus of knowing God. The author is not pessimistic about the human heart or the emotion it represents, despite his parallel emphasis on asceticism. In fact, he clearly articulates a mystical theology in which human emotion represents the pathway to closer union with God. To this end, one of the important recurring images in his work is that of seduction or wooing.

There are two significant passages describing wooing in the *Ancrene Wisse*: in Part Two (on protecting the heart through the senses) and later in Part Seven (on the pure heart). The attempted wooing described in Part Two presents an earthly seduction, the kind of wooing the anchoress is able to avoid if she protects her senses and follows simple advice about discouraging the wrong kind of company and conversations. But it is quite clear from the wider context that it is not the anchoress's capacity for or impulse toward human love that is the problem to be overcome. In Part Two, she should not rebuke in such a way as to invite further conversation with a man who is trying to seduce her:

> For in reply to the rebuke, he might answer in such a way and blow so gently that some spark might kindle. No wooing is so base as that in the guise of a lament—as if someone spoke thus: "I would not, though I died, think of doing anything filthy with you," and swore deep vows: "But even if I've sworn not to, I have to love you. Who's worse off than me? It stops me sleeping a lot. Now I'm very sorry that you know it. But now forgive me that I've told it you. Even if I go mad, you shall never more know how things stand with me." She forgives it him because he speaks so nicely. Then she speaks about something else. But the eye is always on the wood-glade—the heart is always on what was said before. Even after he has gone, she turns over words like this often in her thought, when she should be paying attention carefully to something else. Afterwards he looks for his moment to break his promise, swears he has to, and so the evil grows, getting worse the longer it goes on.
>
> —49

The parallels with the allegorical wooing by Christ in Part Seven are noteworthy, particularly the suggestion that the lover should die for her, and the mercy the anchoress might feel in her heart. The difference between the two seductions is not located in the feeling that is in the woman's heart, but in the source of the wooing. The feeling itself is to be harnessed and redirected toward Christ. The author here seems to be parodying sentiments found in the love lyrics of the period, with their complaints of sickness, sorrow, inability to sleep, and even oncoming madness. The lover's pleasant words enter through the ears, but there is also a gesture on the part of the author toward the rhetorical (and poetic) games that are a part of seduction. The author's reference to the "wood-glade" is obscure, and may simply be a rhetorical maxim. However, it also possible that it refers to a conventional bucolic setting of love poetry.[5]

The anchoress is encouraged instead in Part Two to look at the lady in the Song of Songs and follow her example:

> Look, now, how appropriately the lady in *Canticis*, God's dear bride, by her saying teaches you how you should speak: *En dilectus meus loquitur michi: Surge, propera, amica mea, et cetera*—"Ah," she says, "listen: I hear my beloved speak. He calls me; I must go." And go to your dear lover and complain in the ears of him who calls you lovingly to him . . . You, who should in the bower of your heart ask me for kisses, like my beloved who says to me in the love-book *Osculetur me osculo oris sui*—that is, "May my beloved kiss me with the kiss of his mouth, sweetest of mouths."
>
> —50, 52

The language here is as erotic, or more so, than in the earlier parody of wooing, but importantly draws on medieval allegorizations of the Song of Songs such as those found in the *Sermons* of Bernard of Clairvaux, whose influence on the *Ancrene Wisse* is pervasive (Bernard of Clairvaux 1971–80). Significantly, though, the author of the *Ancrene Wisse* does not develop here the allegory of the bride as soul—he speaks directly of the experience of the lady and her beloved as an analogy of the anchoress (and not simply her soul) and Christ (allegorically) as lover: "These are now two things that are loved very much—sweet speech and bright beauty. Whoever has them together, such Jesus Christ chooses as a lover and as bride" (50; Shepherd 1959: l–li).

The fullest discourse on love in the *Ancrene Wisse* comes in Part Seven, where the author develops his erotic imagery in more allegorical terms and in a way that draws more fully on the conventions of the literature associated with courtly love. Here he sums up the place of mortification and penance by quoting a voice from the Egyptian desert: "For, as the holy abbot Moses said, all the grief and all the hardship we endure in the flesh, and all the good that we ever do, all such things are nothing except as tools with which to cultivate the heart" (177).

The importance of a pure heart is reiterated throughout the work, though it is never fully clear what faculty the author means by the English word "heart" (Middle English *heorte*). He is not writing for philosophers or theologians, and it is most likely that his use of "heart" appeals to an easily accessible understanding of the locus of interior affection. The popularity of the *Ancrene Wisse* in the Middle Ages suggests that there was no difficulty among contemporaries or followers in understanding the writer's intentions. In Part Seven he offers a simple definition of a pure heart: "What is a pure heart? I have said it before: it is that you should not desire or love anything except God alone and those things, for God, that help you towards him. For God, I say, love them, and not for themselves (as with food or clothing, man or woman by whom you are benefited)" (178).

The author's veneration of the Desert Fathers is not mere lip service, but it is clear that he is a world away from them regarding the approach to worldly possessions. The author is not, of course, in favor of attachments to the goods of this world or people, but not only does he see no harm in desiring things or people who might bring us to love God, he sees them as a good to be loved and desired as a means to that end. This emotional bond with the things of the world is not only far removed from the *apatheia* of the Stoic philosopher, but also from the extreme asceticism and Christian *apatheia* of the Egyptian desert. That his was not a widespread view even in his own time is suggested by the author's personal comment ("to me") on the matter: "Those who love most are to me most blessed, not those who lead the hardest life, for love outweighs it" (178). In his generosity, the author points out, God the creator made all that was for the good of humanity and even after Adam's sin, "the earth, the sea and sun" continue to serve even those who are evil (179). For the Christian, it should also be clear that God gave himself to the world in the person of Christ.

To explain the significance of Christ as a gift, the author draws on the sentiments and literary conventions of courtly love to tell a story full of allegorical associations where meanings hover between the symbolic and the literal (Grayson 1974: 173–8). The first parable is brief and emphasizes the theological aspects of redemption:

> Now take good note, my dear sisters, of why he ought to be loved. First, like a man who woos, like a king who loved a poor lady of good family living in a country far off, he sent his envoys before him (they were the patriarchs and prophets of the Old Testament) with sealed letters. In the end he came himself and brought the Gospel like letters patent and wrote in his own blood salutations to his beloved—a love-greeting to woo her with and win her love.
>
> —179

The structure of the parable echoes the story of the owner of the vineyard in Mt. 21.33–41, though there the point is not the great love of the owner of the vineyard, but the great judgment that will come to those who reject and kill the owner's son. Here, and especially in the more elaborate parable that follows immediately in Part Seven, the author borrows the structure of the biblical story and combines it with the ideals of courtly love to produce a narrative that draws together important themes running through the whole work, especially as these concern the emotional relationship between the anchoress and God.

A second longer quasi-romance is introduced as an allegory, with a focus on the lady's situation: "There is a story to do with this, a parable with a hidden meaning. A lady was closely besieged by her enemies, her land completely devastated and she utterly destitute inside a castle of earth" (179).

The author continues to blend the allegorical and the literal in his treatment of the analogy between erotic love and spiritual love. The "lady" here is very much the soul, trapped in the earth-work, that is the body (see Gen. 2.7), but she is also literally the anchoress, enclosed within her anchor-hold. Having begun with the destitute human situation, the tale turns to the point of view of the king: "A powerful king, though, had fallen so extravagantly in love with her that to woo her he sent her his envoys, one after another, often many of them at once, sent her much beautiful jewellery, assistance in provisions, the help of his fine army in holding her castle" (179).

In Christian theology, love and grace are a divine initiative; here the author focuses on the failed human response in terms of emotion:

> She received it all as if she did not care, and so hard-hearted was she that he could never get any closer to winning her love. What more do you want? He came himself in the end, showed her his beautiful face (he being of all men the most beautiful to look at), spoke so very sweetly and in words so joyful that they could raise the dead to life, worked many wonders and performed many mighty acts in her sight, showed her his power, told her about his kingdom, offered to make her queen of all he possessed. All this was of no use. Was not this contempt an extraordinary thing?
>
> —179

The lady is playing the role often found in medieval love lyrics, remaining aloof from her suitor's attentions. It is significant here, though, that the suitor-king makes no demands, but only hopes to be loved in return. The author's rhetorical asides show the trained preacher at work: "What more do you want?," a direct address that focuses on the emotional response of his reader, directly drawing her into the affective strategies of the text.

The king's entreaties and gestures are of no use, so he speaks to her directly, and decides to defeat her enemies once and for all before they kill her:

> Because of my love for you I shall take up the fight myself and set you free from those who want to kill you. I know, though, for certain that in combat with them I shall be fatally wounded—and I desire that heartily, so as to win your heart. Now, then, I implore you, for the love that I declare to you, that you at least love me after the deed when I am dead, even though you would not love me when I was alive.
>
> —180

God's desire (and we see that for the author, God too has emotions), here couched in erotic terms that broadly echo allegorical treatments of the Song of Songs, creates a unique emotional regime within this text: God loves and needs to be loved, and those who refuse to love him are refusing a loving relationship akin to romantic love. The author carefully leaves out of his tale the final response of the lady to the king's noble gesture in dying for her—it is for the anchoress as reader to respond emotionally, because she is the lady. The *interpretatio* provided by the author explains what must have been obvious to any reader (especially as we are told the king rose from the dead): "This king is Jesus, God's son, who in just this way wooed our souls." The enemies are the devils, and so on. But even the *interpretatio* develops into an allegorical tale drawing on secular romance and chivalric conventions:

> And he, like a noble wooer, after many messengers and many acts of kindness, came to prove his love and showed by his knightliness that he deserved to be loved, as knights once used to do. He entered the tournament and for the love of his beloved had every part of his shield, like a brave knight, pierced in battle . . . His beloved should look at it [his crucifix] and see how he bought her love, let his shield be pierced, his side opened to show her his heart, to show her openly how fervently he loved her, and draw her heart to him.
>
> —180–1

This reversion to the gaze on the crucifix in the church returns us to the prayer of the anchoress in Part One, taking communion and contemplating the Cross. The emotional intensity of that moment of union is fused with erotic imagery, seen here in Part Seven: "Thus look, Our Lord woos. Is she not hard-hearted, whom a wooer like this cannot turn to his love, if she thinks carefully about these three things: what he and what she is, and how great is the love of one so high as he is for one so low as she is?" (184).

The physical gaze on Christ's dead body represented on the cross can remind the anchoress of his love for her, and in a homely image, set alight hers for him: "From these two pieces of wood you must kindle a fire of love within your heart. Look at them often" (185). The *Ancrene Wisse* potently blends the physical and spiritual in the emotional center of the anchoress, whose pure human desire is ultimately all that is needed to achieve communion with God: "Stretch out your love to Jesus Christ and you have won him. Touch him with as much love as you have at some time felt for some person, and he is yours to do with all you wish" (187).

CONCLUSION

At the beginning of this chapter I addressed Barbara Rosenwein's definition of an emotional community. Across the early medieval period, the Christian community defined itself by its "common stake, interests, values, and goals." This group was a social community, but one that existed across several centuries and in many different places. Within this community, some people lived the ascetic life as monastics, both men and women. Their common interest lay at the heart of their wider Christian communities—the desire to know God perfectly and to achieve perfection in doing so. They were the superior athletes of the societies they lived in, among whom the hope of salvation was hard enough. But the ongoing process of reflecting on the extreme religious life and writing about it and for it also created an important textual community that was both diachronic and synchronic. The mostly conservative tradition of spiritual writing was not essentially this way—new developments did happen and old texts were reinterpreted to suit changing ideologies in the light of experience. This is radically seen in the *Ancrene Wisse* where an author making extensive use of all that has gone before is relaxed about bringing human experience close to the heart of the search for God, informed by the great spiritual writers of his time. The religious authors of the early Middle Ages, living the solitary life or writing for it, made a lasting contribution to the exploration of what it means to be human and most especially what it means to be a loving individual. The interior life that these authors picked over in fine detail, even obsessively, could not simply rest on presuppositions about feeling, but inevitably developed new ways of understanding human emotional experience.

CHAPTER THREE

Music and Dance

CONSTANT J. MEWS AND CAROL J. WILLIAMS

Music is commonly considered to be a language that specifically expresses emotions that listeners are moved by (Juslin and Sloboda 2010). Nonetheless, musicologists and music historians have tended to neglect the link between music and emotion in music from the distant past. This approach has fostered the assumption that medieval music was simply not expressive and that the relationship between text and melody in song of this time was ordered by principles not easily understood. The other assumption is that medieval writing about music was dry and bloodless and avoided addressing the passions that might be aroused by music. Yet medieval culture generated a rich body of reflection about the ideal of *musica*, even if we are much less informed about the actual performance of music and dance prior to the fourteenth century. This chapter considers a few key moments in that evolving discourse about music between the fourth and early fourteenth century.

The experience of secular music, whether vocal or instrumental, is largely hidden from us prior to the late thirteenth century. Our awareness of the practice of dance is even more limited, other than through hostile comments from preachers about its propensity to lead to immoral behavior. By contrast, there survives a good deal of comment about music and emotions in religious writings relating to worship within the daily liturgy and personal devotions of believers. There was also a body of speculative theory about the philosophical nature of *musica* shaped by Platonic (and thus Pythagorean) thought and classically represented by the *De institutione musica* of Boethius (*c*.480–525) (Boethius 1989). Another body of texts relates to the performance of plainchant as represented by Guido of Arezzo (d. after 1033) (Guido of Arezzo 1978). Only in the thirteenth century would certain theorists explore ways of bringing these two traditions together.

Latin Christian writing on music was profoundly shaped not just by biblical traditions but by classical philosophical views about the emotions. Dance, by contrast, attracted little theoretical attention before the thirteenth century, except in moralizing condemnations of what clearly remained an important cultural practice outside the clerical milieu. Only in the thirteenth century did intellectuals engage widely with the views of Aristotle about emotions constituting an integral part of human nature, so long as they were not taken to excess. Aristotle saw the emotions as complementing reason and opening up realms of moral, aesthetic, and religious values. He used the term *pathē* (passions, emotions) to refer to "anger, fear, pity and the like" which lead to "one's condition becoming so transformed that one's judgment is affected, accompanied by pleasure and pain" (Aristotle 1952: 2.1.8, 623). He produced these views in reaction to those of his teacher Plato who held that emotions could distort or obscure the true way of seeing the world if they conflicted with reason. The Stoics, following similar reasoning, considered emotions to be conceptual errors about the world and one's place in it, ultimately leading to unhappiness. Cicero put aside the notion of "disease" when seeking to define *pathē*, but then developed the notion of emotion as *perturbatio* or "disturbance" of the mind—something flawed that made the life of the foolish wretched and bitter (Cicero 1915: 3.10.35, 102). Such attitudes helped shape Christian perceptions of music as able to arouse uncontrollable emotions and subvert rational behavior, as well as to redeem the human spirit.

THE PATRISTIC LEGACY: AMBROSE AND AUGUSTINE

Music has always been an integral element within the Christian liturgy, which first acquired a fixed ritual structure in the fourth century. Its moral seriousness was frequently contrasted by Christian preachers with the licentious dancing associated with pagan worship. Yet the extent and character of this music was often a focus of debate. All sides agreed that music was powerful in harnessing the emotions. The question was whether or not this power could be controlled and directed toward good ends. Niceta, bishop of Remesiana (370–414), defended its use by tracing the history of singing in both Testaments, emphasizing in particular the psalms: "Can any joy be greater than that of delighting ourselves with psalms and nourishing ourselves with prayer and feeding ourselves with the lessons that are read in between? Like guests at a table enjoying a variety of dishes, our souls feast on the rich banquet of lessons and hymns" (Niceta of Remesiana 1905: 239).

While ascetics often argued for simplicity in musical performance, Niceta presented liturgical music as anticipating the celestial music associated with heaven. His views echo those of John Chrysostom for whom the only acceptable dance was that of the *choreia* that anticipated the dance of the angels: "For where is a dance, there also is the Devil" (Backman 1952: 32; citing *Homiliae in Matthaeum*, 48, PG 58. 492). In this perspective, liturgy provided a sober alternative to the excesses of secular culture.

A key figure in promoting such attitudes in the Latin West was Ambrose (340–397), bishop of Milan. Shaped by Christian Platonist tradition, he composed hymns to make a stand both against the politically dominant Arian heresy, upheld by a number of Christian Roman emperors in the fourth century, and against a pagan backlash, promoted by those who longed to return to older Roman traditions. He is also credited with introducing the Greek practice of antiphonal singing of the psalms to Milan and the cultivation of hymns designed for congregational participation, described by Basil of Caesarea (330–379).[1] Ambrose's hymns were designed for congregational performance, consisting of eight iambic strophes of four lines each, usually with eight syllables per line (Anderson 2001). Singing provided a way of enriching congregational participation and cementing catholic orthodoxy.

Ambrose was convinced of the value of engaging the emotions by using music to pursue spiritual aims. Nonetheless he also warns against allowing the pleasure of the psalms to stir the passions of the body that may weigh down the soul (Ambrose 1919: 1.12.1, 9). Ambrose preached harshly against the seductive power of dance, emphasizing that the only true dance was spiritual: "a certain proper clapping of good actions and deeds, whose sound goes out into the world and results in the glory of good deeds, an honest leaping by which the spirit dances, and the body rises with good works."[2] Liturgy served to direct the body away from sensual emotions.

The emotive power of Ambrosian chant was vividly recalled by Augustine of Hippo (354–430) who describes how he was "keenly moved by the sweet singing of your church.

Those voices flowed into my ears, truth seeped into my heart and feelings of devotion welled up; tears ran down and it was well with me that they did" (Augustine 1981: 9.6.14, 191). For Augustine, words are sometimes not enough to express the ineffable. Speaking of the long melisma added to the final syllable of *Alleluia* and other chants,[3] he reflects:

> The one who sings the *jubilus* speaks no words for it is a song of joy without words; it is the voice of a heart poured out in joy which tries as far as possible to express feeling even when it does not understand the meaning. When you rejoice in your exultation, you burst forth from certain words that can hardly be said or understood to a voice of exultation without words; so that it seems you are indeed rejoicing but it seems your joy is so great that it cannot be expressed in words.
>
> —Augustine 1956: Ps. 59.8, 1394

Augustine's *Confessions* are shot through with passages about the power of music. In an extended apology for his potential enslavement to music, he celebrates the fact that since his conversion, although he can still enjoy the music of devotional hymns "when sung by well-trained, melodious voices," he is no longer bound to it. He reflects that sometimes he treats music with more honor than it deserves, but comforts himself with the realization that "when they are sung these sacred words stir my mind to greater religious fervour and kindle in me a more ardent flame of piety than they would if they were not sung." He follows this thought by observing that "there are particular modes in song and in the voice, corresponding to my various emotions and able to stimulate them because of some mysterious relationship between the two" (Augustine 1981: 10.33.49, 245–6). Here Augustine is reflecting on the classical understanding of ethics and music where habituation to certain modes helped form specific personality traits, as well as responding to his own lived experience of hearing music. He speaks of truth as an interior melody (4.15.25, 72). Only when he listens to this silent melody is he able to rise above the pleasure of the senses. Augustine knows he must do this in order for his soul to find ultimate joy in contemplation of God.

Augustine first expressed this aesthetic formula, deeply shaped by Platonic thought, in his *De musica*, a foundation text of the liberal arts in the tradition of considering music as a science reliant on number and proportion. The treatise was to contain six books on rhythm and a further six dealing with melody, but Augustine only completed those on rhythm. He began the work in Milan around the time of his baptism when, in his state of spiritual excitement, he was particularly sensitive to the power of music to affect the soul and induce or modify behavior. Augustine reasoned that text and music fuse in the hymn, so that while its music is pleasing to the ears, its words reach into the soul (Augustine 1855: 6.17, PL 32. 1191; Brennan 1988). In Book Six of the *De musica*, Augustine considers the relationship between music perception and the soul with a discussion that focuses on close analysis of the Ambrosian hymn *Deus creator omnium*. His objective in this book was to provide an explanation of how the bodily affects or passions, caused when sound hits the ear, could react with the soul. His central idea—that in animating the body, the soul seeks a harmonious balance of all its parts—was classical. While recognizing that music does have a sensory dimension, Augustine teaches that it also assists the soul to imitate the harmony of number in proportion, thus leading it to the love of God. Since God has created all things, all music—whether good or bad—must contain divine order (Augustine 1855: 6.17, PL 32. 1191). Because number generates music, and God has ordered the numbers, music itself has the power to draw back the sinful and suffering soul to a state of beauty. The *De musica* can be viewed as Augustine's justification for his own emotional response to music, one that he always subordinates to reason.

BOETHIUS AND HIS LEGACY

A very different attitude to music, shaped much more by classical thought than by the Church Fathers, was offered by Boethius. He came to the attention of Theodoric the Ostrogoth and rose to consul in 510. In 522, he was called to Ravenna to become Theodoric's *magister officium*. Aware that the ancient learning of the Greeks was under threat, he translated into Latin a large number of sources that have otherwise been lost. Unlike many of his contemporaries, however, Boethius did not merely repeat classical learning—he was a speculative thinker in the Neo-Pythagorean and Neoplatonic philosophical tradition. Thus, of the mathematical works, his *De institutione musica* is not merely an introduction to *musica*, but a preparatory work for the study of philosophy (Bower 2001). Boethius explained that since human behavior is influenced by music, it is essential to understand and control its fundamental elements by which the body and soul come into harmony. He saw cosmic music (*musica mundana*) as an all-pervading force in the universe which determined the courses of the stars and planets, the seasons of the year and the combinations of the elements.

Boethius believed that music was pivotal for individual well-being and drew on Plato's *Republic* (4.424) almost verbatim to point out the moral dangers of the lascivious modes:

> Plato holds that the greatest care should be exercised lest something be altered in music of good character. He states that there is no greater ruin of morals in a republic than the gradual perversion of chaste and temperate music, for the minds of those listening at first acquiesce. Then, they gradually submit, preserving no trace of honesty or justice—either lascivious modes bring something immodest into the dispositions of the people or rougher ones implant something warlike and savage.
>
> —Boethius 1989: 2

Drawing on Plato's *Timaeus* and *Symposium* as well as the *Republic*, Boethius explained how this occurred. First he promoted the sense of hearing since, of the senses, no path to the mind is as open for instruction, and it alone may "actually find pleasure if the modes are pleasing and ordered, whereas it is vexed if they are disordered and incoherent." Then he elevated *musica* above the three other mathematical disciplines, since it "is associated not only with speculation but with morality as well. For nothing is more characteristic of human nature than to be soothed by pleasant modes or disturbed by their opposites." On the grounds that "likeness attracts, whereas unlikeness disgusts and repels," Boethius explained Plato's analogy (*Timaeus* 35b) in terms of the soul of the universe and musical concord: "Thus, when we hear what is properly and harmoniously united in sound in conjunction with that which is harmoniously coupled and joined together within us and are attracted to it, then we recognise that we ourselves are put together in its likeness" (Boethius 1989: 2–3).

Boethius provided a range of examples that demonstrated the power of music to control the behavior of dysfunctional individuals and render them useful members within the community. In his retelling, it was Pythagoras himself who restored the adolescent of Taormina, drunk and overexposed to Phrygian music, from frenzy to a state of absolute calm by ordering that the mode be changed (Boethius 1989: 5–6). The link between music and feeling was established by Boethius, who explained that just as one's physical state affects feeling, the converse is true, so that our physical state is affected by disturbed states of mind. Here Boethius is hinting that emotions are embodied in the process of sensory reception and response. Although he went no further with this idea, he illustrated it by reference to the way the call of trumpets rouses the passions of those fighting in battle, and suggested that if this is true, it must also be true that "a more temperate mode can calm the wrath or excessive desire of a troubled mind" (8). While Boethius says little about dance, he does suggest that moving to music is innate: "How does it come about that when someone voluntarily listens to a song with ears and mind, he is also involuntarily turned toward it in such a way that his body responds with motions somehow similar to the song heard?" (8).

In the *De institutione musica* there is a clinical detachment between Boethius and the object *musica*. When he deals with sounding music, however, whether real or imagined, there is a warmth of emotional response. In *The Consolation of Philosophy*, Boethius uses music to incorporate some Aristotelian ideas on the practice of music into his predominantly Platonic thinking (Chamberlain 1970). In this dialogue, Lady Philosophy speaks in song and it is her maidservant, *Musica*, who sings "now lighter and now graver measures" (Boethius 1957: 2.1, 18). Her task is to delight and refresh the mind after the labor of rhetorical discourse. Boethius responds by exclaiming how "its sweetness has transfixed me" and reflecting that he has been refreshed both by the strength of the reasoning and the delightfulness of the singing (3.1.1, 37). Neumes attached to the many metrical songs within the *Consolatio* in manuscripts from between the ninth and eleventh centuries suggest that singing was an important part of educational instruction, although this practice seems to have declined in the twelfth century.[4]

During the seventh and eighth centuries, Boethius was much less influential than Pope Gregory the Great (*c*.540–604) who never wrote any treatise on music, but who came to be associated with composing the entire chant repertoire of the Church. Gregory was certainly fond of using musical imagery to illustrate his emphasis on the importance of internal harmony, as in his remarks on Job 40.13 about the bones of Leviathan being like reed pipes, which he interpreted as referring to the dangerous power of outward sound to delight the mind but weaken the heart: "While they sound sweetly to the ears, they weaken the strength of the heart in the flux of pleasure" (Gregory the Great 1985: 32.21, 1659). Gregory used the image of a broken organ pipe as a way of describing of how the body should always be in conformity with the heart:

> And however skilled an expert in singing might be, he cannot do justice to his music, unless external services are also in harmony with it, because, of course, an organ that is broken does not spring back properly for a song, even when it is conducted by an experienced hand, nor does its wind produce an artistic effect if a pipe is split with cracks, and is too shrill.
>
> —Gregory the Great 2004: Letter 5.53a, 226; Martyn 2004

Gregory was more interested in the inner integrity of the cantor than his musical expertise. He was troubled by deacons who were more concerned for "the modulation of their voices" than the task of preaching (Gregory the Great 2004: Letter 5.57a, 389). His warnings against excessive musical display, coupled with the gradual imposition of the Rule of Benedict in monastic life, may have helped encourage a shift in the seventh and eighth centuries away from solo cantors to choral singing.

The authority of Boethius in the study of *musica* only became widely established as a result of the reform promoted by Charlemagne in the late eighth century. Reformers

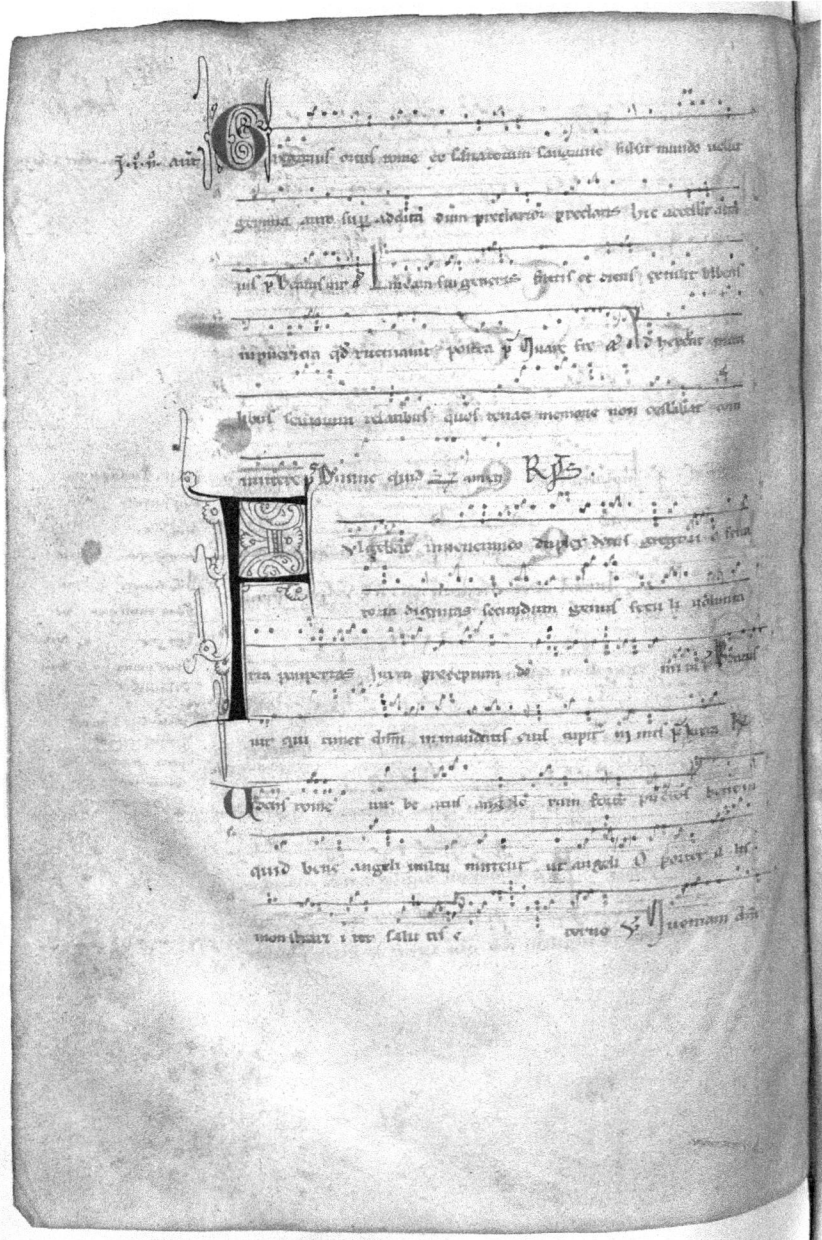

FIGURE 3.1: The responsory *Fulgebat in venerando* showing heighted neumes around the pitch line on F (colored red). This shows an early stage of notation before the staff of Guido of Arezzo. *Antiphonarium Massiliense*, Bibliothèque nationale de France, MS F-Pn lat. 1090, fol. 157ᵛ, thirteenth century.

sought to systematize the body of plainchant that had been transmitted orally in monasteries across Latin Europe, classifying them into one of eight modes or scales, each characterized by a particular melodic shape and final note. Gregory the Great was remembered as having established a *schola cantorum* in Rome, imagined as embodying the ideal of liturgical correctness (Mews 2011). Yet even if this was a great age of innovation in the composition of chant, there was no way of reflecting on their emotional effects without a systematic way of recording their melody. Theorists in the ninth and tenth centuries sought to define the core attributes of what constituted a mode, but remained largely dependent on Boethius for thinking about the abstract nature of music itself in its capacity to lift the spirit more than to stir the body.[5]

GUIDO OF AREZZO AND THE RENEWAL OF CHANT IN THE ELEVENTH AND TWELFTH CENTURIES

A new flexibility in the composition of novel forms of plainchant was made possible in the first half of the eleventh century by Guido of Arezzo, a Benedictine monk and music theorist, best known for his development of a system of precise pitch notation through lines and spaces and for propagating a method of sight-singing that relied on the syllables *ut, re, mi, fa, sol, la*. His *Micrologus* was widely studied throughout the medieval period, not just in monasteries, but also in the University of Paris from the thirteenth century. Next to the *De institutione musica*, it was the most copied and read instruction book on music in the Middle Ages (Palisca and Pesce 2001). Guido assumed the power of music in worship, both for his monastic community and the individual, and understood that power to lie within the classificatory system of *modus* (Atkinson 1988). In the *Micrologus* he linked the expression of meaning and the control of the related emotion of the plainchant text to compositional intent and expressed this with surprising directness: "Let the effect of the song express what is going on in the text, so that for sad things the neumes are grave, for serene ones they are cheerful and for auspicious texts exultant, and so forth" (Guido of Arezzo 1978: 70).

In the preceding chapter "On the Tropes and on the Power of Music," Guido follows closely the pattern set by Boethius, often using the same examples, to support the argument that music had a role to play in the expression of the emotions of the individual. His first example was the familiar story of the physician Asclepiades, who, by the application of carefully selected music, was able to recall a certain madman from insanity (Guido of Arezzo 1978: 69). More telling was his next example: "Also that another man was roused by the sound of the cithara to such lust that, in his madness, he sought to break into the bedchamber of a girl, but, when the cithara player quickly changed the mode, was brought to feel remorse for his libidinousness and to retreat abashed" (69).

In the same chapter, he links particular modes of music to specific character traits so that one man is attracted to the leaping melodies of chants in the Phrygian mode, another to the delightfulness of Hypolydian chants and another to the sweetness of Hypomixolydian chants (Guido of Arezzo 1978: 69).[6] Guido observed that different styles of music suit different individuals, so that:

> what displeases one is cherished by another; and anon, things that blend together delight this man, whereas that one prefers variety; one seeks homogeneity and blandness

in keeping with his pleasure-loving mind; another, since he is serious-minded, is pleased by staider strains; while another, as if distracted, feeds on studied and intricate contortions; and each proclaims that music as much the better sounding which suits the innate character of his own mind.

—Guido of Arezzo 1978: 76–7

Guido's reflection on the subjectivity of human experience of music provided an influential template for encouraging reflection on how music could delight the soul.

The expansion of new monastic communities in the late eleventh and twelfth centuries went hand-in-hand with a flowering of new liturgical writing. Yet there was always a

FIGURE 3.2: Statue of Guido of Arezzo, outside the Uffizi Gallery, Florence, Italy, sculpted by Lorenzo Nencini (*c.*1837). Image courtesy of Wikimedia Commons.

tension between desire for compositional innovation and concern that the core principles of plainchant were in danger of being lost. The founders of Cîteaux, established as an offshoot of Molesme in 1098, were anxious that its monks should confine themselves to chants known in the time of Benedict, a move that eventually promoted a crisis within the order as monks realized that the melodies preserved in the oldest liturgical books they could find (those preserved at Metz) were quite unsatisfying. Bernard of Clairvaux reported this experience in the prologue he attached to a new Cistercian antiphonary developed in the 1140s (Bernard of Clairvaux 1957–77: *Prologus in Antiphonarium*, 3. 515–16; Waddell 1985). Its melodies had to conform to a strict range of rules laid down by the Cistercian theorist, Guy of Eu, summarized in a Cistercian *Tonale* sometimes attributed to Bernard (Maître 1995; Meyer 2003). These included not going beyond a range of ten notes, not mixing authentic and plagal modes in a single chant, and excluding B-flat. Excessive emotion was discouraged. As Bernard put it in a letter to a certain abbot Guido:

> If there is to be singing, the melody should be grave and not flippant or uncouth. It should be sweet but not frivolous; it should both enchant the ears and move the heart; it should lighten sad hearts and soften angry passions; it should never obscure but enhance the sense of the words. Not a little spiritual profit is lost when minds are distracted from the sense of the words by the frivolity of the melody, when more is conveyed by the modulations of the voice than by variations of meaning.
>
> —Bernard of Clairvaux 1957–77: Ep. 398, 8. 378

By contrast, the melodic and emotional range of the melodies of Hildegard of Bingen (1098–1179), who originally grew up alongside the monks of St. Disibodenberg in the Rhineland, did not respect any formal restraints. Liturgical song provided Hildegard with a form of creative expression for her understanding of the spiritual life, encapsulated not just in her hymns and sequences, but in her *Ordo Virtutum* through which her nuns could act out the conclusion to her *Scivias*, her first great visionary synthesis. Soon after Hildegard succeeded in moving her nuns to Rupertsberg, just outside Bingen (*c*.1150), Tenxwind of Andernach criticized her for allowing them to wear extravagant garb on feast days, as if Hildegard was wanting them to act roles assigned to them in the *Ordo*. Her comments suggest this may also have involved sacred dance (Lightbourne 1991).

In the tradition of reformed monasticism inspired by Hirsau, to which Disibodenberg belonged, there was no binding legislation controlling liturgy as in the Cistercian Order. Hildegard felt no inhibition about composing melodies distinguished by leaps far greater than conventional in plainchant, as if addressing extremes of emotional rapture not traditionally articulated. Toward the end of her life, she protested to the ecclesiastical authorities at Mainz against her community being excommunicated for burying a nobleman out of favor with the bishop. The hardest punishment was not being allowed to sing. Adam's voice, before his expulsion from Paradise,

> had the sweetness of all musical harmony. Indeed if he had remained in his original state, the weakness of mortal man would not have been able to endure the power and resonance of his voice . . . The body is the vestment of the spirit, which has a living voice, and so it is proper for the body, in harmony with the soul, to use its voice to sing praises to God.
>
> —Hildegard of Bingen 1994: Letter 23, 78–79

Hildegard's understanding of both music and the body owed more to Gregory the Great than to Boethius, but transformed by the conviction that she could re-create in her own way the voice of Adam in Paradise.

LITURGY, DANCE, AND ECCLESIASTICAL CAUTION

From the time of Ambrose, Christian spiritual writers had used the term *tripudium* (a form of dance) to evoke the notion of joy while condemning secular forms of dance. This hostility toward secular dance was continued by many early medieval preachers who indirectly reveal the persistence of dancing (likely to be of pre-Christian origin) at moments of great festivity during the Church's year. The emotions engendered by such celebrations were perceived as potentially dangerous, if not demonic in character (Mews 2009: 525–7). By the twelfth century, however, we find more positive remarks about dance, as in this passage by Sicard of Cremona, repeating comments made by earlier liturgical commentators:

> And note that the gentiles established circular dances to honor idols, so that they might praise their gods by voice and serve them with their whole body, wanting to foreshadow in them something of the mystery in their own way; for through the circling, they understood the revolution of the firmament; through the joining of hands, the interconnection of the heavens, through the gestures of bodies, the motions of the signs or planets; through the melodies of singers, the harmonies of the planets; through the clapping of hands and the stamping of feet, the sounding of thunder; but what those people showed to their idols, the worshippers of the one God converted to his praise. For the people who crossed from the Red Sea are said to have led a circular dance, Mary is reported to have sung with the tambourine; and David danced before the ark with all his strength and composed psalms with his harp, and Solomon placed singers around the altar, who are said to have produced songs with voice, trumpet, cymbals, organs, and other musical instruments.
>
> —Sicard of Cremona 2008: 6.15, 456[7]

In the mid-twelfth century, John Beleth similarly reports without any reserve the outdoor dancing that took place on certain feasts of the liturgical year, for example on the Eve of the Feast of John the Baptist in midsummer (Beleth 1976: 41A, 137, 267–9). He also describes *tripudia* as dances by clergy that took place during the Christmas celebrations (41A, 69, 130–1). One of them was in the form of a circular dance that took place in certain cathedrals at Easter and involved the throwing of a *pila* or leather ball—a practice attested as late as the sixteenth century in certain French cathedrals (41A, 117a–120a, 219, 223; Mews 2009). In the thirteenth century, William Durand, canon of Narbonne and bishop of Mende, abbreviates Sicard's account, but describes this ritual not as a dance, but as a game played by prelates within their episcopal houses (Durandus 1995–2000: 1.5.14, 62). His comments reflect the increasingly hostile attitude of ecclesiastical authorities to dancing at liturgical feasts, in particular to *choreae* or circular dances being performed at funerals (Denifle and Châtelain 1964: no. 230, 1.230). These critical comments supplement frequent references to the *carole* within vernacular literature between the twelfth and fourteenth centuries. The circular dance continued to be a frequently attested form of entertainment, at least until 1400, within both religious and secular contexts (Mullally 2011).

Musical extravagance inevitably had its own detractors, like John of Salisbury, who lamented that musical virtuosity was degenerating into effeminacy through "womanly

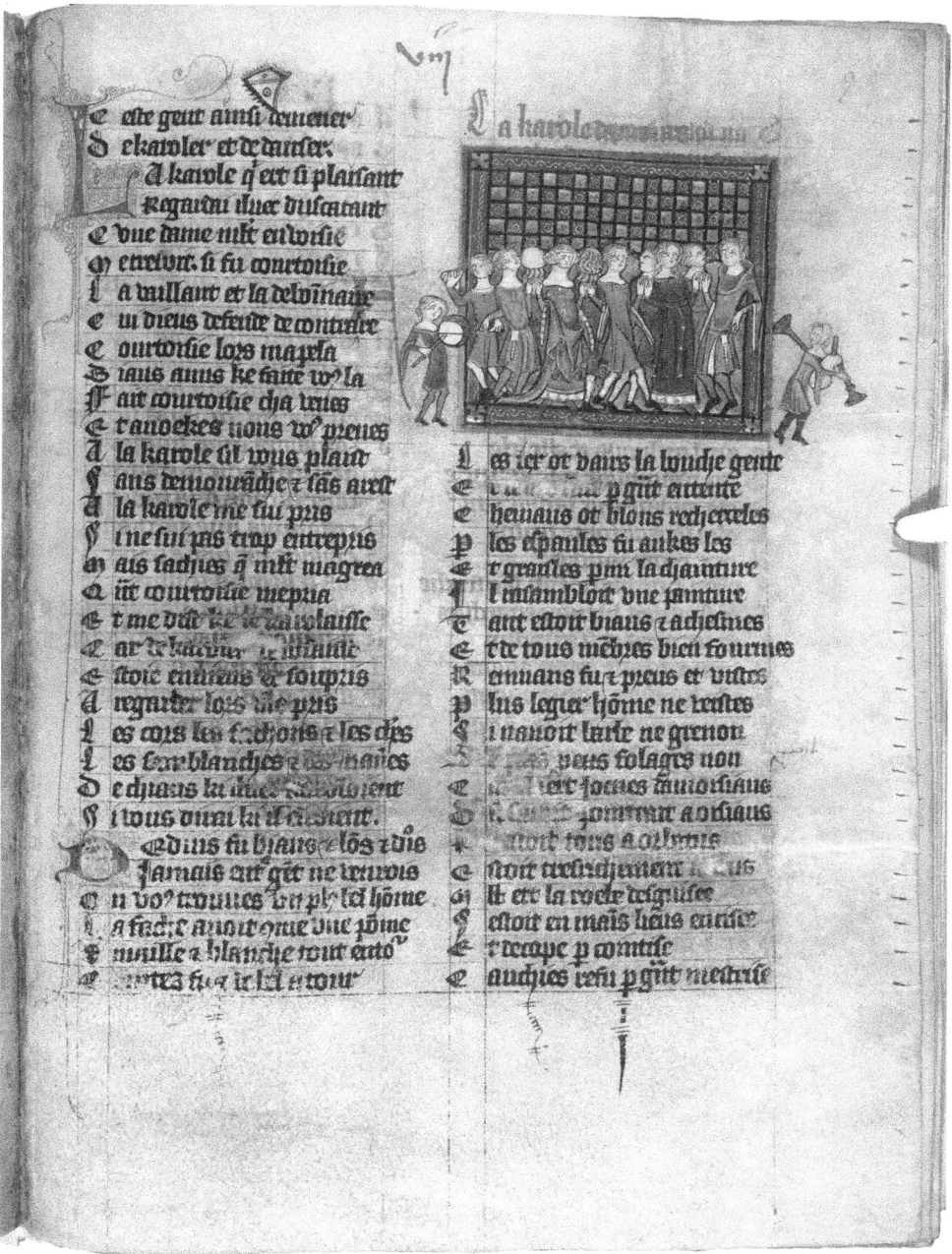

FIGURE 3.3: Detail of Love's Dance (*La karole d'amours*) from the *Roman de la Rose*, depicting ten figures dancing to drum and bagpipes. British Library, MS Royal 20 A XVII, fol. 9ʳ, c.1340. © The British Library Board.

modes of notes" by which certain singers strove to impress during the liturgy, matching songbirds in the facility of their melody (John of Salisbury 1993: 1.6, 48–9; Leach 2009: 30–4). Such complaints imply increasingly sophisticated vocal practices in major churches, such as that of the cathedral at Notre-Dame or chapels attached to a royal court. By the late twelfth and thirteenth centuries, the practice of an early type of polyphonic music based on plainsong (*organum*) involving measured music following a fixed rhythm was introducing very different styles of music from the traditional monophonic *musica plana*, sanctioned by centuries of tradition. Yet while more practical treatises would be written on the subject, such was the authority of Boethius in the theory of music that it took a long time for new ways of thinking to be formulated about its effects on the emotions.

THE IMPACT OF ARISTOTLE IN THE THIRTEENTH CENTURY

When the official curriculum of the University of Paris took shape in the decree of 1215 delivered by the papal legate, Robert de Courçon, *musica* was still part of the quadrivium (along with *arithmetica*, *geometria*, and *astronomia*), taught particularly through the authority of Boethius. Given the great attention in the Arts Faculty on the study of the arts of language, above all dialectic, music received only limited attention, even if students were required to master at least the foundational elements of the quadrivium, studied on feast days, as well as the trivium, studied on ordinary days (Denifle and Châtelain 1964: no. 20, 1. 79).[8] Certain of Boethius's teachings would be challenged, however, in the *Ars musice* of Johannes de Grocheio (*c*.1275), a treatise that sought to discuss the music that was actually being heard in Paris, both secular and religious. Grocheio was fascinated by the project of deepening what Boethius had to say about music by drawing on an Aristotelian conception of music as first of all about sound, "which is found among proper sensibles and is the object of our apprehensive ability" (Grocheio 2011: 0.2, 42). Aristotle's only sustained discussion of music and its effects on the emotions occurs in the eighth book of his *Politics*, a text not known to the Arabs, and so not known to Latin thinkers until William of Moerbeke sent his translation from the Greek to Thomas Aquinas (1225–1274) in the 1260s.[9] Thomas does refer to both Boethius and Aristotle's eighth book of the *Politics* in the *Summa Theologiae* IIa-IIae, 91.2, on which he was working during his last visit to Paris (1269–74), to justify his observation that "the minds of men are disposed in various ways, according to the different melodies of sounds." While Grocheio might have heard indirect echoes of this discussion, he never makes explicit allusion to the *Politics*, whereas he does refer by name to other works of Aristotle.

Grocheio nonetheless criticizes John of Garland and his followers for still following the Boethian tripartite discussion of *musica* as cosmic, human, and instrumental. He sides with Aristotle's criticism of Pythagorean teaching about the music of the spheres in the *De caelo*: "But those who divide in this way either construct their claim or wish to submit to the Pythagoreans or others more than to the truth, or are ignorant of nature and logic" (Grocheio 2011: 5.6, 58). His focus is uniquely on what Boethius called instrumental music, namely that which was audible to the ear: "Nor does it pertain to a musician to discuss the singing of the angels unless perchance when he is a theologian or a prophet. For no-one can have experience of such singing except by divine inspiration" (5.9, 58). Grocheio classifies music by different kinds of acoustic experience, recognizing that types of music are as manifold as idioms, tongues, and cities, or regions. His proposal is to classify music according to what he knows as the use of the people of Paris, dividing this into one branch that he describes as simple or civic, calling it music of the people (*musica vulgalis*), another that is regulated or measured (*musica mensurata*), and a third ecclesiastical branch that draws on both simple and measured forms of music (6.1–2, 60).

Grocheio's reclassification of music according to different genres modeled on the taxonomic principles he had absorbed from Aristotle's *De animalibus* enabled him to acknowledge the important flowering in the twelfth and thirteenth centuries of secular vernacular song within the troubadour and trouvère lyric repertoire. The first specific song that he refers to and which survives today is *Ausi com l'unicorne*, a *grand chans* or, as Grocheio would have it, a *cantus coronatus* attributed to the trouvère, King Thibaut of Navarre (d. 1253). He considers this a genre that celebrates boldness and bravery "and makes for good government" (Grocheio 2011: 9.4, 69).[10] *Ausi com l'unicorne* is a particularly fine example of the *grand chans*, with five stanzas and an envoy, and an unusual allegorical style on the theme of Love's prison. The form demonstrates a clever interweaving of number patterning with seventy-two syllables per stanza. Grocheio has chosen this work as an example of the music of the people—vernacular music—since through "its mediation, the innate trials of humanity may be softened" (9.1, 67).

Grocheio was one of the earliest music theorists to write approvingly of the music associated with dance in secular society. He offers no hint at choreography other than to explain that dance is measured both by the beat of its music and the movement of the performer (Grocheio 2011: 12.5, 73). It was not until the mid-fourteenth century that the fashion for dance manuals emerged, describing how music and dance worked together. This was not Grocheio's interest and his discussion of the dance focuses rather on its function in society. Thus, for example, the sung *estampie* "makes the spirits of young men and women focus on it because of its difficulty and diverts them from depraved thought," and the sung *ductia* "draws the hearts of girls and young men and takes them away from vanity and is said to be effective against the passion which is called love sickness" (9.7, 9.8, 69).

Grocheio's emphasis in talking about these vernacular songs is more on their role in influencing the collective behavior of groups, rather than their impact on individual emotions. His major concern is to describe different types of music—not just popular song and polyphony, but also ecclesiastical music, which he sees as building on these two categories. Underpinning this classification is a vision of the human person as unlike the angels in having physical needs, "such as eating, drinking and sleeping." For that reason, a person needs to worship God at particular times, celebrating the feasts of the liturgical year (Grocheio 2011: 22.3, 90). Grocheio comments on the role of the various elements of the liturgy in moving the faithful to increased devotion. The role of the hymn, for example, is "to rouse their hearts and minds and exhort them to devotion" (27.7, 100). In Grocheio's perspective, music, whether secular or religious, has a function within the community, but is no longer, as it was for so many earlier medieval thinkers, simply an echo of a cosmic or celestial harmony. Grocheio's rebuke to followers of John of Garland for continuing to believe in the notion of cosmic music situates him as a committed Aristotelian at a time when many still followed the authority of Boethius.

In 1270, Bishop Stephen Tempier was so alarmed by the extent of the influence of some readings of Aristotle that he outlawed certain propositions which he believed to be gaining ground in the Faculty of Arts, issuing a much expanded list of 219 heretical propositions in 1277 (Denifle and Châtelain 1964: no. 432, 1. 486–7; Thijssen 1998).

Doctrinal disagreement and divisions within the University of Paris created a three-year schism that only ended when Siger of Brabant was expelled from the kingdom of France in 1275. In his place as dean of the Arts Faculty and thus rector of the University, the papal legate appointed Peter of Auvergne, a senior cleric of the Arts Faculty and canon of Notre-Dame. Peter of Auvergne's strategy to end the schism was to promote the authority of Thomas Aquinas not just as a theologian, but as a philosopher. To this end he completed Thomas's unfinished commentaries on the *De caelo* and *Politica*. Grocheio belonged to a similar generation as Peter Auvergne, committed to promoting an Aristotelian perspective, though without the detailed knowledge that Peter would introduce by expounding the eighth book of the *Politics*.

Peter of Auvergne was profoundly influenced by the teaching of Aquinas that the passions were not disturbances of the soul, but integral to human behavior, ethically dangerous only when taken to excess. In a quodlibetal discussion delivered in 1301, Peter explores the role of "primary qualities" in the body, namely wet and dry, hot and cold, which are normally in balance, but which can create differing emotional states in different situations (Hentschel 2000).[11] Peter extends these reflections, shaped by a strong interest in physiology, to musical harmonies. He makes few comments on particular forms of music besides claiming that the second and eighth ecclesiastical tones stimulate feelings of compassion or mercy. For this reason, the tract and other chants of the Office of the Dead (*cantus mortuorum*) favor these tones.

Aristotle's discussion about music in the eighth book of the *Politics* had been focused around its impact of music on the young. In his quodlibetal discussion, Peter moves to an area that Aristotle had never considered, its impact on the individual soul. Music could legitimately provoke the soul to a sense of rapture. Peter goes beyond Aristotle in reflecting on the personal impact of different types of music. He declares that vocal music is superior to instrumental music, acknowledging that "a well-proportioned musical *harmonia* strengthens moral behavior ('valet ad mores'), but a poorly proportioned one has the contrary effect" (Hentschel 2000: 420). Following Aquinas, Peter accords particular attention to the emotion of delight or pleasure (*delectatio*) as a passion that is not sinful in itself, but rather directs the soul to the highest good.

These ideas, which are attributed simply to the "expositor" of the *Politics*, are elaborated by Guy of Saint-Denis in a chapter of his *Tractatus de tonis*, which seeks to combine theoretical discussion of the nature and effect of the eight tones (into which all chant can be classified) with practical instruction on their melodic character. Guy was particularly interested in what Peter had to say about the soul's appetitive or desiring part as stimulated by the senses in the same way that the will (or intellectual appetite) follows the intellect (Guy of Saint-Denis 2017: 1.4.1, 57).[12] The sensitive appetite varies in individuals according to their particular disposition of qualities (1.4.2, 59). Just as some people are hotter, others colder in disposition, thus some are bold, some jealous, and some wrathful (1.4.2, 59). By the various proportions making up different kinds of music, so is there an impact on the differing constitutions of the human soul, mediated through varying moods (1.4.2, 61). Guy speaks about not just the musical form of a chant, but its capacity to provoke raptures of emotion, occasionally moving beyond the limits of a tone at moments of great intensity:

> Sometimes composers of chants of this kind rush into a kind of unrestrained ascent, either because of the sweetness of the melody they contain, or sometimes because of the matter on which chants of this kind are based. It is just as if they suffer a certain

excess of mind or ecstasy in the manner of lovers or those rejoicing or sometimes of the sad and those who mourn.

—Guy of Saint-Denis 2017: 1.3.20, 51

He continues to provide further examples of chants that step beyond the limits of the tones in order to express specifically an intense emotion. Although Guy's style can sometimes be repetitive and a little pedantic, passages such as this bring the experience of chant to life. While Guy's treatise never circulated outside Saint-Denis, it articulates a broader transformation evident in Latin discourse by the early fourteenth century. Human emotions were now seen not as a disturbances of the soul, but as an integral part of human nature and thus central to the experience of music.

CONCLUSION

Our knowledge of music and dance in Europe between the fourth and early fourteenth century is inevitably extremely selective, since so many melodies were simply transmitted orally, without being recorded in writing. Nonetheless, it is evident that profound changes did take place, especially in the twelfth and thirteenth centuries, involving increased awareness of the need for theoretical reflection to take into account the world of practice. Music and dance had always served as a powerful vehicle for emotional expression. In the twelfth century, we see the beginnings of greater theoretical recognition of the capacity of music (and to a very limited degree of dance) to serve liturgical ends. There was no clear agreement, however, about far how they might do so. By the thirteenth century, vernacular literature opens a window on secular culture that Latin literary culture is unable to provide. Among ecclesiastical authorities, there was always concern that some forms of music and dance might have a distracting influence, creating disturbances of the soul in a way that a later generation might describe as excessively emotional. Yet there were also theologians like Thomas Aquinas who challenged the notion that emotions were inherently sinful, drawing on increased awareness of the teaching of Aristotle. By the early fourteenth century, passions of the soul were being perceived as integral to human identity and experience. Music, whether secular or religious, could be seen not only as articulating cultural values, but as a powerful way of stirring both the heart and the body.

CHAPTER FOUR

Drama

SARAH BRAZIL

The moment in Late Antiquity where we begin our study was a period in which the concepts of emotion and drama were in a state of flux, and both would change irreparably by the turn of the fourteenth century. In line with the Christianization of predominantly Stoic theories of emotion, the foundations on which the dramatic practices of ancient Rome were built had already begun to shift significantly by the time Constantine legalized Christianity in the 313 Edict of Milan. The effect such changes would have on drama cannot be underestimated, though neither should the continual influence of classical models on future forms of dramatic composition. The defining differences between drama in the late antique world and that which developed from principally Christian environments cannot be established in relation to either the level of interest in emotion or how feeling might be conveyed—the critical distinction lies in the purpose served by the emotions, not the emotions themselves.

Identifying the ways emotion was performed in drama across the years 350–1300 cannot be easily reduced to a set of anticipated modes of expression. Such a lack of conformity undoubtedly stems from the enormous variety and variability of drama to be found across such a large period of time. The purpose of this chapter is consequently to offer an entry point into how such a question was approached by the many playwrights in this period. Temporal as well as geographical features play a role, as do the influences taken up by the crafters of dramatic texts. Drama could use music, gesture, or language to convey particular emotional states, but even the same types of drama do not strictly adhere to one mode or another.

Like art, drama in this period could draw on codified gestures and stylized expressions of emotion, particularly ritualized ones, as in the case of grief or sorrow. Such conventions must be taken into account and contextualized in order for their full dramatic value to become apparent. Playwrights could choose for dramatic purposes to locate emotion in facial expressions, which is seldom the case for art in this period. Alternatively, music could signal the emotional climax of proceedings, as it did in certain liturgical sequences, and highly emotive language could convey the feelings of characters even when music did not follow the trajectory of the action. What a reader of drama from this period must bear in mind, then, is to set aside expectations.

The development of drama from 350 onward is necessarily marked by Christian perspectives. Although this impacts the extent to which late antique drama can be heard on its own terms, it is an accurate reflection of the tensions developing between the Church and popular entertainments, the result of which would be the suppression of Roman forms of drama. Moreover, the types of commentaries on Roman drama considered in this chapter inadvertently allow access to the emotional impact of performances on the audience, evidence that is largely missing from later dramatic counterparts. While giving different, and often indirect access to late antique drama, such commentaries also offer tantalizing evidence suggesting that emotional engagement with drama was valued as much in this period as it would later be.

DRAMA OF THE LATE EMPIRE: MIME, PANTOMIME, AND CHRISTIAN DENUNCIATION

The Christianization of the Empire was to change the landscape under which Roman dramatic performances had previously thrived, though this was not immediately the case in practice. Roman entertainments, including dramatic forms, lingered for several centuries across the Empire, but by the seventh century had largely been suppressed, if they still were in practice at all. The forms of drama that prevailed from the late fourth century are perhaps slightly unexpected. Indeed, the dramatists that spring to mind when one thinks of Roman drama—Plautus (c.254 BCE–184 BCE), Terence (195 BCE–159 BCE) or even Seneca (4 BCE–65 CE)—were themselves antiquities by the mid-fourth century. Ronald W. Vince notes that "The last recorded performance of a new Roman play was in 31 B.C.," and that "By the first century of the Christian era, mime and pantomime had replaced the literary drama" (Vince 1984: 73, 79). These newly dominant forms, themselves descended from ancient models of comedy and tragedy, are at the heart of many polemical stances on drama, often for varying reasons. T. D. Barnes offers a succinct definition of both, outlining core differences between each one:

> The *pantomimus* was a solo performer, always a man, who played both male and female roles; he danced, without speaking or singing, to the accompaniment of a choral ode; and the subject matter was mainly mythological, though it might sometimes be historical . . . In contrast, mimes were performed by several players, female as well as male; the performers spoke and sang, usually without a chorus, but did not dance; the plots were taken from or modeled on everyday life.
>
> —Barnes 1996: 169

Both forms remained at the center of Roman Christian life for at least two centuries after Constantine, and Barnes points to the fact that "theaters were built in Constantine's new and aggressively Christian city of Constantinople" to confirm their continued relevance in the Christianized Roman Empire (1996: 164).

Pantomime had long been recognized as a form of drama that was emotional and emotive. The second-century rhetorician Lucian (c.125–after 180) wrote the tract *On Dancing* in order to discuss the moral value of pantomime. He describes one of the strengths of the dancer as the ability to embody and convey a wide variety of emotional states depending on the story at hand:

> In general, the dancer undertakes to present and enact characters and emotions, introducing now a lover and now an angry person, one man afflicted with madness, another with grief, and all this within fixed bounds. Indeed, the most surprising part of it is that within this the selfsame day, at one moment we are shown Athamas in a frenzy, at another Io in terror; presently the same person is Atreus, and after a little Thyestes; then Aegistus, or Aerope; yet they all are but a single man.
>
> —Lucian 2008: 393

Lucian's criteria for pantomime are bound with the capacity of the dancer to capture the specific emotive power of each myth and to express this clearly to the audience via gesture. The sheer range of emotions conveyed by an individual is a testament to his capacity to excel within generic specifications, and Lucian distills each episode to the defining emotion of a specific character, be it grief or anger. Edith Hall notes that the

FIGURE 4.1: Lid of a box, fragment, ivory. Thalia, Muse of Comedy with lyre, masks, and sword, Trier. Antikensammlung, Staatliche Museen zu Berlin, 2497, fifth century. © bpk / Antikensammlung, SMB / Ingrid Geske.

Greek rhetorician and grammarian Athenaeus's account of a famous dancer, Pylades, "described [his] dancing style as exalted (*ogkōdēs*), and emotive (*pathētikē*)—two terms which had long since been associated with the tragedy of Aeschylus and Euripides respectfully" (Hall 2008: 10). This overlap of terminology relating pantomime to classical tragedy signals the new genre's capacity to arouse emotion, and it is on these grounds that church authorities would launch attacks.

Augustine's hostility to pantomime, among other dramatic forms, is a supreme example of the Church's condemnatory stance on Roman drama. His rejection of enacted performances of mythological characters and pagan gods is unsurprising; what is noteworthy is that the ground on which he builds his argument is emotional impact, elsewhere thought to be intrinsic to the success of such performances. The abuse of spectators' emotional faculties was considered one of the predominant reasons why such entertainments needed to be rejected by the conscientious Christian. In Book Three of the *Confessions*, Augustine derides the redundant evocation of Christian emotions such as compassion (*misericordia*) in the face of human suffering, because there is no possibility of performing acts of kindness in response to the elicited inclinations:

> But what is the real meaning of compassion in imaginary events and stage plays? The audience is not being summoned to assist, but merely invited to feel distress; and the deeper their distress, the more they appreciate the performer of those representations. If, on the other hand, the usual human disasters, either historical or fictitious, are performed in a way that does not cause the spectator to feel distress, that spectator walks out in critical disgust—whereas if they do feel distress, they stay in their place, completely absorbed, and revel in their own weeping.
>
> —Augustine 2014: 1. 93–5

In the midst of decrying such practices, Augustine admits that an audience's barometer for dramatic success resides in the capacity of the performer to move the audience to an emotional response. Yet what such an audience, and the young Augustine himself, considered to be excellent drama is what incurs the mature bishop of Hippo's scorn. Donnalee Dox argues that Augustine identifies such emotional responses to fiction as "superficial" and "vicarious" (Dox 2004: 14). Furthermore, Augustine frames his spectatorship of drama as part of the misuse and misdirection of his affective faculties. This emotional outpouring is dismissed as redundant.

In a different sphere of the dramatic spectrum lies mime, designed to provoke laughter from its audience by presenting comic scenes "often centred on sexuality and slapstick within the context of adultery" (Foka 2015: 69), or by performing parodies of the ancient gods (Weiss 2004: 29). With such an initial description of mime, it might seem a rather base form of drama. Ruth Webb, however, cautions against such simplistic readings, instead claiming mime as a powerfully subversive cultural force: "The mimes' depictions of transgressions, sexual and otherwise, and their depiction of 'licit and illicit things,' shone a pitiless spotlight on the boundaries between the acceptable and the unacceptable in society, revealing, in the process, that those boundaries were constructed on fictions and conventions" (Webb 2008: 137).

Webb's careful examination of the place of mime within the social fabric of the late antique world reverberates in relation to the manner in which performances evoked and provoked specific emotional responses from audiences. Once again, this capacity incurs staunch rejections, but surprisingly, also engenders defenses. Among the detractors once again are church authorities, with Augustine and John Chrysostom, archbishop of Constantinople, writing vehement condemnations of the theatrical spectacle. Chrysostom's attack is aimed at Christians who attend Roman entertainments such as chariot races and drama, and is preserved in the sermon titled *Against those who have abandoned the church and deserted it for hippodromes and theaters*. Like Augustine, Chrysostom suggests that emotional responses to drama undermine the faith of Christian spectators. He specifically mentions the presence of women on stage, who were known to perform in the genre of mime (the Empress Theodora had in fact performed mime before marrying the Emperor Justinian). Their acting is argued to enflame the flesh of the male spectators with desire (*epithumias*), leading to what Chrysostom terms "the destruction of temperance" (*sōphrosunēs*) (Chrysostom 1862: 267). The result is the enslavement of the unwitting spectator by lust long after he leaves the theater.

Augustine is equally severe in relation to mime in his *Confessions*. As Webb notes, his discussion of such performances not only considers their capacity to provoke laughter, but also their ability to entice audiences to "empathize and identify with the characters and their forbidden desires" (Webb 2008: 136). As in the case of drama with a tragic subject matter, such empathic responses prove equally troublesome:

> but back then, at the theaters, I used to be united with the lovers in their pleasures, when they were reveling in sinful behavior though they were playacting the misdeeds on the stage for entertainment. When the protagonists got themselves lost, it made me feel sad as if I was full of real pity. Yet both contrasting cases caused me to experience delight.
>
> —Augustine 2014: 1.95

Augustine's retrospective narration of his misspent youth highlights the thoroughly unchristian experience of emotion aroused through watching illicit love affairs. What is remarkable about this example, however, is the emotional complexity that Augustine articulates, which follows the reversal of fortune the stage lovers undergo. The likely discovery of an affair causes the youth to feel sadness ("*contristo*"), but their previous condition causes him joy ("*congaudeo*"). The verbs chosen further express the responsive nature of these emotions, as "*congaudeo*" is a form of joy that is contingent on being shared with others, while "*contristo*" conveys the effect of sadness of an external force upon a specific object. The prefix *con* (or *cum*) emphasizes that these emotions are defined by their ability to be shared by a group. Their oppositional nature, moreover, is further complicated by the sum of their parts, which for the young Augustine is an overall feeling of delight ("*delecto*"). But undermining this summative emotion is its inadequacy; what one should feel for those unaware of their sinfulness, Augustine contends, is pity.

While mime had its detractors based on emotional grounds, it also had defenders whose rhetorical strategies were not radically dissimilar. Choricius of Gaza, writing his *Apologia Mimorum* in the sixth century, challenged the church condemnations and legal prohibitions that targeted the practice. Such prohibitions expressed an increasing hostility to mime upon moral grounds, which culminated in it being officially banned under the Emperor Justinian (Foka 2015: 68; see also Krueger 1906). Choricius's strategy of defense, however, was to argue that mime shows were moral affairs with a pertinent educational value. As Foka explains: "while mimes are broadly based on adultery . . . the committers of these moral faults are always punished at the end" (Foka 2015: 74). Following this predictable plot-line, Choricius argued that such outcomes had the effect of "societal shaming through punishment," which in turn was argued to have "a disciplinary effect upon its audiences" (74). Choricius insisted that the power of mime to shame spectators led to moral edification. Contrary to Augustine and Chrysostom, then, such an argument pushed for a defense of mime based on its targeted evocation of emotions.

Whether condemnatory or celebratory, the responses to Roman drama that have been briefly discussed were often based on direct experiences of such performances. Later Christian condemnations of drama would not relate to the practice as an "institution and a cultural practice" but as a "historical category" (Dox 2004: 37). As Dox puts it, "Medieval thought [would place] ancient theater solidly in the realm of society, idolatry, and representational perfidy" (58). It would take the refashioning of dramatic practices in unprecedented ways to recuperate drama as an imaginative mode which had a viable place in a predominantly Christian world.

THE TRANSITION TO MEDIEVAL DRAMA

Scholarship of medieval drama has often been reticent to make any links between the drama of Late Antiquity and what was to emerge from both inside and outside of the monasteries of western Christendom. The general narrative has tended to insist on complete severance rather than to nuance the many links that remained between the old forms and the new. Such a fragmentary narrative does a great injustice to a complex and under-documented period, and what evidence does exist suggests greater complexity still. Roman dramatic forms continued to influence dramatists who mined the works of Terence, among others, for elements of style and even plot that they could integrate into their own works. Stylistic and formal influences are not the only points at which the drama of Late Antiquity and the Middle Ages overlap, however. While Church Fathers were vehement in their rejection of drama on the basis of its capacities to evoke particular emotions and desires within an audience, the various genres of drama that emerged from the ninth to the thirteenth centuries were keen to draw on the language and gesture of emotion in their performances, as well as relying on music in certain instances to convey feeling. Indeed, once the subject matter shifted to a Christian context, the value of emotions was weighted along different criteria. This is not to say that emotion in the plays was never unproblematic, but that the types of censure issued by the likes of Augustine and Chrysostom were no longer applicable in the Christianized West.

LOCATING EMOTION IN LITURGICAL DRAMA

The way in which emotion was integrated into liturgical performances is something that varies widely from sequence to sequence. What must be borne in mind, however, are the high levels of stylization which intentionally remove such performances from the realm of naturalism. One of the earliest and most widespread liturgical plays, the *Visitatio Sepulchri*, first recorded in the tenth century, offers tantalizing evidence as to where emotion can be found in such a performance. However, it also cautions us to bear in mind the liturgical parameters within which such a performance was crafted and to expect codified emotive displays. Musicologist Susan Rankin writes of the astounding success of this early monastic composition, noting that by the end of the tenth century "it had been integrated into the liturgies of institutions in southern and central France, southern England, and along the Rhine in German-speaking countries, as far east as St Gall" (Rankin 1990: 311). This sequence, which involves a sung antiphonal exchange between the three Marys and at least one angel, was performed either before the Introit of Easter Mass or before the closing hymn of Matins (313). In spite of the sequence's frequent brevity, it is an evocative piece, capturing the transition from despair to joy, enacted through the revelation of the Resurrection. In relation to the earliest extant version of the sequence, recorded in the Aquitaine Troper (first half of the tenth century), Rankin identifies the emotional climax of the play as lying in its musical structure:

> The high points in the musical composition are in fact literally those where the melody moves away from its otherwise low tessitura: for the angel's words "Non est hic surrexit" and for the women's response "Alleluia resurrexit Dominus." With both musical climaxes emphasizing announcements that Christ is risen, the object of the entire dialogue emerges as the communication of this news to the celebrating community . . . the celebratory "Alleluia" is not just that of the Marys returning from the tomb . . . but of all those present in the church.
>
> —Rankin 1990: 312–13

The purpose of performing the movement from despair to joy is to carry those present along a similar trajectory.[1] As Rankin indicates, the power of these ritualized emotional displays is that all present can share the experience. Indeed, the *Regularis Concordia*, a tenth-century treatise that prescribed regulations for all English monasteries and convents in accordance with Benedictine Rule, records the earliest English *Visitatio Sepulchri* and emphasizes this point in its own account of proceedings: the congregation should be "rejoicing *with* (the women) at the triumph of our king" ("*congaudens pro triumpho regis nostri*") (Bevington 1975: 28). What is being described, via the term "*congaudens*," is strikingly similar to the experience of theater that Augustine recalls with the sole purpose of condemnation. Drama, then, is circumscribed in both instances as something designed to provoke specific emotional responses in an audience. The difference here, and one that Augustine would likely approve of, is that emotion in the *Visitatio Sepulchri* is directed toward God.

Other ways in which emotion was performed in the *Visitatio Sepulchri* were also integral to the power of the sequence, with gesture regularly taking a central role. The clearest examples are those where a specific emotional state was mediated in performance. The initial movements of the various Marys, as seen in the directions in the *Regularis Concordia* and the Fleury Playbook, do exactly this. The English manuscript details that they are to begin the sequence by moving "haltingly, in the manner of seeking for something," ("*pedetemptim ad similitudinem quaerentium quid*"), while in Fleury they "go forward haltingly as though sorrowful" ("*pedetemtim et quasi tristes*") (Bevington 1975: 27, 39). These movements imply the absence of a clear trajectory in both a physical and spiritual sense. The lack of fluid motion, a stock theological motif for spiritual disorder, is used to great effect within the frame of liturgical procession. The disjointed motion achieved via the stopping and starting is, as the Fleury example demonstrates, intended to convey sorrow, loss, and spiritual malaise. The power of this sequence, however, lies in the sudden reversal of such a condition, showing that the depths of despair can quickly turn to joy through the intervention of the divine.

FIGURE 4.2: The Three Marys at the tomb, Benedictional of Aethelwold, British Library, Add. 49598, fol. 51ᵛ, 963–984. © The British Library Board.

EXTREME EMOTION IN LITURGICAL DRAMA: GRIEF AND ANGER

Some of the most evocative pieces of drama created throughout the high Middle Ages took inspiration from scriptural events that centered on intensely emotional experiences. In addressing this tendency, John Stevens invokes the "angry Herod" and "mourning Rachel" as key examples (Stevens 1986: 348). Both characters embody excessive emotional responses to particular events, but in the case of Rachel, this extreme display is not completely censured, though neither is it sanctioned. Unlike Herod, whose emotional register ranges from sequence to sequence but is likely to attract systematic condemnation for his heinous acts, Rachel's scenario is more difficult to evaluate. On the one hand, she is regularly compared with the Virgin Mary in her sorrow for her lost son, and yet she is continually reproached for crying by at least one interlocutor. The ways in which several liturgical dramas respond to the challenge that both excessive emotions provide, then, is indicative of the place of such emotion within frameworks that cannot simply be reduced to theological or devotional.

To begin with the example of Rachel is also in many ways to begin with the Virgin Mary, for it is difficult to assess the responses that grief might have engendered in one without a comparison with the other. The sung complaint of Mary, the *Planctus Mariae*, was performed in numerous liturgical plays from the high to late medieval period, and expressed the depth of the Virgin's sorrow at the death of her son. This established tradition of maternal sorrow gained steady ground only in the twelfth century—by contrast, many early Church Fathers had insisted on a "vision of a Virgin firm and resolute on the Golgotha" (Sticca 1987: 50). Indeed, the Virgin's own emotional experience throughout Christ's Passion was an issue of theological speculation: the death of her beloved son, and his salvation of the world as a consequence of this death, resulted in many theologians theorizing that she simultaneously experienced a "natural *grief* (*dolorem*)" and "a supernatural *joy* (*gaudium*)" (Sticca 1987: 51). This complex response to grief taps into what Jan Ziolkowski terms "the Christian ambivalence about the death of children" and death in general (2010: 95). The early Church reacted harshly to elaborate ritualized mourning practices, particularly around the Mediterranean, but, as historians note, they were largely unsuccessful in stopping such culturally ingrained responses to death (Nagy 2000: 44). However, the Virgin Mary, a figure capable of embodying the paradox of virgin and mother, was also able to take on the role of a grieving mother who was beyond reproach. In grieving for her son, Mary became instead a model of Christian piety:

> To dwell upon the sufferings of Jesus was an exercise encouraged by many Christian theologians from late antiquity and later. Even as theologians condemned sorrow . . . many argued for the conscious cultivation of a private and interior contrition (wholesome or "fruitful sorrow") that was essential to penance . . . Lamentation could be part of penance, which was itself a means of reaching God.
>
> —Ziolkowski 2010: 90

The *Planctus Mariae*, originally a separate piece that was "probably to be performed on Good Friday during the adoration of the cross" (Ziolkowski 2010: 100), was integrated into numerous Passion plays and Ziolkowski points out that "the laments of Mary have been credited as being the first steps toward dramatization of the Passion" (99). An example, thought to date from the thirteenth century though recorded in a fourteenth-century manuscript, manifests the power of such a performance. Alongside 127 lines of sung lament, the manuscript includes "seventy-nine indications of gesture that appear above the lines to which they pertain. Characters beat their breasts eighteen times in lamentation. Other gestures of despair or misery include striking the hands together, dropping the hands limply, putting hands to the eyes, and wiping away tears" (100). The extraordinary expressiveness of this culturally codified display of grief might elsewhere have incurred church sanction, yet as these recognizable gestures were directed solely toward God, they instead proved to be exemplary.

While the lament of Mary flourished within liturgical dramas of the later medieval period, by contrast the lament of Rachel faded from the thirteenth century onward (Boynton 2004: 319). Yet in the eleventh and twelfth centuries, Rachel's role in the plays containing the Massacre of the Innocents was so substantial as to lend her name to it, as in the Freising *Ordo Rachelis* (late-eleventh century). This play, as well as the *Slaughter of the Innocents* episode recorded in the Fleury Playbook (twelfth century), drew on a ninth-century sequence composed by the monk Notker the Stammerer of St. Gall. This sequence, often praised as the most beautiful of the forty sequences of Notker's cycle, features the figure of Rachel and at least one other interlocutor. The ensuing dialogue highlights the complex and numerous theological roles that the figure of Rachel embodied. Here Rachel occupies the role of a literal, grieving mother, functions as a type of Mary (*virgo mater*), and fulfills the allegorical role of *Ecclesia* allotted to her in medieval exegesis (Boynton 2004: 320). Furthermore, as her interlocutor insists, the death of her own son must be connected to the death of Christ and his life-giving salvation.

The plays that draw on this sequence inherit much of the complexity that surrounds the figure of Rachel. Her excessive grief, exhibited in her incessant crying, makes her a figure that can simultaneously engender empathy and censure. For the twelfth-century theologian Aelred of Rievaulx, Rachel is an example of the will imperfectly controlling the affect and the interior battle that results: "Attachment demanded sons, but reason resisted attachment, so that [the sons] might not be recalled" (Aelred of Rievaulx 1990: 152, 1855: 542: "*Affectus filios requirebat, ne revocarentur, affectui ratio obsistebat*"). Piroska Nagy and Damien Boquet add: "Therefore, according to Aelred, love solely according to reason and love solely according to emotion exist, but they are incomplete as long as reason and emotion do not combine their forces in the same movement" (Boquet and Nagy 2015: 207–8). The ideal scenario therefore, and precisely what Rachel does not illustrate, is a balance between reason and emotion, thus marking her refusal to be consoled as contrary to reason.

The *consolatrices* (consolers) in the Fleury *Slaughter of the Innocents* embody much of the tension inherent in responses to Rachel as they offer tenderness in the midst of censure. In this episode, Rachel's grief culminates in a swoon, after which two *consolatrices* support her before she falls. Despite such a tender gesture, the grief of Rachel remains problematic, and in the very act of carrying her, the figures reprimand her ("*Consolatrices excipientes eam cadentem dicentes*"). Akin to the theological issue of whether Mary experienced both joy and sorrow during Christ's Passion, the Fleury *consolatrices* impose a similarly complex internal response on Rachel: "Do not, virgin Rachel / restrain your tears of sorrow. / Although you grieve, rejoice that you weep. / For, truly, your sons live blessed above the stars" (Bevington 1975: 70).[2] While she is not told to cease crying, Rachel's tears are transformed through interpretation into signs of joy. The rest of the play's action supports this transformed meaning. It does not end, as in Freising (and Notker's sequence), with a sustained focus on the grief of Rachel, but shifts to a tableau of the holy family's escape to Egypt, before the sung exultation "*Gaude, gaude, gaude, Maria Virgo*" closes proceedings (Bevington 1975: 72). The interpretation of ephemeral death as eternal life underlines the reading of joy in sorrow, yet the inconsolable figure of Rachel herself precludes a wholly unproblematic resolution to the action.

The "Magi plays" (or *Officium Stelle*) which were performed as part of the liturgical office regularly feature the kind of emotional disjuncture that the Fleury *Slaughter of the Innocents* encapsulates. The anger of Herod is often structured in opposition to the joy of the other characters, with all emotions stemming from his hearing the angel's prophecy of Christ's birth. The excessive display of emotion is thus a sign that this character, as with Rachel, lacks adequate control over his emotional faculties. The manner in which Herod's anger is conveyed varies from play to play. Unlike the biblical verse Mt. 2.16–18, in which his anger manifests only after the realization that he has been tricked by the Magi, in the liturgical plays Herod often displays anger in their presence. There is evidence, however, that such portrayals of excessive emotion are shunned. Rankin notes that "The Rouen play gets rid of Herod altogether," while "Two of the three Nevers versions omit Herod's discussion with his scribes, and several versions do not have the final Compiègne episode showing the enraged Herod ordering his soldiers to kill the young children" (Rankin 1990: 324). Nevertheless, a multitude of liturgical sequences do feature a *Herodes iratus* who frequently performs his anger through stylized gestures that indicate his lack of control over it.

Hans-Jürgen Diller has observed that "Herod's wrath [leaves] no noticeable effects on the other characters . . . it is merely an expression of his evil disposition which is directed against the newborn king" (Diller 1992: 43). The critic also points to the fact that most of Herod's furious actions are contained within stage directions: "In the Montpellier manuscript and in Bilsen he brandishes swords, in Fleury and Freising he throws the prophetic books to the ground, but in none of these plays does the dialogue betray any symptoms of emotional disturbance" (42). This conflict between Herod's gestures and the effect they have upon the action of the play points to the importance of stylization over plot coherence. More important in the eyes of the crafters of these plays is the singularity of Herod, who is often circumscribed by this overwhelming and dramatically alienating passion.

An exception to this otherwise valuable observation is found in the aforementioned Fleury *Slaughter of the Innocents*, which features a Herod whose rage is particularly

FIGURE 4.3: Battle of Patience and Anger (*Pacienciam ira percutit gladio*), Prudentius, *Psychomachia*. Bibliothèque du Palais des Arts, Lyon, MS 22, fol. 7ʳ (lower), eleventh century.

violent. Having been told that the Magi have tricked him, Herod responds by attempting suicide. This action is described in a stage direction: "*Then let Herod, as if demented, having seized a sword, contrive to kill himself; but let him be finally prevented and pacified by his followers [as he is] saying*: Let me quench my burning vehemence by destroying myself!" (Bevington 1975: 68).³ The actions Herod performs in trying to kill himself are evident in his speech, further circumscribing his character as at the mercy of this violent rage.

This curious attempt at suicide is reminiscent of Prudentius's early fifth-century allegorical poem, the *Psychomachia*, in which the battle between Patience and Wrath ends with a victory for Patience after Wrath kills herself. Patience is characterized as being in perfect equilibrium, both in terms of interior and exterior. Her face is described as "*vultu . . . inmota*," meaning that her expression is immovable, and her breast (which encapsulates the heart, considered the seat of emotion from as early as Galen (130–210 CE)) is termed "calm" ("*securo pectore*"). Patience displays no response to either internal movements or external stimuli. Wrath, in opposition, is circumscribed by the overwhelming presence of one emotion. She is physically presented as swelling ("*tumens*") and foaming at the mouth ("*spumanti fervida rictu*"), and her anger is further evident in word and action, as she berates Patience by weapon and speech ("*teloque et voce*") (Prudentius 1949: 1.286). Wrath, moreover, proves to be entirely self-destructive, and after failing to pierce the implacable armor of Patience, turns her sword on herself. The destructiveness of this overwhelming emotion can thus be linked to Herod's own experience of it at the news of the birth of Christ. That suicide is the only perceived solution of the Fleury Herod to his fury at the Magi's actions equates him with the allegorical figure of Wrath. He is a character whose reason is incapable of controlling his emotions and, as with Rachel, proves to be exemplary in his failure to do so.

HROTSVIT OF GANDERSHEIM AND THE ROMAN LEGACY

Terence had a complex reception throughout the Middle Ages. His six plays had long been standard texts in Latin instruction and this function continued from the classical through to the medieval period (Augoustakis 2013: 398). While Church Fathers such as Jerome were firm supporters of Terence, the Roman playwright did not escape the Christian censure aimed at other forms of classical drama. Even though Augustine considered these works preferable to the theater of his own day, he nevertheless objected to Terence's depiction of immoral and shameful conduct (Zampelli 2013: 152). In spite of, and also because of the ambivalent status of drama in her own time, Hrotsvit of Gandersheim took up the models of this condemned genre in order to prove it capable of service to her Christian agenda. Katharina Wilson compares Hrotsvit, abbess of a Benedictine monastery in the tenth century, with Jerome and Augustine who had used pagan literary traditions for Christian purposes. In doing so, Wilson argues that Hrotsvit adopted dramatic exemplars "for apologetic and instructive purposes—as weapons to defeat an opponent on his own grounds" (Wilson 1988: 85). Hrotsvit's plays are an extraordinary product of tenth-century Christian devotion and "mark an important moment in the history of Western theatre" as she revised the genre to produce plays that were themselves beyond reproach (Zampelli 2013: 155). Hrotsvit is all the more remarkable when one considers that liturgical drama had not yet reached her cultural milieu by the time she had penned her six plays (this number is likely in line with Terence's own corpus), thus leaving her without a Christian form of drama to draw on for guidance (Wailes 2013: 122). Indeed, unlike the sung verse integrated into liturgical proceedings, Hrotsvit's plays are composed in rhymed prose intended to be spoken and may have been designed, at the very least, for performance through recitation. Moreover, it is important to keep in mind that her monastery was not some remote backwater; among a prospective audience or readers could be counted the Holy Roman Emperor, Otto I, and his court, as well as Brun, archbishop of Cologne, and Wilhelm, archbishop of Mainz (McMillin 2013: 323).

Hrotsvit's engagement with emotion and its intended manifestation in her plays is strikingly different from the drama developing elsewhere in tenth-century Europe. Beginning in her Preface, Hrotsvit gives insights into the role that emotion will play in her writings. Throughout this Preface she employs a sophisticated modesty topos in order to justify her groundbreaking compositions. The manner in which she does so, however, displays an acute attention to the concept and experience of modesty itself. Indeed, one might surmise that such a posture is necessitated by Hrotsvit's dramatic subject matter. Her plays feature a sustained interest in desires of the flesh and its negation through chastity. Hrotsvit explains the drive to engage with such themes as deeply ambivalent, causing the chaste abbess much embarrassment ("*verecundari*") which she explains is manifested through blushing ("*rubore*"). Despite such difficulties, however, she insists that it was necessary to overcome her own modesty ("*erubescendo neglegerem*") (Hrotsvit 1970: 233) in order to reach her object which is "to glorify the innocent to the best of my ability" (Hrotsvit 1923: xxvii). Hrotsvit uses this rhetoric of emotion with great care, first by eliciting the image of her own blush and then by displacing it in the service of the women who were so often degraded and silenced in Terence's plays. This stance, moreover, continues throughout the more traditional modesty topos. In explaining her experience of composing such texts, Hrotsvit writes that she has been "torn by conflicting affections" ("*Inter haec diversis affectibus*") (Hrotsvit 1970: 236). This conflict, she claims, arises from her dual role as conduit of God and dramatic innovator: "I rejoice from the depths of my soul that the God through Whose grace alone I am what I am should be praised in me, but I am afraid of being thought greater than I am" (Hrotsvit 1923: xxix). Hrotsvit, as a woman composing in a genre in an unprecedented way, is careful not only to situate her authority in relation to God in a precise emotional capacity (joy), but also draws on this device in order to anticipate and reject being honored as an authority in her own right (fear). The dialectic between joy and fear works to mitigate any attacks that might be leveled at her for her dramatic endeavors. Such self-effacing claims are as carefully constructed as the tried and tested topos of modesty. As a woman and servant of God, it is a fitting and necessary stance to take because, as Linda A. McMillin asserts, Hrotsvit is "aware of the audacity" of her dramatic output (McMillin 2013: 311).

Unlike the careful and often unnatural stylization of liturgical drama, the feelings of Hrotsvit's characters are often located in eminently readable facial expressions. Her play *Gallicanus* provides an excellent example. Here the Emperor Constantine's face proves to be the site where other characters gain access to his emotional states. Confronted with the task of having to marry his chaste daughter Constance to his most valuable general, Gallicanus, Constantine's expression is described by Constance as "strangely grave and sad" (Hrotsvit 1923: 6, 1970: 246: "*solito tristior*"). Constantine states that he is greatly distressed, and in repeating the emotion "*tristitia*" (sadness) confirms that his daughter has correctly read his emotional condition. This tender interaction between father and daughter evinces their intimacy and the emotional proximity between the two ensures a happy outcome for both. Similarly, Gallicanus, who is to be converted to Christianity, is also marked as a positive character by his own capacity to read emotions correctly. He does so upon Constantine's return from consulting with his daughter. Noting with hope that the Emperor's expression is now "serene and glad" (Hrotsvit 1923: 8, 1970: 248: "*vultu admodum sereno*"), Gallicanus interprets this change as potentially indicating a favorable response to his marriage request. Indeed, in a citation borrowed from Jerome, Gallicanus explicitly places the outward manifestation of emotion in the face according to common wisdom: "It is said that the face is the mirror of the soul" (Hrotsvit 1923: 9, 1970: 248: "*ut dicitur, speculum mentis est facies*"). While Constantine's relaxed expression does not indicate what Gallicanus had hoped for, it is the beginning of a happy resolution for all, and the conversion of the general ensures a life devoid of fleshly pleasures.

The other key use of emotion in Hrotsvit's corpus is evident in plays of virgin martyrdom. In *Dulcitius* and *Sapientia*, the martyrs are characterized as joyful in the face of torture, looking beyond transitory pain to the bliss of everlasting life. Sapientia, the mother of three martyred daughters, reassures Faith: "Oh, my daughter . . . I am not dismayed—I am not distressed! I bid you farewell rejoicing. I kiss your mouth and eyes, weeping for joy" (Hrotsvit 1923: 146).[4] The calm resolution of all martyrs opposes the fury of the pagan powers that persecute them. Indeed, Hrotsvit's virgins are precisely what Rachel fails to be—with a focus resolutely on heaven, their emotional condition of serene joy identifies them as fitting brides of Christ. Via the medium of drama, Hrotsvit foregrounds the path to eternal life, which for the abbess was consistently found through the defense of chastity against all earthly obstacles.

PERFORMING EMOTION IN THE ELEVENTH AND TWELFTH CENTURIES

There are a host of medieval plays that shun generic categorization and this last section will be devoted to three of them, including the Hildesheim *Tres filie* (manuscript from first half of eleventh century), Hildegard of Bingen's *Ordo Virtutum* (*c*.1151), and the *Jeu d'Adam* (recorded in a mid-thirteenth-century manuscript but itself likely mid-twelfth century). All plays could have been performed inside a church, but no records of performance survive to locate any of the three precisely. What unites this collection of plays, however, is that they integrate emotion into their performances, although each one offers a different perspective on how this can be achieved, whether via gesture, facial expression, music, or thematically.

Tres filie can be generically linked to the saints play, although it also exhibits sufficient liturgical features for critics to surmise that it could have been performed within church space (Dronke 1994: 53). It tells the story of the good deeds of St. Nicolas, whose earliest Latin *vita* was composed by John, Deacon of Naples (*c*.875), itself used to produce a liturgy just before 966 (Dronke 1994: 53). Peter Dronke notes that the saint had a "flourishing existing cult" in Hildesheim and that Nicolas was the patron saint of the local bishop, Godehard (1022–1038) (53). However, the extant text is located "amid scholastic, not liturgical, texts," so practical issues related to performance remain speculative (62). The plot of the play is intricately linked to the emotional condition of the father, which provides the structure around which the rest of the action operates. It opens with his expression of distress at his family's impoverishment. He then implores his daughters for advice, and each gives her best council to relieve his suffering. The dialogue, moreover, is

FIGURE 4.4: Ambrogio Lorenzetti, *Miracle of the Poor Youth, Scenes of the Life of Saint Nicholas*, c.1332. Galleria degli Uffizi, Florence. Image courtesy of Wikimedia Commons.

designed to convey the love between father and daughters, with each speaker using some form of the address "*cara*"/"*care*" (dear one, beloved) throughout.

Although the first daughter's advice is offered as a means of stymying the father's lamentations, in suggesting that she will prostitute herself for the good of the family, she only exacerbates her father's emotional turmoil. His heart is now "griefstricken" ("*cor lammentabile*"), his body to be shattered by the sighs of hers (Dronke 1994: 67.32–35). Instead of resolving the grief of the father, the first daughter suggests a scenario where her suffering and degradation will not be limited to her body. The second daughter reiterates this notion of contagious distress, advising her father "not to heap sorrows upon sorrows" ("*doloribus dolores addere*"), and not to secure eternal as well as ephemeral misery (67.37). In turn, this advice "pleases" ("*placet*") (67.51) him, as does that of the third daughter who declares that "those who fear God lack nothing" ("*Nichil enim . . . deum timentibus*") (69.61–2). Her final plea not to despair ("*Neu desperes*") (69.66) is then followed by the intervention of St Nicolas, and his gift of gold. The father then leads the rejoicing ("*gaudete*") (70.81), and the final words of the play are directed toward God, "*Te deum*." The movement from despair to joy, connecting earthly love to eternal love, is achieved through the progressively excellent advice of the daughters, which leads to the intervention of the saint. Indeed, the family are rewarded for isolating the correct emotional stance to take—to fear God, shun despair, and avoid shameful sorrow.

Hildegard of Bingen's *Ordo Virtutem* is an altogether more lavish affair than the domestic drama of *Tres filie* and features an epic battle for the salvation of the soul. The reversal of the initial condition of the allegorical figure Anima (the Soul) is established in directions that accompany the speech headings. Beginning as "Felix Anima," she quickly becomes burdened by the weight of attaining salvation and begins lamenting ("*conqueritur*"). This reversal in condition is compounded by her designation as "*Infelix Anima*" (Dronke 1994: 162). Dronke notes that these "guiding phrases" are likely "directions to the singer of the role of Anima to convey these emotions by her voice and bearing" (153–4). Moreover, the extent to which a character's emotional state or moral condition is evident in their vocal performance is emphasized by the fact that the Devil is the only character who does not sing, but instead shouts at Anima ("*Strepitus . . . ad Animam*") (164). Unlike liturgical drama, where musical notation can often efface extreme emotion, Hildegard's *Ordo* intertwines the one with the other. In this drama about the soul finding its way to the love of God, which in essence describes the function of the faculty of the affect, Hildegard makes the role of emotion integral.

The *Jeu d'Adam* features vernacular dialogue accompanied by copious Latin stage directions. It was possibly performed in a church or even a cathedral and offers enticing indications of how emotion might be performed in the twelfth century (Chaguinian 2015: 382). Evidence demonstrating the role of facial expressions is found in the first section of the adjacent Latin text, which gives remarkable details related to performance. Indeed, one of the first directions mentions a screen that only allows the audience to see the actors' bodies from the shoulders up ("*possint videri sursum ad humeros*") (Bevington

FIGURE 4.5: God confronts Adam and Eve, mosaic, Cathedral of the Assumption, Monreale, Sicily, twelfth–thirteenth century. © Professor Richard Stracke.

1975: 80). The importance of the face, then, is tantamount. Indeed, we are told as much a few lines later, for Adam is said to stand closer to God than Eve, with a "peaceful countenance" ("*vultu composito*"); Eve's face, meanwhile, is said to be "not quite sufficiently humble" ("*vero parum demissiori*") (80). Although the instructions regarding facial expressions are vague, they are intended to convey an interior state that is related to the main action of the Fall: as well as her physical positioning, Eve's facial expression clearly foreshadows her susceptibility to temptation.

Meanwhile, correctly performed gestures, prescribed within these Latin directions, carry the most evocative moments of the play. At the moment of the Fall itself, gesture is vital to the meaning of the action. Unusually, Adam and Eve are dressed at the beginning of the play. Once Adam eats from the apple, he disappears behind the screen in order to strip off his clothing of paradise and instead "put on poor clothes sewn together with fig leaves" ("*induet vestes pauperes consutas foliis ficus*") (Bevington 1975: 96). The timing of this vital costume change performs the loss of grace, and calls on an exegetical tradition of a lost original garment in order to express the catastrophic change to the embodied and spiritual condition of the first parents (Brazil 2015). Their own despair in response to this change is also conveyed through specific actions and postures. They are to "hide in a corner of paradise, as if knowing how wretched they are" ("*latebunt in angulo paradise, quasi suam cognoscentes miser[i]am*"), and when they stand in front of God, they are no longer upright, but "somewhat bent forward and extremely sad" ("*aliquantulum curvati et multum tristes*") (Bevington 1975: 98). Both of these postures are invested with precise meanings, connecting interior emotional states to exterior bodily manifestations and allowing the audience to access the internal distress of the first sinners.

CONCLUSION

As the discussion of various forms of drama from 350–1300 has shown, emotion is regularly central to dramatic performance. This prevalence of emotion in drama should come as no surprise, given that drama is an imaginary form that relies heavily on the presence of bodies in order to communicate the narrative. Bodies are undeniably defined by their capacity to feel—to love, despair, grieve, rejoice, be angry or ashamed. All the plays discussed use the body to convey emotional states, whether stylized or not. All bodies, regardless, are circumscribed by the codifications produced by particular societies or inherited from others. Yet other factors are also crucial to the performance of emotion in pre-fourteenth-century drama. Music has been shown to have an especially important place in conveying particular feelings or emotional states, but equally it can be unreflective of moments of extreme and heightened emotional intensity. The dynamism of the dramatic output that has been considered across this chapter should stand as a testament to the vivacity and variety of theatrical forms before the mystery, morality, or saints plays of the later Middle Ages, which often overshadow their earlier counterparts. In the history of how emotion was performed in drama, this extraordinary collection of texts and commentaries should not be overlooked.

CHAPTER FIVE

The Visual Arts

KATHERINE M. BOIVIN

It is easy to overlook emotion in the visual arts created in Western Europe between 350 and 1300 CE. With notable exceptions, faces remain impassive, and it is primarily in stylized gestures that emotions can be read. But what at first glance may appear an artistic disinterest in emotion is actually a carefully constructed and complex approach to emotion, the experience and nature of the soul, and the belief in redemption.

Of course, the experience of emotion was as much a part of medieval life as it was of life in any other culture. Medieval men and women felt joy and despair, love and anger, fear and hope. However, these emotions, as well as the manner in which they were externally displayed, were socially constructed within their particular cultural context (Rosenwein 2002, 2010; Rubin 2009: 80; Meyer 2013: 9). In the visual arts of medieval Europe, ostensible emotion only appeared in a limited number of scene types. In these, emotion primarily functioned in the service of narrative or moral judgment. Only in the last two centuries of our period did attitudes toward emotion shift considerably and images become more emotive.

The relationship of emotion to the visual arts, as it was both depicted in images and elicited in response from the viewers of images, was conditioned by shifting cultural contexts. Gestures that looked the same might in different contexts express different ideas or emotions. Therefore, instead of attempting to identify specific emotions and their visual expressions, this chapter sketches general consistencies and changes in the approach to emotion over the course of the millennium. In doing so, it aims to raise relevant considerations for the further study of emotions in the art of the medieval period.

The era from 350 to 1300 may be roughly divided into three artistic periods: the art of the fourth through seventh centuries, generally classified as late antique or early Christian art; early medieval art of the eighth through eleventh centuries; and the art of the high Middle Ages of the twelfth and thirteenth centuries. The culmination of many of the trends discussed in this chapter falls in the late medieval period (fourteenth and fifteenth centuries) and so will be covered in the following volume of this series, having been briefly prefigured here.

The Oxford English Dictionary defines emotion as "Originally: an agitation of mind; an excited mental state. Subsequently: any strong mental or instinctive feeling, as pleasure, grief, hope, fear, etc., deriving esp. from one's circumstances, mood, or relationship with others." The connection of emotion to the mind rather than simply the body is important and we shall return to it below. In her book *Emotion and Devotion*, Miri Rubin takes the OED's list of emotions as a point of departure: joy, love, anger, fear, happiness, guilt, sadness, embarrassment, hope (Rubin 2009: 80–1). This list, coupled with the four principal emotions discussed by Augustine in the fifth century—desire, joy, fear, and grief—provide a basic framework from which we will work, though the list could be greatly expanded and nuanced (Augustine 1972: 551).

As a modern culture, we are conditioned to look for emotions in the face, but in the visual arts of medieval Europe, emotions were rarely displayed through facial expressions before the 1300s (Sauerländer 2006: 3, 17). Instead, gesture played a critical role in communicating the emotional content of a piece. Much of the scholarship on emotions in medieval art has approached the topic through an exploration of the role of gesture. The work of Moshe Barasch characterizes typical medieval gestures and their communicated emotions as they relate to and differ from the tradition of antique art (Barasch 1976, 1987). François Garnier's book *Le Langage de l'image au Moyen Âge: Signification et symbolique* (1982) acts as a handbook for identifying the meaning of a wide range of gestures and postures with the premise that gesture functioned as a legible visual language. Gestures, however, often had multifaceted communicative roles, making them difficult to interpret precisely without consideration of their particular context. Indeed, in medieval art, gesture can function to communicate action, express emotion, and pronounce judgment all within the same image. To untangle one function from the other is not only tricky, but risks reducing the intended complexity of the image.

Many formulaic gestures expressing emotion were adopted from classical imagery during the medieval period. These gestures were adapted repeatedly, on the one hand to suit a wider range of contexts and meanings, and on the other to address changing theological agendas. Consequently, gestures lost in precision but gained in communicative complexity. The variety of gestures found in classical art was reduced to a more limited corpus, but individual gestures appeared in a wider range of contexts (Barasch 1976: 20; Steinhoff 2012: 39).

As Barasch has demonstrated, the many violent emotional gestures found in late antique art appeared in a more limited range of contexts as the Middle Ages progressed. From the sixth through twelfth centuries, dramatic gestures were extremely rare in the visual arts with the exception of a period during the ninth century commonly called the "Carolingian Renaissance." During this period of revived interest in antiquity, the depiction of emotions following classical models experienced a brief resurgence (Barasch 1976: 23, 34). In many ways, it was in the Carolingian Renaissance and subsequent Ottonian period that many of the image types destined for the later depiction of emotion began to develop. The ties between this early medieval art and Byzantine art have been explored by numerous scholars, but the role of depicted emotions in the relationship between these artistic cultures deserves further study. Although it falls outside the purview of this series, it is worth noting that the depiction of emotions in Byzantine art has recently received some attention (Maguire 1977, 2012; Meyer 2013). This scholarship offers an excellent starting point for further study of emotions in the art of the West.

It is striking that many of the clearest representations of emotion, as well as the clearest elicitations of emotive response to medieval art in Western Europe, take the form of image types developed around or after the year 1300: the Pietà (the image of Mary mourning over the dead body of her adult son), the Man of Sorrows (the image of Christ presenting his wounds) and the Sorrows of the Virgin Mary (the image program depicting scenes from the life of Mary and Christ in which Mary sorrowed). These new image types, however, relate closely to shifting trends in the twelfth and thirteenth centuries and cannot be understood in isolation. Scholarship has appropriately focused on the cultural context for these images, including textual sources as well as related devotional practices (Ziegler 1992; Büttner 1983; Decker 2008; Weilandt 2007).

Broadly stated, perhaps the most general trend over the course of the millennium under study was a shift from an intellectual approach to the religious image toward a more emotive approach. The serene pastoral image of the Good Shepherd gave way to the ominous scene of the Last Judgment. The triumphant, upright Christ on the cross became a suffering, sagging corpse.[1] As emphasis on Christ's divinity gave way to an exploration of his humanity, emotions—both depicted and elicited—played a more central role in the visual arts. Above all, this shift engendered a changed relationship between beholder and beheld, viewer and image. In place of a concern that visible signs of the divine might be read and understood intellectually came an interest in the power of mimesis—the affective association of the devout viewer with Christian heroes. Particularly through religious images, medieval viewers were encouraged to contemplate, approach, or better understand the order of the world and the nature of the divine. As we shall see, emotion played an important role, particularly in the art of the high Middle Ages, in engaging the viewer in this discourse.

For the purpose of this chapter, I have chosen to focus on a selection of religious scenes with unambiguous emotional content, whether explicitly stated in the source texts, clearly implied by the story, or apparent from the corpus of images themselves. They are also image types that have engendered some of the most important scholarship to date on emotions in the visual arts of the period. In what follows, I will begin with a discussion of how emotion was depicted through the use of gesture in medieval art, specifically in scenes of the Massacre of the Innocents. I will then consider more closely how the representation of emotion could act to pronounce judgment on the subjects of the depicted scene and, by implication, on the viewer, specifically in scenes of the Fall and the Last Judgment. Finally I will explore the idea of mimesis, the expectation that the pious viewer should experience the emotions represented in an image as a way of approaching the divine, specifically in images of the Virgin Mary.

GESTURES OF EMOTION: THE MASSACRE OF THE INNOCENTS

The representation of emotion in medieval Europe inherited much from classical antiquity. In part, this may be because the externalized expression of emotion during the period looked much like the display of emotions at other times or in other places. The practice of mourning the dead in medieval Italy, for instance, shared much in common with mourning practices of earlier antique cultures as well as with contemporary practices of the Byzantine Empire (Gertsman 2012; Meyer 2013). Not only was mourning primarily the purview of women in these cultures, but it also seems to have involved similar formulaic gestures of grief such as tearing the hair, beating the breast, and wailing.

Many of the gestures common in actual mourning practices also appeared in the visual arts of the medieval West. One of the scenes in which classical gestures expressing emotion was most commonly employed throughout the period in question was the Massacre of the Innocents. In his Gospel, Matthew tells the story of King Herod who, threatened by the tidings that a new king had been born in Bethlehem, sent soldiers to kill all male children two years old or younger:

> Then Herod, when he saw that he was deceived by the wise men, was exceedingly angry; and he sent forth and put to death all the male children who were in Bethlehem and in all its districts, from two years old and under, according to the time which he

had determined from the wise men. Then was fulfilled what was spoken by Jeremiah the prophet, saying: "A voice was heard in Ramah, lamentation, weeping, and great mourning, Rachel weeping for her children, refusing to be comforted, because they are no more."

—Mt. 2. 16–18

Like most medieval images, representations of this story generally communicated emotional content through hands, not faces. While Herod is described in the text as "angry," it is interesting that this anger is often left out of medieval images of the Massacre. Instead, the emotional focus is on Rachel and her fellow mourning mothers. As a narrative device, this emphasizes the consequence of the Massacre rather than its instigation, but it also reserves the expression of emotion for women rather than men. In high medieval art, Herod's anger does occasionally receive indirect expression in the exaggerated features with which he is rendered. These features—a large hooked nose, darker skin, or a grimacing mouth—also categorize devils and Jewish people during the same period and, as we shall see, belong to a deep-seated belief that the external expression of extreme emotion reflects an evil soul. More consistently, however, it was the wild gesticulations of a group of huddled mothers that became the focus for the depiction of externalized emotion.

In an illumination from the Ottonian Codex Egberti (tenth century), for instance, the scene is shown with dramatic gusto (see Figure 5.1). At the left, the crowned "Herodes" points his soldiers toward a group of rotund, nude male infants at the center. Under the heading "*pueri occiduntur*" ("children are killed"), half of the boys already lie slaughtered with heads severed and breasts pierced. The remaining three children seem to float for a frozen moment between the advancing soldiers and their distraught mothers. The four representative mothers stand huddled in a group before the gates of "Bethleem" at the right of the image. One woman reaches out both hands toward her son. Another turns away and covers her face with her hands. The remaining women appear frazzled, having bared their chests and uncovered their hair. One looks away, her hands raised palm-outward, while the last sinks to her knees, holding her clenched fists to her chest, either pulling her hair or beating her breast.

From both the social context and the visual tradition, it is clear that the gestures of the women in this image communicate intense emotion. The biblical text indicates that the emotions express lamentation and mourning, but it is difficult to affix a precise term to the represented emotions. In his book on the language of the image in the Middle Ages, for example, Garnier identifies the gesture of both arms raised with palms facing outward as an expression signifying astonishment or fear.[2] In the image of the Massacre, the corresponding emotion for this gesture might more appropriately be termed grief or sadness, but whatever the signified emotion, the gesture clearly expresses a strong negative reaction to the killing.

Read from left to right in this manner, the scene unfolds in three stages: Herod's order, the massacre, and the emotional response of the women. Laura Jacobus has pointed out that representations of the Massacre of the Innocents that divide the story into three scenes share much in common with the earliest known dramatic performances of the Massacre from the eleventh century. The texts of these dramatic *Ordo Rachelis*, which were typically performed by clerics in Latin, presented the Massacre as part of God's plan (Jacobus 1999: 39–40). The mourning of the women, who thought only of their immediate loss, not of the redemption to come, became a warning against excessive emotion.

THE VISUAL ARTS 87

FIGURE 5.1: Slaughter of the Innocents. Stadtbibliothek/Stadtarchiv, Trier, Codex Egberti, MS 24, fol. 15ᵛ, tenth century. Photograph: Anja Runkel.

The passage of Jeremiah's prophecy quoted by Matthew in his account of the Massacre of the Innocents not only acts as a typological link between New and Old Testament stories, but also sets up the negative evaluation of the mourning women during the Massacre. With its following verse, the passage reads:

> Thus says the Lord: "A voice was heard in Ramah, lamentation and bitter weeping, Rachel weeping for her children, refusing to be comforted for her children, because they are no more." Thus says the Lord: "Refrain your voice from weeping, and your eyes from tears; for your work shall be rewarded, says the Lord, and they shall come back from the land of the enemy."

—Jer. 31.15–16

God thus admonishes Rachel and, by implication, the mourning mothers at the Massacre, since their children will be redeemed. The women, with their excessive wailing, will not be comforted even by God and the promise of salvation. The medieval audience of the Codex Egberti illumination, conditioned by actual mourning practices and the tradition of visual representations of mourning to read the gestures of the depicted women as intensely emotional, would have understood the negative implications of the scene.

To complicate matters, however, a second, positive reading might be added to the grieving women of the scene. While the dramatic performances of the *Ordo Rachelis* generally emphasize the inconsolability of the women as a negative, the audience was simultaneously encouraged to draw a parallel between the sadness of the mothers and the sorrow of the Virgin Mary at her son's crucifixion. This sorrow was a positive emotion, inasmuch as it affected the pure and blameless Mother of God. The conflicting implications of these two associations—on the one hand the negative commentary on excessive emotion as evincing disbelief in salvation, on the other the positive connection to the virginal Mother of God caring for her son—make interpretation of depicted emotion in scenes of the Massacre of the Innocents complex (Jacobus 1999: 44).

The use of liturgical dramas for the interpretation of images has proven fruitful, particularly for the art of the twelfth century and later (Sauerländer 2006: 11; Barasch 1987: 11). Though rare, the inclusion of stage directions, for instance, can provide clues regarding specific gestures that were used in both dramatic performances and artistic renditions of a biblical story. The applicability of these dramatic texts, however, depends on the context. Jacobus has shown that in general in the later Middle Ages, the focus of images of the Massacre of the Innocents strayed away from the theological implications articulated in contemporary dramas (Jacobus 1999: 43).

Representations of the Massacre of the Innocents accompanied by wailing mothers appear throughout the thousand years from the fourth through the fourteenth centuries and in a range of media: an ivory plaque in Berlin (*c*.410–20) includes distressed mothers as witnesses of the massacre, as does Giovanni Pisano's marble representation of the scene from the pulpit of the church of San Andrea in Pistoia (completed in 1301) (Weitzmann 1979: 446–8, entries 406, 407; Carli 1986). Over the course of the millennium and across a large geographic area, the witnessing mothers are depicted with a range of expressivity and emotional intensity. During the Carolingian Renaissance (ninth century) and other periods of revived interest in classical arts, renditions of the scene seem to increase in dramatic expressivity. At other times, the gestures of sorrow remain more restrained, recounting Matthew's narrative without displaying extreme emotion. Differences may relate in part to the shifting balance between positive associations with Mary and negative associations with emotional women (Jacobus 1999: 44). The most dramatic representations of despair appear in images of the Massacre from the end of our period, and from the fourteenth and fifteenth centuries when Mary became increasingly important. Reasons for this are closely connected to cultural changes such as the rise of mystical movements and the new interest in mimesis which will be discussed further below.

JUDGMENT OF EMOTION: ADAM AND EVE AND THE LAST JUDGMENT

From the start, Christianity adopted and adapted the Stoics' emphasis on the virtue of moderation, a value that strongly conditioned the role of emotions in the visual arts as well as in other domains (Largier 2008: 365). With the Christological belief that the greatest joy (or greatest sorrow) was to come after judgment in a second life, extreme displays of emotion were quickly interpreted as evidence of a sinful or troubled soul. Emotion was not considered an involuntary sensation, but an act of will for which a person might be judged. In his *City of God* (early fifth century), Augustine writes of the four

> most familiar disturbances of the mind: desire and fear, joy and grief, which may be called the origins of all sins and moral failings . . . The important factor in those emotions

is the character of a man's will. If the will is wrongly directed, the emotions will be wrong; if the will is right, the emotions will be not only blameless, but praiseworthy. The will is engaged in all of them; in fact they are all essentially acts of will

—Augustine 1972: 551, 555; see also Wetzel 2008: 350

With this understanding of emotion as consensual and tied to the blameworthy or praiseworthy nature of the will, the depiction of emotions in the visual arts of the medieval period became a means of communicating more than just a feeling or experience: it became a visualization of the morality of the subject.

We have already encountered examples of how the expression of extreme emotion, such as the inconsolable wailing of the mothers of the Innocents, might be construed as negative. Those who truly believed in Christ's resurrection would recognize that the joys and sorrows of human life on earth were temporary. This negative assessment of excessive emotions was articulated by numerous early Christian and medieval writers, including Ambrose (fourth century), John Chrysostom (fourth century), and Alcuin (eighth century) (Barasch 1976: 35). Only two types of intense emotion were truly laudable: grief at one's own sins, and the unconditional love of God (Maguire 2012: 8). These emotions were virtuous, but they were also hard to depict. It was important that such timeless and honorable sentiments not be confused with quotidian emotions that arose in response to particular moments or events which demonstrated a "wrong" will; moreover, although these positive emotions were absolute and supreme, they should not mistakenly be read as overpowering or excessive.

The medieval solution to this conundrum in the visual arts was to depict with composure those who loved God. Since saints and holy figures were virtuous, there was no need to show their grief at sins committed. The experience of the divine, which was a higher, spiritual sensation than earthly emotions, was depicted as resolute calm. Using the example of the painted cycle of Berzé-la-Ville (first half of the twelfth century), for instance, Gil Fishhof has argued that since spiritual exaltation resulted from the presence of God, the notion of joy might be conveyed simply through the position or gaze of figures arranged in an image program (Fishhof 2013: 29, 32). Of course there were changing fashions in artistic style that at times add beauty, elegance, or even an angelic smile to these depictions of divine love, but, for the most part, medieval happiness, joy, and divine love were not visually expressed so much as indicated by a stoic immunity to earthly emotions (Sauerländer 2006: 7). To the modern viewer this seeming impassivity often reads as an absence of emotion, when in actuality it was a way of representing a higher spiritual experience.

The antithesis to the visual composure of the virtuous was the uncontrolled externalized emotion of the sinful. The connection between perverse will and the expression of emotion is epitomized by high medieval representations of the Last Judgment. The appearance of images of the Last Judgment in the eleventh century and their rise to prominence in the twelfth century demonstrate the extent to which expressivity became associated with sin (Christe 1999: 7). However, in the centuries before the development of this image type, sin had already been visualized as the external display of emotion in images of the Fall. In the most direct biblical story about the consequences of sin, Adam and Eve disobey God by eating the fruit of the Tree of Knowledge of Good and Evil. Before they eat the forbidden fruit, Adam and Eve "were both naked . . . and were not ashamed," but after eating "they knew that they were naked" and hid themselves (Gen. 2.25, 3.7–8). The primary emotion Adam and Eve experience in this episode, according to the biblical text, is shame. For Augustine, the predominant passion of the fallen couple is that of grief—defined as the soul's lack of God (Wetzel 2008: 355). From the OED's list of emotions quoted earlier we might also add feelings of guilt and embarrassment to Adam and Eve's experience, but whatever the identification of the emotional response, it was visually represented in medieval art through a number of gestural formulas.

Images of Adam and Eve are already quite common in the catacombs (third through fourth centuries) and continue throughout the medieval period. An illumination in the Vienna Genesis (sixth century) showing Adam and Eve after the Fall depicts them with drawn brows, lowered gazes, and cowering postures (Figure 5.2). They carefully cover their genitals with leaves in shame. Other representations seem to add grief to shame. In a register of stained glass from a window in the Cathedral of Soissons (c.1200–25), the angel brandishes his sword and directs the flanking figures of Adam and Eve out of Eden (Figure 5.3). Adam covers his genitals with leaves with one hand while raising his other hand dramatically to his brow. Eve turns away and raises her hand to her cheek in a traditional gesture of grief (Garnier 1982: 181–3). This gesture of grief also appears in representations of the scene from other chronological and geographical contexts, for example, in the famous bronze doors of Hildesheim Cathedral (cast in 1015). The fact that Adam and Eve so often display emotion (though this emotion is at times subtly expressed) serves not only to identify the biblical figures and communicate narrative content but also to establish an association between the very experience of emotion and the commission of sin: it was not until after the Fall that Adam and Eve experienced "any agitations of the mind," so the depicted agitations act as evidence of their sin.[3]

It is not surprising, then, that the gestures of Adam and Eve after the Fall were often repeated in scenes of the Last Judgment where sinners are shown being dragged down to and tortured in hell (Barasch 1976: 37). Whereas Adam's and Eve's sin and subsequent shame were generally shown as part of a biblical narrative, the sins of the damned at the Last Judgment were less specific. On occasion, the nature of the sin might be indicated (a money bag, for instance, demonstrated avarice), but for the most part, no story or reason was given for the damning judgment handed these souls. Instead, the damned represented universal examples of evil and its consequences. While many of their gestures already appear in Roman art, the judgmental function of these gestures is particularly medieval. It was new to use emotional gestures outside a narrative context to visualize the state of a person's soul (Barasch 1976: 20, 33).

In addition to emotional gestures, it is largely in representations of the Last Judgment that we find a revival of expressive faces. In the so-called Fürstenportal, the monumental north portal of the Cathedral of Bamberg (c.1230), for instance, the pinched faces of sinners contort in toothy grimaces as a demon drags them to hell (Figure 5.4). The excessive facial expressions of the damned contrast with the controlled, closed-mouthed, and serene smiles of the blessed within the same composition. Appropriate hand gestures support the contrast in facial expressions as well, with the good folding their hands in prayer while the damned wring their hands or cup their cheeks in despair. This display of emotions stands out, even within the portal composition, for the flanking apostles and prophets in the jambs maintain stoic expressions and even triumphant Ecclesia and blindfolded Synagogia stand beautifully composed.

The viewer standing before the portal was thus confronted by a range of possible emotions, some of them grotesque in their excessive expressivity, others serene and contemplative. It is clear from medieval images of the Last Judgment—their placement, insistence on gruesome tortures, and attempted universality—that these were images meant to elicit an emotional response from the viewer. The implication of these scenes was that the viewer too would be judged and would join either the blessed or the damned.

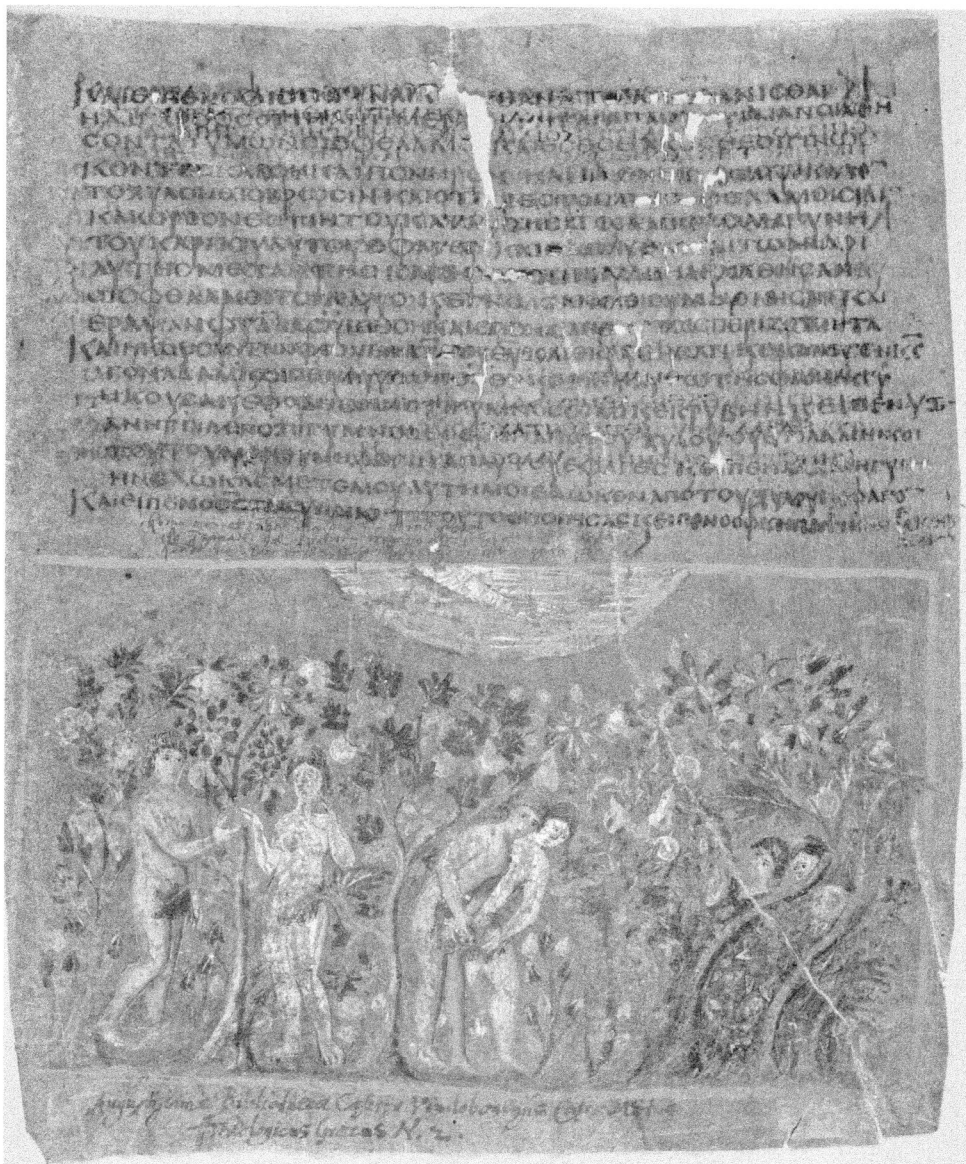

FIGURE 5.2: Adam and Eve after the Fall, Vienna Genesis, Vienna, Österreichische Nationalbibliothek, cod. theol. gr. 31, fol. 1ʳ, sixth century. © ONB/Wien.

FIGURE 5.3: Expulsion from Eden, stained glass, Cathedral of Soissons, c.1200–1225.
© Madeline H. Caviness, 1979.

FIGURE 5.4: Last Judgment Tympanum of the Fürstenportal, Cathedral of Bamberg, c.1230.
© Katherine Boivin.

FIGURE 5.5: Lintel frieze from the Last Judgment Portal, Cathedral of St-Lazare, Autun, c.1130. © Andrew Tallon, 2010.

I would like to end this section by considering the spatial relationship between image and beholder. The spatiality created by image programs in medieval churches was predicated upon the participation of the viewer, on her movement through the space, and her experience of the images. We have touched on some of the formal and theological sources for the treatment of emotion in medieval art, but to this we must add the participatory and therefore experiential nature of much of the art.

One of the most expressive representations of the Last Judgment is found in the north portal of the Cathedral of St-Lazare in Autun (c.1130).[4] The lintel frieze shows the dead rising from their graves and gesticulating in an impressive array of emotions (Figure 5.5). From hands raised palm-outward expressing awe, to hands clasped to cheeks in either elated amazement (gazing upward) or horror (bent cowering), to the wringing of hands and tearing at breasts in visible distress, the awakened dead are undoubtedly portrayed in the throes of intense emotion. Such expressions continue in the tympanum above, where the blessed are lifted into an architectural representation of the heavenly Jerusalem to Christ's right, while the damned are tortured in the flames of hell to his left.

As Mary Carruthers has recently argued in her book *The Experience of Beauty in the Middle Ages*, we should not dismiss the aesthetic power of medieval images which would have evoked sensations in the audience (Carruthers 2013: 11, 15). It is not difficult to imagine the range of emotional reactions a viewer might have to the dramatic scene of judgment at Autun. The strong contrasts, energetic lines, and extreme gestures of the scene still affect modern viewers. However, it was not in isolation before this portal that the medieval visitor to the Cathedral of Autun was expected to have a highly emotional experience.

Marian Bleeke has argued that the Eve Fragment from the lintel of the east transept portal of St-Lazare once participated in an evocative spatial program that also prompted emotional reactions from visitors. Viewers were meant to see and experience two emotions in a specific temporal and spatial order. These emotions were notably those of the women who witnessed Christ raising Lazarus from the dead. In the east portal, Eve's gesture of touching her cheek with her hand expressed grief and conditioned pilgrims on their way to the shrine of Lazarus within the apse (twelfth century, now destroyed). Within the shrine of Lazarus, the feelings of sorrow and grief, modeled by Eve in the portal, would give way to shock and surprise, modeled by images of Mary and Martha, witnesses of the miracle. For women in particular, Bleeke argues, the Eve sculpture "may have provided a trigger for a gendered expectation of a strong emotional response" (Bleeke 2012: 16, 24, 26).

This example of Autun, where several components of the image program depicted emotion with the intent of eliciting the same in response from the viewer, is just one of many. Over the course of the high medieval period in particular, the expressive emotionality of images steadily increased. The judgment associated with externalized expressions of emotion persisted, but broader social developments added a stronger emphasis on the positive potential of emotional experience as well. Andrew Tallon has described how "an entire world of popular piety that was saturated in emotion saw its birth during these centuries" (Tallon 2008: 118).

Although it is impossible thoroughly to explore these social changes in the scope of the present chapter, it is worth mentioning a few major events which likely impacted the role of emotion in the visual arts. These included the call to Crusade, which encouraged Christians to take up the cross as Christ had done, the formation of the mendicant orders, which promoted a humble life following the model of Christ, and the rise of the cult of Mary, which encouraged men and women to identify with the experiences of the Virgin (Uibert-Schede 1960: 12–15; Ziegler 1992; Largier 2008: 374; Rubin 2009: 79; McNamer 2010; Steinhoff 2012: 37).

Imitation of Christ's suffering was seen as a way the human soul could attain absolute love of God, for this imitation or mimesis produced an emotional intimacy with the divine (Largier 2008: 374). The most extreme examples of this in medieval society were penitents who inflicted physical punishment on their own flesh, whether through self-flagellation, wearing a catena (a chain strapped around the thigh), or fasting (Tallon 2008: 119). As Niklaus Largier has described it, "to be crucified with Christ meant not only to contemplate the suffering body of the savior but at the same time to emulate it, to make it present through the imagination, to feel the suffering in terms of sensation and emotion, and to embody it psychologically and physically" (2008: 374). One of the best models in the visual arts for the way the medieval public was to engage in this emotional oneness with the divine was the figure of the Virgin Mary. Her roles of loving mother, sorrowing parent, and supreme intercessor made her an effective and affective tool of devotion.

MIMESIS OF EMOTION: THE VIRGIN MARY

Much has been written by historians, theologians, and art historians about the rise of the cult of Mary in the eleventh and twelfth centuries (Carroll 1986; Clayton 1990; Maunder 2008; Fassler 2010). Particularly in the high Middle Ages, the Virgin Mary became increasingly central in the visual art of the church. For instance, as we have seen, the emotional response of mothers depicted in scenes of the Massacre of the Innocents was often positioned as a parallel to Mary's sorrow at her son's crucifixion. Mary was also seen as a counterpart of Eve: the pure virgin would help rectify original sin.

Miri Rubin, one of the leading scholars on the role of emotions in medieval art, has discussed how the Virgin Mary provided a "site for reflection on the expression of emotion" (Rubin 2009: 79; Belting 1994: 416). Rubin sketches a major shift toward increasing expressivity in representations of Mary that encouraged mimesis, or imitation, on the part of the viewer. As interest shifted from the intellectualized divinity of Christ toward his experienced humanity, medieval art became more expressive. Emotion was potentially the most effective way of representing the humanity of both Christ and Mary, and it was through this humanity that the faithful were afforded access to the divine.

This shift is illuminated by comparison between a Romanesque Throne of Wisdom and a Gothic Pietà. Both image types share formal characteristics—the Throne of Wisdom shows Mary enthroned with Jesus seated on her lap; the Pietà shows Mary seated with the corpse of her dead son cradled in her lap—but they diverge in the manner in which they engage the viewer. Consider, for instance, a Throne of Wisdom from Auvergne (second half of the twelfth century), now at the Metropolitan Museum of Art in New York, and the so-called Röttgen Pietà (c.1325), now in the Rheinisches Landesmuseum Bonn (Figures 5.6 and 5.7).

In the Throne of Wisdom, Mary sits upright, her head in line with her body and her gaze straight ahead. The rigidity of her posture is reinforced by the rhythmic folds of her garments. Her stiff hands create a protective barrier between the gesturing Christ-child and the viewer. The only softness of the piece is reserved for Mary's face. Here, slightly slanted eyes, heavy lids, and a pouting mouth express a quiet sadness. The interpretation of this image requires an intellectual engagement from the viewer: she must understand that Christ represents the Logos, the Word of God made flesh, here enthroned upon his mother's lap (Forsyth 1972). Mary's sadness must be understood as prescience of the coming sacrifice of her son, Christ's gesture as an acceptance of this fate.

In contrast to what I call the intellectual appeal of the Throne of Wisdom, the Röttgen Pietà engages the viewer primarily through emotion. Mary sits with her head inclined, her mouth open, and her brows contorted in angry grief. Christ's emaciated body, with its oversized head, angled neck, and gushing wounds, extorts a visceral response from the viewer. Even without knowledge of the story or identification of the figures, the violence of death and the complex emotional response of a mother are palpable.

Both pieces express emotion, but they do so in different manners and with different intents. The Throne of Wisdom presents a special mother and child, a holy group with divine foresight; the Pietà captures the dramatic expression of a human relationship and of violent suffering. While the Throne of Wisdom maintains a formal and intellectual distance from its audience, the Pietà draws the viewer in through its emotionality. The consequence of this new approach in the visual arts, particularly in the depiction of suffering and sorrow as a positive experience bringing one closer to God, was the creation of a number of new image types. As Rubin states, "the tendency to dramatize Mary's suffering allowed her to be seen in some alarming new positions: fainting, leaning, falling, sometimes pulling at her son's body" (Rubin 2009: 98).

Many of the late-medieval images of Mary in dramatic poses grew out of the long-standing tradition of representing Mary at the Crucifixion. Whether in narrative scenes of the Passion or in emblematic figure groups of Christ on the cross, Mary acts both as a witness of the event and as a model for the viewer (Rubin 2009: 90; Belting 1990). Although the intensity of her display of emotion fluctuates throughout the period, she generally expresses sorrow through gesture and posture. On the cover of the Lindau Gospels (*c*.880), now in the collection of the Morgan Library in New York, Mary appears in a pose of melancholy, crouched over with her chin resting on her hand; in a wall painting in the Basilica of San Isidoro in Léon (second half of the twelfth century), Mary raises her hand to her cheek in a gesture of sorrow similar to that of Eve in the images in Soissons and Hildesheim discussed above; and in a monumental wooden statue of the mourning Virgin (thirteenth century), now at The Cloisters Museum in New York, Mary clasps her hands close to her face in grief. One of the most direct appeals to the viewer to mimic Mary's depicted emotion is found in the sculpture of the west rood screen in Naumburg, Germany (*c*.1250) (Jung 2000, 2012). Here, Christ on the cross divides the central entrance to the west choir into two doorways. Mary, on Christ's right, shows her sorrow in her swollen eyes, slanted brows, and downturned mouth. She appeals to the approaching viewer with her gaze as she gestures with one hand on her heart, the other toward her dying son. The clear invitation is to see and feel what she does at the scene of the Crucifixion. The mimesis of Mary's experienced emotions is clearly positive.

FIGURE 5.6: Throne of Wisdom/Enthroned Virgin and Child, Auvergne, c.1150–1200, The Metropolitan Museum of Art, 67.153. © The Metropolitan Museum of Art, gift of J. Pierpont Morgan, 1916. Image source: Art Resource, NY.

CONCLUSION

The end date for this volume, the year 1300, falls in the middle of a burgeoning trend in the depiction and elicitation of emotions in medieval art. The development of new affective image types, like the Pietà or Man of Sorrows, would be unthinkable without the cultural and aesthetic shifts of the twelfth and thirteenth centuries, particularly the new positive call for mimesis. New means of representing emotion, such as the depiction of tears and the revival of expression in the face, had their roots in these changes.

The paintings of Giotto, often cited since Vasari as the start of a new Renaissance approach to the image, also exemplify the continuity between the art of the thirteenth and fourteenth centuries. In the Scrovegni chapel in Padua (c.1305), for instance, Giotto

FIGURE 5.7: Röttgen Pietà, c.1325, Rheinisches Landesmuseum Bonn.

painted some of the most affective images of the turn of the fourteenth century. Here we find scenes of the Massacre of the Innocents, the Lamentation, and the Last Judgment. While the degree of expressivity and naturalism, particularly in faces, is novel, the individual gestures of sorrow and despair are familiar (Barasch 1987: 40, 42). In the Lamentation, Mary tenderly supports Christ's torso on her lap (Figure 5.8). Her arms lovingly encircle his neck, her eyes and mouth turn downward in sorrow, and she bends her head as if to kiss his face. The other women who surround Christ show their grief by throwing open their arms, bowing their heads, or wringing their hands. These women could as well be mothers in a scene of the Massacre of the Innocents for their gestures of despair. In the context of the Lamentation, however, their grief is unambiguously positive. But in the same chapel, we also find cases where extreme emotional gesticulation identifies vice. The personification of Wrath, for instance, bares her breast dramatically, in stark contrast to her counterpart Temperance who stands composed and well covered. Following a long tradition, Giotto has used a dramatic gesture as the visualization of vice.

Changes in the representation of emotion in the visual arts around 1300 thus do not offer a sharp break from the preceding centuries. Nevertheless, the altered relationship

FIGURE 5.8: Giotto di Bondone, Lamentation (The Mourning of Christ), Cappella degli Scrovegni all'Arena, Padua, 1304–1306. Image courtesy of Wikimedia Commons.

FIGURE 5.9: Penitence, Devotion, and Contemplation, British Library, London, MS Yates Thompson 11 (previously Add. 39843), fol. 29ʳ, c.1290. © The British Library Board.

between viewer and image and the increasing call to mimesis and self-association was central to a major shift toward the privatization of the image. Not surprisingly, women, and female religious in particular, were some of the primary subjects and audiences of this new art. An illustrated manuscript (British Library, London, MS Add. 39843, fol. 28, *c*.1300; see Figure 5.9) containing instructions for nuns on how to attain the three states of the pious soul calls these states "fear," "hope," and "love" (Belting 1994: 412–13). Emotions are more than simple feelings—they are means of approaching the divine. The accompanying images show a nun kneeling before an altar on which statues and then visions appear. The early and high medieval composure that demonstrated supreme joy in the divine has given way, not to any extreme emotional expression in the face, but instead to an intensely personalized experience of the divine. The insistence on the universality of depicted emotions has shifted to an emphasis on their individuality.

CHAPTER SIX

Literature

JUANITA FEROS RUYS

The category of "literature" in Late Antiquity and the Middle Ages differs from modern understandings of the term. There was less of a focus on texts designed for "leisure" reading, such as novels today, but rather a strong didactic intention to teach, impart knowledge, and improve and edify the individual, either spiritually or socially. For this reason, texts that formed the literature of the premodern world could be drawn from a variety of genres, including first-person life-writings, allegories, saints' lives, miracle tales, guides to the religious life, sermons, and texts of advice. It is not until the latter part of the period under discussion here, from around the mid-twelfth century, that we begin to see texts designed for imaginative pleasure, with the rise of stories about knights, quests, and the pursuit of love, which would become a key feature of literature in the later Middle Ages.

Texts that constituted literature, regardless of their genre, could be written either as prose or as poetry. Literacy rates in the premodern world were not high, and for many people access to texts came through listening to them being read aloud, rather than reading themselves. Moreover, as this period predated the invention of cheap forms of textual transmission such as paper, access to physical texts was limited. In Late Antiquity, texts were often written on papyrus, and from the early Middle Ages, on specially prepared animal skins known as parchment. Skins were expensive and time-consuming to prepare for writing, and all texts had to be painstakingly written by hand. For these reasons, texts were scarce and not widely circulated. This contributed to literary texts frequently being composed in poetic form, since poetry was more easily remembered than prose and memorizing texts overcame the limitations that lack of literacy and scarcity imposed on the circulation of texts. Accordingly, poetry was a much more common literary form in the premodern world than it is today.

For the period under investigation here, 350–1300, the primary language used across Europe was Latin. Latin was the language of the Roman Empire, which was still in existence at the beginning of this period, and it became a Europe-wide *lingua franca* in the course of the Middle Ages, being the main written language in the countries we now know as England, France, Germany, and Italy. Latin was also the language of the Roman Catholic Church which had spread across Europe in association with the Empire, particularly after the Emperor Constantine's adoption of Christianity in 313. For the early medieval world, then, the bastions of literacy were the monastic houses of the Catholic Church, which meant that much of the surviving literature of the period was written in Latin and focused on religion and spirituality.

One of the first great vernaculars of Europe was Old English, which flowered in the British Isles between the eighth and tenth centuries. By the high Middle Ages, new national vernaculars across Europe were also becoming important vehicles of literacy. As will be discussed below, a literature of personal piety and devotion, and a literature of romance and adventure developed in such emerging languages as Old French, Middle High Dutch, Middle High German, and early Italian.

Because the literature of the period covered in this volume was so strongly influenced by Latin intellectual traditions, it inherited the Roman approach to emotions, and this was overwhelmingly Stoic. Stoicism had its roots in Ancient Greek philosophy, but was particularly associated in the medieval world with the influential Roman thinkers Cicero and Seneca. Stoicism also meshed well with the ascetic streak of early Christianity, with its focus on desert eremitism, self-control, and the sublimation of the body's wants and desires. The primary aim of Stoicism was to produce individuals who could weather whatever confronted them with equanimity, rather than be tossed about by their emotions, as if on a sea. Stoicism aimed at self-mastery of one's emotions and the arrival at a state of dispassion or impassibility.

For the period under discussion here, then, we can see an arc of development in the way the emotions were theorized in relation to the Christian subject and represented in literature. From Late Antiquity into the high Middle Ages, the Latin Stoic approach emphasized the primacy of reason over the impulses of the emotions. Meanwhile, the vernaculars, and especially the literature of Anglo-Saxon England, began to explore the ways that emotions could shape a human life and its course. By the high Middle Ages, a new approach to spirituality in the form of mysticism was being developed, and it became particularly associated with spiritual writings by women in various European vernaculars. Together these developments meant that personal experience came to be positively revalued as a means of knowing oneself and God, and emotions came to be represented in literature not as obstacles to the pious life, but rather as the potential pathway to understanding and sharing in the ineffable love of God. This also underlines that an understanding of literature in the medieval period is inseparable from an understanding of religion and spirituality.

LATE ANTIQUITY

In Late Antiquity, the administrative and intellectual frameworks of the Roman Empire were still in place across Europe, stretching into the Near East and North Africa, and Latin was a language that was still widely spoken (in a vulgar form at least) as well as written. There are three texts written in Latin between the late fourth and early sixth centuries that are crucial for indicating the way emotions were being thought about and represented. These were not only extremely popular in their own time as forms of literature, but continued to be widely read and influential on other writings throughout the next thousand years. These are the *Psychomachia* of Prudentius, Augustine's *Confessions*, and Boethius's *Consolation of Philosophy*. All three were written by subjects of the Roman Empire, and evince a strongly Stoic approach to the emotions.

Prudentius, Psychomachia

The *Psychomachia* of Aurelius Clemens Prudentius is an allegorical battle between personified virtues and vices, all figured as female,[1] written around the turn of the fourth century in 900 lines of poetry. It functioned as a school-text for young boys to learn Latin, with the idea that they would imbibe the moral lessons of the text along with their grammar. One of the lessons the boys would have learnt was about emotional control.

The poet begins by asking Christ how best a person can battle the sedition that arises through the disturbance of one's inner feelings ("*exoritur quotiens turbatis sensibus intus seditio,*" 278).[2] The poet imagines the individual as a battlefield, with warfare taking place within a besieged body against the lusts of the heart ("*obsesso in corpore,*" "*ludibria cordis,*" 280). At this point, a number of actors enter the drama, all virtues and vices, though interestingly, many of the vices also figure emotional states.

On the positive side is Patience (Patientia) who enters the fray with perfect stoic equanimity. She is sober and unassuming in stance ("*modesta*") her face gives nothing away, being set in a look of unemotional seriousness ("*gravi vultu*"), and she is unmoved ("*inmota,*" 286) by the scenes of violence before her. Against her is contrasted the figure of Wrath (Ira) who is immediately marked as a vice through her excessive emotional complexion. She is swelling with anger ("*tumens*"), and foaming from her wide-open mouth ("*spumanti fervida rictu*"). Unlike Patience's carefully fixed gaze ("*defixa oculos*"), Wrath's eyes are bloodshot and darting about wildly ("*sanguinea intorquens . . . lumina,*" 286). Wrath is particularly enraged by Patience's stoic impassibility, and as she hurls a javelin at Patience, she mocks her, telling her to accept the blow in her calm breast ("*securo pectore*") and not to cry out in pain ("*nec doleas*"), since she knows that Patience would find showing such emotion shameful ("*turpe,*" 286).

As Wrath continues to assail Patience with increasing savagery ("*more furentis*"), the latter remains unharmed and unmoved ("*quieta*"). At last in fury ("*effera,*" 288) and despair at her failure, Wrath turns her weapons upon herself instead. In the premodern Christian world, suicide was the ultimate sin, the only one for which there could be no forgiveness, so Wrath's capitulation in this way provides the reader with a stark warning about the dangers of excessive emotion. Patience then stands over Wrath's dead body and declares that she faces the savage fury of all evils with equanimity and overcomes them through calm perseverance. A number of similar battles then ensue, before Prudentius returns at the end with the moral lesson, personalizing the warfare for each reader as the battle which rages within our own body and soul. He warns that the feelings in our shadowy hearts can pull us in two directions at once. The answer is to endure in patience until Christ comes to settle the battle on our behalf.

Augustine, Confessions

The *Confessions* of Augustine, written in the late fourth century, is generally regarded as one of the earliest autobiographies in Western literature, although it differs in significant ways from the modern genre of that name. Augustine gives us an intimate portrait of his boyhood and adult life, including powerful evocations of the emotional journeys he travels through his close friendships, his love for his mother, and his experience of having his emotions manipulated in the theatre (discussed in more depth by Sarah Brazil in Chapter Four in this volume). Yet his primary concern is always how the individual can live in right relationship with God, and key to this question is the role the emotions should or should not play in the Christian's journey to God. Augustine's thoughts on this are clearly indebted to Stoicism, evident through his categorization of the emotions into the Stoics' four primary types—happiness, sorrow, fear, and hope (X.14, 221)[3]—and his ideal of *apatheia* as the absence of, or perhaps freedom from, emotion. Augustine also adheres to the early Christian doctrine of God's impassibility, or remoteness from emotional disturbance, as he addresses God saying: "You grieve for wrong, but suffer no pain. You can be angry and yet serene" (I.4, 23).

FIGURE 6.1: Chastity pierces Lust with her sword (*Pudicicia transfigit libidinem gladio*), Prudentius, *Psychomachia*, British Library, Cotton MS Titus, D XVI, fol. 7ʳ (lower), St. Albans, England, 1120. © The British Library Board.

In one of the most moving episodes in his *Confessions*, Augustine reveals to us the sorrow he felt at the death of his good friend. He tells us that "I hated all the places we had known together, because he was not in them" (IV.4, 76), and "wondered that he should die and I remain alive, for I was his second self" (IV.6, 77). He tells of the "tears and sighs that allowed me neither rest nor peace of mind," because "[m]y soul was a burden, bruised and bleeding" (IV.7, 78). Yet at the same time, he knows that emotions left unbridled can be dangerous, so he struggles against them, for sins arise "when the soul fails to govern the impulses from which it derives bodily pleasure" (IV.15, 86). Although Augustine knows that God counts and cherishes every hair of a Christian's head, yet a person's hairs "are more easily counted than his feelings and the emotions of his heart" (IV.14, 84).

A similar outpouring of grief and soul-searching occurs later when Augustine relates the death of his beloved mother, Monica. He tells us that "a great wave of sorrow surged into my heart" (IX.12, 200), but that he struggled to prevent it spilling over into tears because lamentation was not the proper emotional response for the death of a good Christian woman. Instead, he wrestled repeatedly with his sorrow, which would recede only to return with even greater force, confessing that "[i]t was misery to feel myself so weak a victim of these human emotions, although we cannot escape them, since they are the natural lot of mankind" (IX.12, 201). In the end, Augustine could not restrain his tears and they "streamed down," making "a pillow for my heart" (IX.12, 202). Yet afterward he accused himself of having been "guilty of too much worldly affection" (IX.13, 203), believing that he should rather have shed tears for the souls that will die remote from God.

Augustine attempts throughout his life story to understand the place of God in all this human affective upheaval. He argues that God is not best sought through the evidence of the senses, as important as this is, but by the proper analysis of that sense perception by reason (X.6, 213). This then leads him to a unique discussion of how memory intersects with emotions, and a further insight into how emotions can be tempered so that they do not impact on human life. This is because, as Augustine realizes, he is capable of *remembering* having experienced an emotion without actually reexperiencing it, so that "even when I am unhappy I can remember times when I was cheerful . . . I can recall past fears and yet not feel afraid" (X.14, 220). This draws him to contemplation of how the emotions get into the mind in the first place—how they are both ideas and (sometimes involuntary) experiences. In the end, however, Augustine has to conclude that this is only so much sophistry, since none of it will lead to God—God is not image, emotion, memory, nor even the mind itself, since these are all susceptible to human ratiocination, while God is not (X.25, 231). In this revelation, Augustine particularly stresses that God is not an emotion "such as is felt by living men when they are glad or sorry, when they have sensations of desire or fear." Augustine then moves beyond the question of the individual feeling human person, and indeed beyond the genre of life narration, to end his memoir with a meditation on the goodness of God encompassing all creation.

Boethius, Consolation of Philosophy

Anicius Manlius Severinus Boethius wrote the *Consolation of Philosophy* in around 524, while he was exiled and in prison awaiting the death sentence for treason against the Gothic king Theoderic. Boethius was a senator and consul at the very end of the Roman Empire; he belonged to a time and milieu in which the Christian faith readily coexisted with classical forms of philosophy. The *Consolation* is composed in five books, each of which intersperses prose with poems, the whole conceived as a dialogue between the figure "Boethius" (who is more of a literary character here than an authentic self-portrait) and Lady Philosophy who consoles him in his sorrow.

As the text opens, Boethius is attempting to console himself on his reversal of fortune by taking "shelter in sad songs" and "elegies that wet my face with tears" (35).[4] Lady Philosophy at once appears and banishes the Muses of Poetry, who are exacerbating Boethius's sorrows with their sad words, describing them as "over-dramatic little whores" who only play on Boethius's emotions ("*scenicas meretriculas*," my trans.). She explains to Boethius that the Muses have "no medicine to ease his pains, only sweetened poisons to make them worse," because they kill "the rich and fruitful harvest of reason" with the "barren thorns of passion" (36). Philosophy criticizes the "great tumult of emotion" to which Boethius has succumbed, leaving him "torn this way and that by alternating fits of grief, wrath and anguish" (49). Instead, she advises Boethius to eradicate his emotions: "rid yourself of joy and fear, put hope to flight, and banish grief. The mind is clouded and bound in chains where these hold sway" (52).

Throughout the dialogue, Philosophy appears physically impassible, much like Patience in the *Psychomachia*, having "dignity of countenance and gravity of expression" (116). As

Boethius complains about his fate, Philosophy reminds him that he has enjoyed more than his fair share of good in life. She also recalls that "[i]t is the nature of human affairs to be fraught with anxiety" (62), and because this cannot be changed, all that can be done is to change the way one views one's fortune. Accordingly, in line with Stoic thought, Philosophy advises Boethius that "all luck is good luck to the man who bears it with equanimity" (63). She advises him that human happiness is both mutable and transient ("bitter-sweet"), so that true happiness should be sought within, not through external things.

In Book 4, Philosophy outlines the negative impacts that emotions have on the human person—lust engenders greed, wrath defeats sense, sorrow depresses, and hope torments with false promise—and she characterizes them as multiple tyrants, all trying to rule the one human heart (123). If Boethius allows this, he will lose the sovereignty of his own soul and fall captive to his passions (150). In the final book, Philosophy points out the unique position of humans within the scheme of creation. All animals have "mere" sensation. Higher-order animals also have imagination, but only humans top this with reason (161). Our senses "cannot perceive anything beyond matter" (158), but reason can. As a result, it is incumbent upon us to apply our reason to our lives, and not merely react according to the passivity of our feelings. Philosophy ends her speech with a declaration of God's Providence in all things.

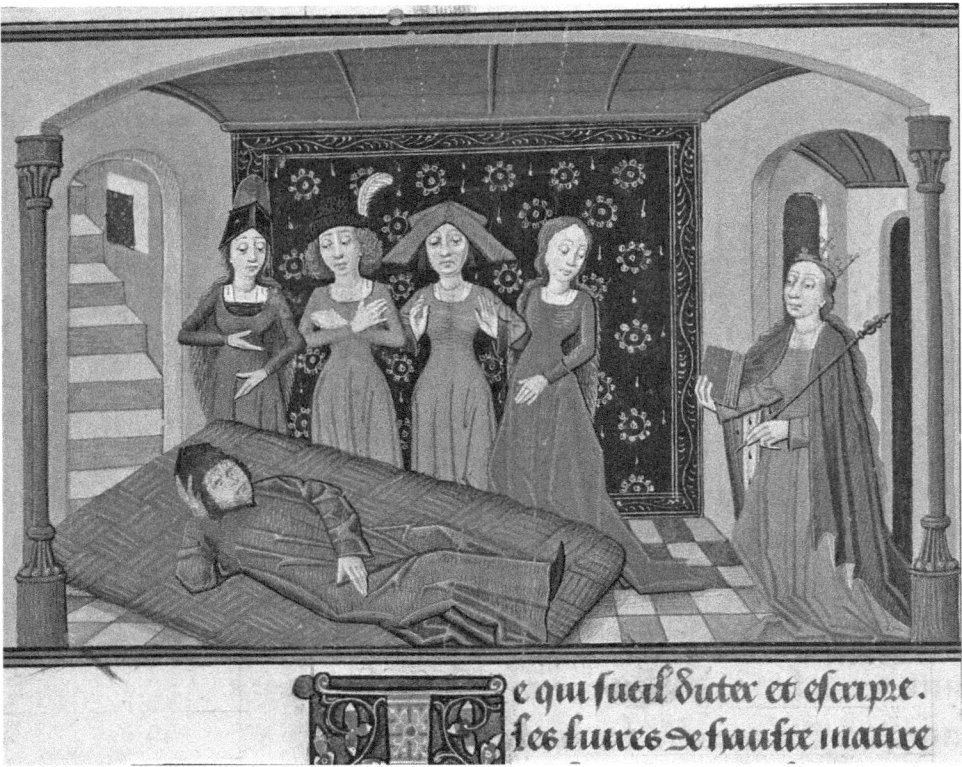

FIGURE 6.2: Boethius, Philosophy, and the Muses. Miniature from Boethius, *De consolatione philosophiae* (*Consolation of Philosophy*). Bibliothèque municipale, Rouen, France, fifteenth century. Photo by Leemage via Getty Images.

CAROLINGIAN RENAISSANCE

Under the leadership of the great Frankish king Charlemagne in the late eighth century, there was a renewed focus on Latin literacy and literary writings. This "renaissance" (or "renewal") as it has been called, lasted for around a century through the reigns of Charlemagne's successors. It saw many highly gifted scholars drawn from across Europe to the Carolingian[5] court where a critical mass of expertise and innovation stimulated an extraordinary literary output. While great advances were made in the genres of instructional works on grammar, rhetoric, and dialectic, scriptural commentaries, medieval forms of the encyclopedia, and historiography, the innovation of literary culture in the Carolingian Renaissance is best characterized by the explosion in poetic forms at this time. Peter Godman has spoken of "those genres—from dream-poetry to verse-epistles—in which early Carolingian poets excelled" (Godman 1985: 35), and poetry provided the vehicle for history, devotional texts, and biographies. Carolingian poets delighted in play, building into their poems word games, such as acrostics in which the first letter of each line of verse would spell out a name, word, or phrase.

One very influential poem of this period was Notker's Rachel sequence, which, as Sarah Brazil notes in Chapter Four of this volume, would initiate the numerous Rachel and Marian sequences of the high Middle Ages with their moving depictions of maternal love and sorrow. In Carolingian poetry, however, the most emotive descriptions coalesce around the idea of exile, a theme that appealed to writers in the Carolingian court not only because many of them had traveled far from their home countries to the court, but also because it offered an allegory of the Christian life in the world, awaiting return to the true home in Heaven. One such beautiful lament is "*Clangam filii*" (Godman 1985: 322–5) which depicts the sorrow of a swan who has flown too far from land and is now "*exsulata*," exiled. She is caught in a storm, sure to be plunged into the waves at any moment. The poem expresses the fear and sadness of the lost bird as she suffers anguish ("*angor*") and groans aloud ("*gemens*") in her distress. As the swan is lifted at last by a new breath of wind, symbolizing the Holy Spirit, she is filled with joy and happiness ("*Hilarata /Ac iucundata*") and, singing sweetly, she heads toward the beautiful lands that signify Heaven.

One Carolingian poet who particularly explores the emotional world of the Christian subject is Gottschalk. In "O mi custos" (Godman 1985: 233–47), Gottschalk exhorts Christ to look upon him "so that I, a wretch, may weep most bitterly" ("*possim flere miser amarissime*"), tears being a sign of remorse and repentance. He then asks the Holy Spirit to shake him up so that his feelings may be unsettled ("*me tuo . . . more conturbandum commove*"). Throughout the poem, Gottschalk begs for the release of his feelings in mourning and lament, as these will attest to the softening of his heart by God. At the same time, he beseeches Christ to be emotionally moved on his behalf, as this will be the saving of him: "Groan, groan, good Jesus, and be disturbed in spirit, /weep with kindly tears for the death of your slave." In this poetry, then, we see a striking rejection of Stoic equanimity and a focus on the repentant powers of emotion, an idea that will appear again in the writings of the mystics later in the Middle Ages.

A rare maternal voice that emerges from the Carolingian period belongs to Dhuoda, a Frankish noblewoman who wrote a text of advice to her teenage son William in 843. He was at that time absent from her, being held as a political hostage in order to ensure the loyalty of her husband to the Emperor. Dhuoda's text is multi-generic, combining prose and poem, and including traditional advice, numerology, etymology, genealogy, and prayers. Perhaps most striking are the acrostics Dhuoda builds into her verses, which spell out her great love for her son. The acrostic at the beginning of her text reads: "Dhuoda sends greetings to her beloved son William: Read" (Dhuoda 1998: 42–7), while at the end it reiterates: "Verses to William my son" (220–3). Within the text itself, Dhuoda explicitly expresses her great love for her son. She begins by noting that women tend to take joy in the company of their children, but that for her, this pleasure is withheld. Although she is anxious ("*anxia*") at William's absence, she rejoices ("*gaudens*") that she can be of use to him through the advice she sends. At the end she declares that she has all but forgotten herself, overcome by the sweetness of her great love for him and her longing for his beauty (224–5). Dhuoda thus offers us a rare first-person view into the emotional life of an early medieval woman.

ANGLO-SAXON LITERATURE

One of the most powerful and varied early vernacular literatures of Europe was the Anglo-Saxon, and perhaps its most famous text was the great epic poem *Beowulf*. It has been transmitted in a single manuscript dated to around 1000, but was probably composed, based on oral elements, in the eighth century. The epic genre tends to be concerned with heroic action and stirring speeches rather than feelings or introspection, and this remains true of *Beowulf*. Nonetheless, the affective erupts into the narrative in interesting ways, particularly associated with the monstrous elements of the poem.

When the monster Grendel is first introduced into the story, we are told that he suffers at the loud rejoicing ("*dream . . . hludne*," 38)[6] in the great hall of Heorot, and he attacks at night while the men inside "have no thought of sorrow" ("*sorge ne cuðon*," 40). It is, however, with sorrow ("*sorh*") that the king Hrothgar relates to Beowulf the humiliation Grendel has wreaked upon Heorot through his hate-filled thoughts ("*heteþancum*," 56). On the night that Beowulf stands watch against him, Grendel approaches, "bereft of joys" ("*dreamum bedæled*"), "swollen with rage," and "angry at heart" ("*yrremod*," 68). This excess of emotion is the affective expression of his inner evil will ("*inwitþancum*"). However, when confronted with Beowulf's power, his only thought is to flee, having become fearful in spirit ("*forht on ferhðe*," 70). Interestingly, following Grendel's defeat, his mother—although also monstrous—is shown sorrowing his loss, as she "brooded on her misery" ("*yrmþe gemunde*"). Gloomy at heart ("*galgmod*"), she goes to Heorot to avenge her son ("*sunu deoð wrecan*," 94–5), and in a touchingly maternal act, she takes Grendel's arm, which has been hung up in the hall as a war trophy, back with her to her lair. When Beowulf descends into the lake to fight her, she is still shown as motivated by maternal sorrow, since "she wished to avenge her child, her sole offspring" ("*wolde hire bearn wrecan, angan earferan*," 108–9).[7]

This association of powerful emotions with dark and demonic figures continues in the more overtly Christian poetry of the Junius XI manuscript. Again this manuscript is dated to around 1000, but with contents likely composed in the late eighth or early ninth centuries. Two of its poems—*Genesis B* and *Christ and Satan*—contain evocations of the Devil which imbue him with a range of affective states. *Genesis B* is a 615-line interpolation within the longer poem *Genesis A*. It makes us privy to Satan's wrath that human beings created out of the earth should be intended by God to replace the fallen angels in Heaven. The poet—can we see an anticipation of Milton here?—notes how Hell is now for Satan both an internal state as well as his external prison: "It welled within him, his mind around his heart, just as heat surrounded him outside, wrathlike punishment" ("*Weoll him on innan, /hyge ymb his heortan, hat wæs him utan, /wraðlic wite*," 14).[8] The swelling of heat about the heart was for medieval theorists of the passions the key somatic indicator of anger, so the poet here describes Satan as though he is a physical embodied being. Satan himself declares of Adam's presumptive elevation: "That to me is the greatest misery" ("*þæt me is sorga mæst*," 14). Interestingly, given the doctrine of God's impassibility in medieval theology, Satan's plan to deceive Adam and Eve rests on his assumption that their disobedience will engender God's anger, as he declares that God "will become wrathful in spirit" ("*Þonne weorð he him wrað on mode*," 15) and then "become infuriated with them" ("*þonne he him abolgen wurðeþ*," 16).

Satan in *Christ and Satan* is a more craven figure. As the narrative repeatedly circles back to him in Hell with his fellow demons, he is shown as sorrowing, and at times fearful, contemplating his future pain and suffering. In one memorable passage, he utters the lament "Alas" ("*Eala*") nine times in a row, bewailing the world he has lost (74).[9] He describes himself as "sick and sorrowful" ("*sic and sorhful*") as he laments the bitter harms and evils ("*bitres niðæs beala gnornian*," 77) that he has brought upon himself. Yet the wailing of the demons is nothing compared with their fear when Christ arrives to harrow Hell, for then "all were terrified with dread" ("*Þa wæron mid egsan ealle afyrhte*," 80). Interestingly, as with *Genesis B*, the suffering of the demons is depicted as a function of God's wrath ("*Him wæs drihten god wrað geworden*") which induces fear and terror ("*egsan gryre*," 82) in Satan. Both these Anglo-Saxon poems thus depict a Satan who is far more affectively labile than will be the case for many more centuries in the Latin medieval tradition.

For truly affecting—even haunting—Old English poetry we have to turn, however, to the elegiac laments of the Exeter manuscript. Short poems like *The Wanderer*, *The Seafarer*, and *The Wife's Lament* (all most likely composed around the mid-ninth century) are drenched in powerful emotions words. Spoken in the first person, they powerfully evoke feelings of loss, sorrow, grief, abandonment, and exile, made all the more acute by the wild and windswept *mise-en-scène* of deserted beaches and desolate forests, and their narrative allusiveness as we struggle to understand how the speaker has come to be there and what exactly they have lost. The speaker of *The Wanderer*, who is "anxious at heart" ("*modcearig*"), tells us that he must lament his cares alone ("*Oft ic sceolde ana . . . mine ceare cwiþan*," 75).[10] The word sorrow ("*sorg*") recurs as the speaker describes the pain of exile, and he locates this pain in his soul's enclosure ("*ferðlocan*"), his breast-chamber ("*breostcofan*") and his spirit ("*modsefan*," 75). He then broadens his view to encompass the transience of the world and all temporal things, declaring that everything is burdensome in the realm of earth: "*Eall is earfoðlic eorþan rice*" (78). In the poem's call for patience and acceptance, its editor, Anne L. Klinck, finds the influence of Boethius's *Consolation of Philosophy* at work (Klinck 1992: 6).

The speaker of *The Seafarer* immediately relates the pains of his exile in which he suffers "bitter breast-cares" ("*Bitre breostceare*"). Although his surroundings are icy, his cares complain hotly about his heart ("*þær þa ceare seofedun hat ymb heortan*," 79). Yet he also points out that while those at home might seek pleasures or honors, for him his lonely wanderlust is an eternal longing ("*longunge*," 80). In this exilic state, his spirit is able to roam wild and free, beyond the bounds of his body, out upon the waters: "*min hyge hweorfeð ofer hreþerlocan, / min modsefa mid mereflode*" (81). As with *The Wanderer*, the poem concludes with a meditation on the passing glories of life and the need to rest in the love of God. These two poems thus partake in the motif, discussed earlier with regard to the Carolingian era, of earthly exile as inevitable, a separation that will only be resolved in the Christian's homecoming to Heaven.

No such resolution appears possible, however, for the female speaker of *The Wife's Lament*. She tells us from the first line that she is utterly sorrowful (*"ful geomorre"*). Her lord has departed, leaving her alone which distresses her deeply (*"forþon is min hyge geomor,"* 93). Yet the poem then takes a more disturbing turn in the wife's description of where her husband has ordered her to live—in an earthen cave (*"eorðscræfe,"* 94). Not a few critics have read this as the wife's confession that her husband has in fact murdered her and buried her body. This idea is supported by the wife's next statement that many of her friends also live inside the earth—once they were living, but now they dwell in death. There is no resolution for the wife. She spends her days in contemplation of her many miseries and sorrows of mind (*"earfoþa fela . . . modceare"*) and the poem ends with the lament that "Woe is him" who must await his love with unsatisfied desire (*"Wa bið þam þe sceal / of langoþe leofes abidan,"* 94).

HIGH MIDDLE AGES

If we had to characterize the twelfth century in terms of a single emotion, it would be love. Innovative new ideas on love arose and circulated throughout European society—Latinate and vernacular, spiritual and secular—reinvigorating classical and biblical tropes and bringing the erotic into play in new and innovative ways.

Latin love letters and lyrics

In what has been described as the "Twelfth-Century Renaissance," a wave of Latinate poetic innovation swept France, bringing with it a freedom of expression, a desire to reclaim and reinvent classical Latin forms and a focus on various kinds of love. Running through this literary output was a sense of play allied with a desire to push boundaries and apply old forms in new ways. One outcome of this was satiric poetry (sometimes called "Goliardic") that lambasted individuals and mocked conventions. Another was increasingly extravagant and personalized ways of expressing friendship (*"amicitia"*), especially in the salutations of letters exchanged between monastic men. Writers particularly looked for inspiration to the Roman poet Ovid, who had written the *Ars amatoria* (*Art of Love*), and took pleasure in taking on different roles or "personae" in their compositions. The erotic increasingly came into play in these texts, and as writers were both male and female, we find poems and letters that play with both heterosexual and homosocial desire.

An exchange of verse letters between Baudri, the Abbot of Bourgueil, and Constance, a nun of the convent of Le Ronceray, provides evidence of this. Despite their respective monastic vows of chastity, their letters play suggestively with erotic imagery. Baudri tells Constance that he writes to her of love (*"amor"*) and he encourages her to touch his bare page (*"nudum folium"*) with her bare hand (*"nuda manus"*), and then to hold it in her lap (Bond 1995: 170–1). Constance assures Baudri that she not only touched his text with her bare hand, she also slept with it beneath her left breast (*"sub ubere leuo"*), this being closer to her heart (182–3). And yet Baudri makes it clear that this is mere rhetoric, and that in reality "I do not want to be your husband, nor you to be my wife"—what he desires is friendship only (*"amiciciam,"* 172–3). The letters are a literary exercise, a rhetorical pastime through which both correspondents can play at the expression of emotion from the safety of distant enclosed spaces.

Intriguing in this regard are three letters preserved in a mid-twelfth-century manuscript (Munich, Clm 19411) which appear to express homoerotic desire between women. In one, the writer, who ends her letter by sending the greetings of the rest of her convent, says to her addressee that "I desire to love you till the moon falls from the sky" (Dronke 1968: 476–7). In a second, the writer employs all the conventional tropes of lovesickness, telling her beloved that "you alone are my love and desire" ("tu sola amor et desiderium"), and that she would happily give her life for hers (478–9). In the third, the writer not only grieves night and day for her beloved, she also recalls "the kisses that you gave" and "the sweet words with which you refreshed my little breasts" ("*quam iocundis verbis refrigerasti pectuscula*," 480–1). While we can read this latter description as metaphorical—"your words calmed my heart"—it also hints at actual caresses. This reveals that there was a willingness in the learned community of this period to play at emotional positions, that women were as invested in this ludic writing as men, and that in this discourse, women did not hesitate to refigure the usual rhetorical tropes of heterosexual desire into evocations of homosocial love.

Collections of Latin love lyrics abound in the twelfth century. Perhaps the most famous, the *Carmina Burana* includes a range of traditional love lyrics, such as the advent of spring inspiring the renewal of love, the pastoral in which the young man seduces (read rapes) the young shepherd girl, and poems of love variously unrequited, cruel, fulfilled, rejected, or deliberately unconsummated ("*amor purus*"), directed toward women who are either virginal, prolific, or professional.

But another collection troubles the dismissal of such letters as mere exercises. The *Epistolae duorum amantium* (*Letters of Two Lovers*) appear to be genuine (though still rhetorically constructed) letters and fragments of letters that were exchanged between a male scholar and his female pupil, tracing an arc from the first beginnings of desire through misunderstandings to possible pregnancy and separation. These have recently been identified as the lost love-letter correspondence of the famous twelfth-century couple Abelard and Heloise (Mews 2008; Newman 2016). These letters differ from other contemporary collections by being multi-generic (each correspondent writes both verse and prose), having an explicit Christian focus, and actively interrogating the nature of love and its relationship to both biblical ideals and Ciceronian notions of friendship. The woman correspondent in particular is very concerned with how love can retain integrity and virtue, and her ideal of love is remarkably stoic in complexion, as she argues that it should "restrain all lusts, repress carnal loves, temper joys, and root out sorrows" ("*cupiditates omnes refrenat, amores reprimit, gaudia temperat, dolores extirpat*," Mews 2008: Letter 49, 252). For the woman, love is true when it values the beloved above all else and takes no heed of the things that the world values. The *Epistolae* thereby give us a glimpse into how two medieval Latin-literate Christian individuals attempted to synthesize intellectual ideals of love with its disturbing and embodied physical experience, and particularly how this life experiment was mediated in words by a learned woman.

Mystic and erotic spirituality

This combination of life experience, spiritual disposition, and an openness to love also came to imbue religious writings in the twelfth century, particularly those of Cistercian men. At the center of these devotional writings was the Old Testament book of the Song of Songs. This deeply erotic text, which appears to describe an intense, though thwarted, sexual relationship between a young man and woman, was now reinterpreted as expressing the soul's love for God, or Christ's love for his Church. A key Cistercian writer of the period, Bernard of Clairvaux, undertook a series of meditations on the Song of Songs,

FIGURE 6.3: Hildegard of Bingen receives a vision from God and dictates it to her scribe and secretary. Illumination from Hildegard of Bingen, *Liber Scivias*, Rupertsberg Codex (*c.*1175, now lost). Image courtesy of Wikimedia Commons.

grounding his teachings in both personal experience and a mystical reinterpretation of heterosexual love as spiritual longing. He claimed that the path of study was "the book of our own experience," and he imagined spiritual conversion as a series of three kisses given in turn to the feet, hands, and mouth of the Beloved (God).

This mystical turn in spirituality was soon taken up and pushed to new extremes by women writers of the thirteenth century who often wrote from outside official Church structures, translating the discourse from Latin into a range of vernaculars. The key concept flowing through these texts was the love of God as sublime, ineffable, and all-consuming. In its most perfected form, this kind of love overcame reason, destroyed the will, and even annihilated the individual soul in its ultimate union with God. These texts, informed by the vocabulary of secular courtly love, spoke extravagantly of infinite longing, the violent wounds of love, the ecstasy of union that ended in nonbeing and a kind of holy madness in the quest for the Beloved.

Like many of these visionary women mystics, Hadewijch was a Beguine,[11] living in northern Europe in the thirteenth century. Her writings, in Middle Dutch, comprise poems, visions in prose and letters, and reveal a familiarity with both the courtly literature of her day and ecclesiastical writings on the Song of Songs. Mother Columba Hart has observed that Hadewijch played fluidly with gender roles in her poems, sometimes figuring herself as a knight errant while God, or else Love personified ("*Minne*"), was pictured as the Lady to whom her service was owed (Hart 1980: 19). Throughout Hadewijch's writings run the themes of love's suffering, love's fire, and the embodied experience of the lover. This is evident in her poem, entitled by modern editors "Love's Seven Names," in which she characterizes Love as chain, light, live coal, fire, dew, living spring, and—perhaps most surprisingly—Hell. This is because:

> In Love nothing else is acquired
> But disquiet and torture without pity;
> Forever to be in unrest,
> Forever assault and new persecution . . .
> In the deep, insurmountable darkness of Love
> This outdoes the torments of Hell.
>
> —Hart 1980: 356

To the one who has experienced love, Hadewijch concludes, it is understandable "That Hell should be the highest name of Love" (Hart 1980: 357).

Also a Beguine was Mechthild of Magdeburg (c.1210–82), whose *The Flowing Light of the Godhead* (*Das Fließende Licht der Gottheit*) was most likely written in Middle Low German, although it survives in earliest form in a Middle High German manuscript. It is multi-generic, containing "tales, dialogues, poems, visions, prayers, ecstasies, liturgical and, more particularly, lyrical reminiscences" (Zum Brunn and Epiney-Burgard 1989: 46), giving speaking voices to a range of allegorical figures including Love and Pain. The text speaks of the power of love and employs imagery from the Song of Songs, particularly when God implores the Soul to stay and become naked with him. When the Soul demurs, God instructs: "you are so 'co-natured' in me that nothing can be interposed between you and me" and he advises her to cast off fear, shame, and all such exterior virtues. All she should feel, God advises, are "your noble desire and your insatiable hunger, which I shall satisfy eternally" (ibid.: 59–60).

Although Beatrice of Nazareth (1200–68) also commenced her training in a beguinage as a child, she took orders as a Cistercian nun in her teenage years. Devoted to the idea of Love's suffering in the pursuit of the Beloved, Beatrice experienced the traditional torments of the female mystic, including violent self-mortifications, demonic temptations, and even a spell of "holy madness." Along with a number of highly sensory visions, Beatrice left behind a short treatise in Middle Dutch entitled *The Seven Manners of Love* (*Van Seven Manieren van Heiligher Minnen*). These include all the intense suffering that characterized mystic discourse, leading to the annihilation of the self. For instance, in the Third Manner, the questing soul feels "as if she dies while living, and dying feels the heavy pain of hell."[12] In the Fourth she is subsumed: "The beauty of love has eaten her. The power of love has consumed her. The sweetness of love has plunged her into nothingness." Building toward its apogee in the Fifth, love then becomes overwhelming, "immoderate," and it "breaks out in the soul in such a way, that it seems to her that her heart is repeatedly being painfully wounded." The Lover experiences this as an intensely psychosomatic phenomenon: "It seems to her as if her veins break open, her blood is being heated, her marrow atrophies, her legs weaken, her chest scorches, and her throat dries up, so that her face and all her limbs . . . participate in this primal rage of love."

As can be imagined, having women, and particularly women not enclosed within recognized monastic structures, writing texts that idealized spiritual love as unbounded, intensely embodied, and unashamedly sexualized, deeply disturbed the male ecclesiastic elite. There is evidence that Mechthild was impelled to become a nun later in her life because of growing concerns over her writing, while women like Beatrice gained some security from writing within Cistercian structures. The question came to a head, however, with the Beguine Marguerite Porete. Marguerite's *A Mirror of Simple Souls* (*Le Miroir des âmes simples anéanties*) was written in Old French as a Boethian dialogue between allegorical figures, interspersed with poetry, in a vocabulary indebted to courtly love. Described as "a daring attempt" to portray the "affective capacities of the soul" (Babinsky 1993: 27), the text argued that Reason had to become the servant to Love, which was a complete inversion of the earlier medieval subordination of feeling to reason. The aim of the annihilated soul was then to transcend feeling and Love argues that such a soul "is so enflamed in the furnace of the fire of Love that she has become properly fire, which is why she feels no fire" (107). Similarly, the annihilated soul "feels no joy, for she is joy itself. She swims and flows in joy, without feeling any joy, for she dwells in Joy and Joy dwells in her" (109). Marguerite's text concerned the authorities, however, and was publicly burned; some time later, Marguerite was arrested. Imprisoned, interrogated, and excommunicated, Marguerite refused to acknowledge the authority of her inquisitors or to give assurances that she would stop circulating her writings. She was therefore sentenced to death for heresy and burned at the stake in Paris in 1310 (20–4). This death, which still shocks over seven hundred years later, makes an appropriate close to the period under discussion in this volume, marking the life-and-death consequences that literature could have for its makers in the "persecuting society" that emerged in the course of the thirteenth century (Moore 2007).

Arthurian romances

The rise of courtly romances, and particularly the creation of the Arthurian tradition, is marked by intensity of emotion. Within these texts, emotion becomes a driving force—often *the* driving force—that moves the action forward. These texts explore the inner lives—the psychological motivations—of their characters through an analysis of their feelings. Chrétien de Troyes, often viewed as the originator of the Arthurian tradition, wrote five romances in the second half of twelfth century, composed in rhymed couplets in Old French. Two of them, *Erec and Enide* and *The Knight with the Lion*, explore the struggle a knight might experience between the pleasure of romantic love and his need to pursue honor. Having fallen madly in love with his wife, the knight Erec has no further taste for tournaments, but while he "turned all his attention to embracing and kissing" Enide, his followers "were grieved by this and often lamented among themselves, saying that he loved her far too much." The nobles claimed that "it was a great shame and sorrow" that Erec had given up fighting and when Enide learns that she is the cause of her husband's loss of repute, "she could not refrain from weeping" because "she felt such pain and sorrow" (Kibler 1991: 67). This sets in motion the many adventures Erec then undertakes with Enide by his side.

Throughout the tale, the emotions described are deeply somatic: Enide weeps until her tears fall upon Erec; later as she listens to the noise of his battle, she is struck with such fear that "there was no vein in which the blood did not curdle, and her face became pale and white as if she were dead" (Kibler 1991: 83). Chrétien's description of Yvain's love for his lady in *The Knight with the Lion* is even more deeply embodied, and appears at times to anticipate the poetry of writers like John Dunne. Chrétien tells us that Yvain "left his lady so reluctantly that his heart stayed behind." He then takes this conceit to extravagant, even humorous, levels, adding that "Once the body is without the heart, it cannot possibly stay alive," and "[y]et now this miracle happened, for Yvain remained alive without his heart, which used to be in his body but which refused to accompany it now" (328).

Chrétien left his fifth romance, *The Story of the Grail* (about the knight Perceval), unfinished, and it became the source from which the German writer, Wolfram von Eschenbach, crafted his masterpiece *Parzival*, composed in rhyming couplets in Middle High German in the first decade of the thirteenth century. An emotionally insightful episode occurs early in the story (Bk. III) where Parzival's mother, Herzeloyde, has taken him as a child to grow up deep within a forest, far from the court, so that she might never lose him to the knighthood. Wolfram intuitively captures the competing emotions as the child begins to explore his surroundings and his mother watches him prepare to grow apart from her. Parzival loves to hunt birds with his little bow and arrow—a sign of his natural nobility and knightliness—but also regrets killing the beautiful songbirds so much that "he would weep and tear at himself, wreaking vengeance on his hair" (Edwards 2006: 51). Meanwhile, Herzeloyde, watching Parzival's enchantment with the birds, is overcome with jealousy and orders them all destroyed. When Parzival first encounters armored knights in the woods, he is filled with wonder, and Wolfram beautifully captures his perplexity as he attempts to figure out what kind of beings they are. Finally, when the youthful Parzival leaves the forest to become a knight, his mother runs after him and, as he disappears from sight, dies of grief (55).

The story of Tristan and Isolde, although later incorporated into the Arthurian cycle, began as a separate story. At its heart it is a tale of emotions, since it is founded upon the love triangle of Isolde, her husband Mark, and the knight Tristan, and the complex and evolving moral and affective responses each has to this situation. The story was most famously told by Gottfried von Strassbourg who wrote his *Tristan* in rhyming couplets in Middle High German at the beginning of the thirteenth century. Gottfried enters deeply into the psychology of love, its compulsions, and jealousies. When Tristan and Isolde look at each other "they enmesh their eyes and hearts . . . so intimately that they often failed to disengage them" before Mark, who is always watching them, catches sight. He in turn "conceived such anger, such envy and hatred" that "now pain and anger had robbed him of measure and reason," because "[i]t was death to his reason that his darling Isolde should love any man but himself" (Hatto 1967: 258). Later when Mark finds Tristan and Isolde lying asleep together, but separated by a drawn sword between them, his feelings are complex and confused: should he be pained that they are together or joyful that they appear not to be sexually involved? Gottfried invokes psychological allegory to explain Mark's emotions: "Love, the Reconciler, stole to the scene, wondrously preened and painted. Over the white of her face she wore the paint of golden Denial, her most excellent cosmetic" (Hatto 1967: 272).

The story, of course, cannot end well, but the conclusion with all its unresolved emotional complexity is perhaps best expressed in the fragmentary text that formed Gottfried's main source. The Old French *Tristan* of an Angevin writer known only as Thomas, written probably contemporaneously with Chrétien's romances of the mid-twelfth century, sums up the unhappy denouement. Almost like a montage from a soap opera (another genre driven almost entirely by emotion) it scans the various bedrooms of the main characters, finding Mark sexually enjoying Isolde but in torments of jealousy and fear, Isolde paying Mark his dues but longing for Tristan and jealous of Tristan's new wife, Tristan encumbered with a new wife (another "Isolde") whom he does not love but cannot leave and suffering sexual jealousy over Mark's access to his former Isolde, and the new Isolde desperately in love with her husband but a frustrated and angry virgin in his bed (Hatto 1967: 316–18). In the end, falsely convinced by the new Isolde of his former Isolde's death, Tristan turns his face to the wall and gives up his spirit with the

FIGURE 6.4: Tristan and Isolde. Paris, Bibliothèque nationale de France, MS Fr. 2186, fol. 5ᵛ, c.1250–75. Photo by FALKENSTEINFOTO/Alamy Stock Photo.

words "Dearest Ysolt." When his beloved Isolde in fact arrives, she presses her body to his and dies of sorrow and pity at his side (352–3).

This resolution of courtly love in death was driven to dangerous new extremes of suicide both contemplated and attempted in Chrétien's *The Knight of the Cart*, the first tale to introduce the adulterous love of Lancelot and Guinevere. When Guinevere thinks that Lancelot is dead, she is "crazed with the thought of killing herself" and "repeatedly grabbed at her throat" (Kibler 1991: 259). On hearing of Guinevere's life-threatening demise, Lancelot is so distraught that he attempts to strangle himself with his own belt, a scene that Chrétien spells out in disturbing detail (259–60). Suicide was an unforgivable Christian sin and a capital crime in Europe at this time, so having it evoked as a reaction to emotional distress highlights the dangers of emotion-guided action in this period. Increasingly in these romances we see that deep emotions are able to be resolved—or even not resolved so much as just simply ended—only in death. This marks an interesting comparison with the spiritual writings discussed earlier, where the great love of the mystic ends in the annihilation of the soul—but in union with God. By contrast, in these secular romances, great earthly love ends in the destruction of the bodies of the lovers in the grief and sorrow caused by their parting.

LOOKING FORWARD TO THE FOURTEENTH CENTURY

Chrétien's *The Knight of the Cart* makes explicit the conflicting emotions with which courtly characters must contend, evoking them as personifications who verbally dispute

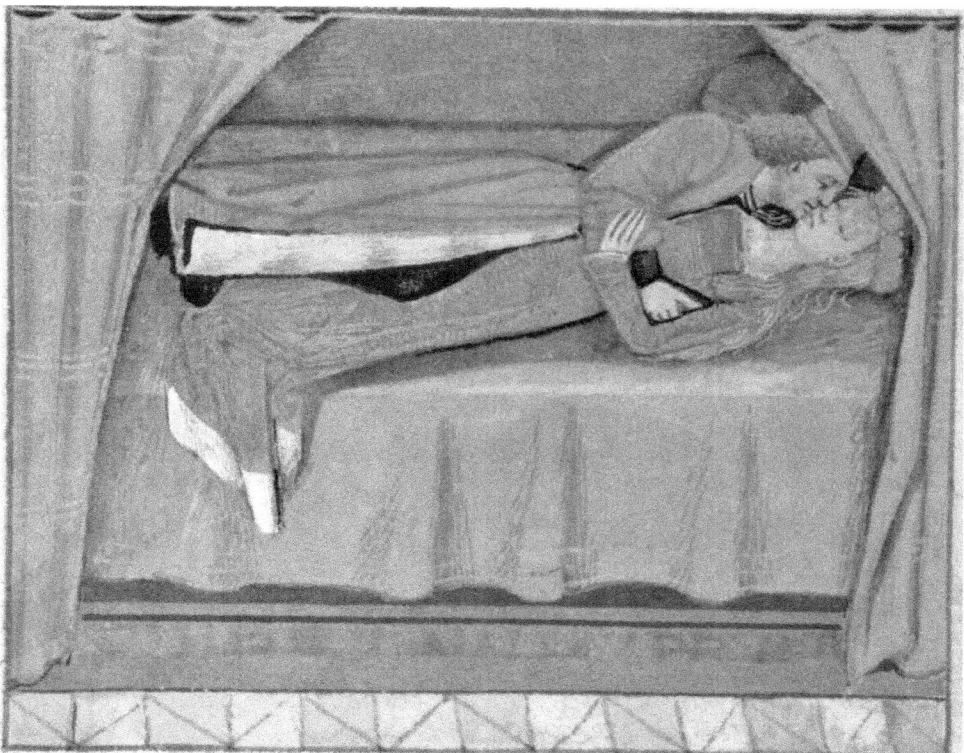

FIGURE 6.5: "The Lover enjoys the Rose," Guillaume de Lorris / Jean de Meun, *Roman de la Rose*, Oxford, Bodleian Library, MS Douce 195, fol. 155ᵛ. © The Bodleian Libraries, The University of Oxford.

with their human agents. When Lancelot is required in Guinevere's service to mount a cart driven by a dwarf—two cultural markers of shame—he momentarily hesitates. Reason and Love then contend with him as to the right course of action (Kibler 1991: 212). Later, when a maiden requests that he give her the head of a knight he has just defeated, Lancelot finds himself obliged to negotiate the competing demands of Generosity and Compassion (242).

These personifications lead us finally to the great allegory of the *Roman de la Rose* (*Romance of the Rose*) and the conclusion of our story of emotions in literature in the period 350–1300. This complex text, a dream narrative in Old French, was begun in the 1230s by Guillaume de Lorris, who composed around 4,000 lines of verse, then completed in 1275 by the great scholar Jean de Meun whose continuation took the poem to nearly 22,000 lines. In its opening by Guillaume, we see the erotic passion and questing motif of the Arthurian tradition at play, as the Dreamer relates how he has come to write this romance "in which the whole art of love is contained" (Dahlberg 1983: 31). Having fallen asleep, the Dreamer imagines that he comes upon a beautiful enclosed garden inhabited by personifications of affective states such as Hatred and Joy. Within the garden are rosebushes and the Dreamer finds himself irresistibly drawn to one particular bright red rosebud, perfectly formed and sweetly scented. As the Dreamer struggles through the thorns to grasp the rose, the God of Love notches an arrow in his bow and strikes the Dreamer with it. The Dreamer then suffers all the psychosomatic torments of love as he quests for his Rose.

From this straightforward quest-romance beginning, Jean de Meun turned the text in a much more philosophical direction. Jean had translated Boethius's *Consolation of Philosophy* into French, and its Stoic philosophy colors Reason's discourse to the Lover. Reason, who is pictured as the mother of Shame, the figure who prevents the roses from being plucked, speaks for over 3,000 lines, dissuading the Lover from his quest. She quotes Cicero's *De senectute* on the advantage of old age in quelling desire and Cicero's *De amicitia* on the greater value of friendship over romantic love. In particular, she reminds the Lover that Boethius teaches us to live not for this world, but the next, and that Socrates practiced Stoic equanimity so that he was "neither happy in prosperity nor sad in adversity" (Dahlberg 1983: 117). Although Nature subsequently supports the Lover's quest, the focus of her argument is not the primacy of emotions, but rather the necessity of sexual desire and consummation. In the end, the Lover's claiming of the Rose is an unemotional affair, depicted in a sustained metaphor of the breaching of the Rose's virginity which conveys no emotional resonance with the event. Simply, the Rose is claimed and the Dreamer awakes.

The *Roman de la Rose* therefore makes a fitting end to this survey of emotions in the literature of Late Antiquity and the early and high Middle Ages. It cycles from the questing romance of the twelfth and thirteenth centuries back to the Stoic philosophy of Late Antiquity and reestablishes reason as a powerful force in the restraint of the emotions after its obliteration in the writings of the women mystics in the face of love. The *Roman* then moves in a much more medicalized direction—we might even say a Scholastic direction, given the Scholastic attention to the Aristotelian natural sciences—to focus on the necessity of sex, rather than romantic love, for the continuation of the line. The poem's allegorical structure would lead the way to other late medieval allegorical texts such as *Piers Plowman*, while its treatment of grand themes written over many thousands of lines of verse in a European vernacular would reach fulfillment in the great fourteenth-century *opera* of Dante, Boccaccio, and Chaucer.

CHAPTER SEVEN

In Private: The Individual and the Domestic Community

LISA PERFETTI

PRELUDE: PRIVATE OR PUBLIC, INDIVIDUAL OR COMMUNAL?

In the contemporary West, we are accustomed to distinguishing between private and public, between the thoughts and behaviors we confine to ourselves or to our immediate circle of friends or family at home and the interactions that we perform in front of others. But this is a distinction that was less clear in the Middle Ages. Matters of state were often discussed in the intimate spaces of the household in the presence of family members, including women and children. Aristocratic women, associated with the "domestic sphere," were in charge not only of raising children but managing the affairs of a substantial household, making them managers as well as mothers. Personal correspondence, which we largely view as private, was often edited and circulated for others to read. The educated clerics who wrote about political and church life in the eleventh and twelfth centuries envisioned "a profound and divinely ordained resonance between public and private," and they used the gestures and emotions of family life to construct their image of the ideal Church and describe proper relations between members of lay and religious communities (McLaughlin 2010: 227). A woman's impassioned pleas to her husband to avenge the death of a kinsman is an event that might happen between spouses behind closed doors, but end up entailing public consequences of great magnitude. With the difficulty of distinguishing between public and private thus understood, this chapter will nonetheless address topics conventionally associated with the private realm—family relationships, friendship and marriage, and parenting—and explore the emotional standards and areas of debate relating to personal relationships.

Another question is how to define "the individual" (Morris 1972; McGuire 2011: 98). Related to the blurring between public and private is the overall tendency for emotions to be construed in the medieval period less as "individual" expressions of "authentic" feelings and more as events situating a person in a network of relationships. Whereas dominant attitudes in the twenty-first century in the West view the individual as having his or her own valid aspirations and ideas, the medieval period saw the individual as intertwined with a web of familial and communal relationships and the responsibilities those entailed. Some scholars of emotion have identified a binary between individualism and collectivism as the most important factor that creates variation in emotions across cultures (Triandis 1994). The choice of life partner, which we think of as an individual choice, was viewed among the European nobility more as a means of creating familial and political alliances. William Ian Miller's work on honor in the Icelandic sagas suggests that emotions were viewed as a "social state"; the grief of a father who loses a child—which would most likely be viewed today as an individual and private affair—was a condition that positioned him relationally to others, whether in the domestic or public sphere (Miller 1993a: 83). The grief of a wife for her husband in an Anglo-Saxon poem might signify personal individual loss, but also a mourning for kin structures that are decaying as norms of personal loyalty to a centralized sovereign edge out traditional forms of alliance based on family ties (Ingham 2003: 30).

A last dimension related to framing the subject of inquiry in this chapter is that of the influence of religious doctrine. It seems completely reasonable to us to distinguish between emotion and ethics, to view our feelings as separate from our behavior, and to consider religious teachings as a key factor in cultural difference rather than fundamental to our common identity as humans. In the medieval period, however, debates raged as to whether, or at what precise point, a feeling would count as a sin. Building on classical philosophy's interest in emotions as connected to virtue, early Christian authors begin to categorize some emotions as sins, with Pope Gregory's development of the Seven Deadly Sins in the sixth century—with pride (*superbia*) at their root—as perhaps the most notable legacy. As a result, by the early medieval period, some emotion words could do "double duty," indicating moral states as well as feelings (Rosenwein 2006: 49). And it was not uncommon for advice literature to exhort the individual to avoid not only certain behaviors, but states that we would consider emotions.

The impact of this religious discourse on the lived experience of people throughout the medieval period cannot be overemphasized. Barbara Rosenwein has remarked:

> As Christians deliberately turned pagan definitions of good and evil upside down, old emotional habits had to change. Parenting, education, and the availability of hallowed models—first of the martyrs and later of the saints—helped make this transformation possible. Christ's kingdom was not of this world: that essential fact was absorbed in different ways by different groups. But one thing is certain: Christianity had the potential to effect seismic shifts in the emotions that were valued or disdained as well as the norms of their expression.
>
> —Rosenwein 2006: 42

Emotions situated the individual in the larger ethical and moral universe, even when those feelings transpired in the domestic rather than public sphere, even in utter solitude in a private chamber. Whether cursing in anger at one's spouse at home or spewing vitriol at a political enemy in public, an individual's emotional outburst could be said to be indicative not of his feelings, but of his sinfulness. Under God's constant watchful scrutiny, emotions at home were always in some sense performed. Most importantly, because clerical discourses increasingly came to emphasize the individual's guarding against emotions that were sinful, every thought or feeling was not to be "let out" or naturally expressed but rather suppressed or redirected (Knuuttila 2004: 177–255).

At the same time, we must be cautious not to universalize specific clerical pronouncements about emotional states, since variations in emotional standards occurred not only across time but geographical region. As Rosenwein notes, there may be a common set of "building blocks" in Christianity, but like the notes of a musical scale, they can be rearranged in different ways to produce different musical expressions among different "emotional communities." Moreover, an individual can navigate between these communities, adapting to the different standards and norms of expression (Rosenwein 2006: 201). Rather than attempting a chronological account of shifting emotional standards, the rest of this chapter will lay out a conceptual framework for interpreting emotion discourses in individual accounts. Contemporary readers must then determine the available networks of emotional communities at play in any given "private" moment of domestic experience.

AFFECTIVE TIES AND THE CONCEPT OF FAMILY

The modern notion of family in the West typically denotes a private unit of people related to each other by blood or marriage. The term *familia* in the medieval period, by contrast, encompassed a wider group of servants and dependents. Authors of texts of moral instruction in the Carolingian period, for example, emphasized the responsibility of the man or woman of the house for the welfare and instruction of the wider household (Stone 2012: 175). Studies of family structures, particularly in the early Middle Ages, have only recently started to emerge, and rarely are the affective ties between household members analyzed, a lacuna explained not only by the difficulty in locating evidence that demonstrates these ties (particularly in peasant families, for which there are fewer records), but also the assumption that emotions are either universally shared or unworthy of attention (McLaughlin 2010: 12). Specific examples of the affective ties between spouses and between parents and children will be discussed below. Before examining these, however, it will be useful to consider some overall features of the concept of the family in the Middle Ages.

Generally speaking, the medieval family was hierarchical and relations between family members reflected a worldview in which hierarchy was fundamental to a well-ordered universe. There was an asymmetrical view of affective bonds, whether in family or society, and relationships of emotion and power were differential, juxtaposing the "humility, fidelity, and obedience of subordinates and the justice, generosity, and discipline (tempered with mercy) of their superiors" (Stone 2012: 213). Gender was one key dimension of this hierarchical view. Beliefs about women's innate weakness calling for their subordination to men, inherited from classical Antiquity and refashioned by Christian thinkers, tended to view women as more susceptible to their emotions, especially vulnerable to excessive or inappropriate laughter or weeping (Perfetti 2005). Writing aimed at women, whether as wives, mothers, or daughters, therefore, emphasized the importance of controlling emotion. This was not limited to women, of course—every Christian was required to monitor closely thoughts and feelings that could be sinful or lead to sin—but beliefs about women's susceptibility to the passions meant that they were expected to be especially vigilant.

A good example may be found in a set of German poems between aristocratic parents and their children commonly called *Der Winsbecke* and *Die Winsbeckin*, possibly dating around 1210 (see Figure 7.1) Whereas the father's advice to his son is rooted primarily in practical advice about an array of responsibilities (warfare, behavior at court, household management), the mother's advice to her daughter is primarily oriented toward her domestic role as a virtuous woman to be sought by men; whereas the son is viewed as an active agent, the daughter's agency "is largely confined to imposing self-control and restraint upon herself" consisting more of an "honorable passivity" (Rasmussen 1997: 140).

FIGURE 7.1: Mother instructing her daughter, *Die Winsbeckin*, c.1300–1340. Große Heidelberger Liederhandschrift (Codex Manesse), Zürich. © Heidelberg University Library (Universitätsbibliothek Heidelberg), Cod. Pal. germ. 848, fol. 217ʳ.

Regarded as less in control of their emotions generally, women were consequently urged to suppress emotions, such that the ideal woman might be described as either lacking in emotion or feeling primarily on behalf of others.

The representation of women sacrificing their own desires out of feeling for the wants and desires of others runs counter to twenty-first-century sensibilities which accord more importance to defining one's aspirations, fulfilling one's dreams, and seeking happiness. Yet the self-abnegation of women in medieval texts is inflected by medieval notions of sacrifice that determine virtue. An instructive example comes from one of the lais of the twelfth-century author Marie de France. Often thought to be the last and culminating of the twelve lais in the manuscript, *Eliduc* tells the story of a woman, Guildelüec, in a marriage of mutual love and respect whose husband, Eliduc, unwittingly falls in love with another woman. When Guildelüec comes to understand the love that has arisen in her husband, she neither feels jealousy nor sees herself as wronged. Rather, she orients her emotion toward both her husband and his beloved, who appears to be dying. When the maiden is miraculously revived, Guildelüec explains: "Truly, I am his wife and my heart grieves for him. Because of the grief he displayed, I wanted to know where he went, and came after him and found you. I am overjoyed that you are alive and shall take you with me and return you to your beloved. I shall set him free completely and take the veil" (Marie de France 1999: 125). Notable in this passage is how the emotion words are those of others (her husband's grief) or on behalf of them (she grieves for her husband and is overjoyed that the damsel is alive). The convenient solution of retiring to a convent—although not permissible at any point in Christian teaching (Stone 2012: 267–74; McLaughlin 2010: 43–7)—seemingly demonstrates the wife's abnegation of her individual happiness. Yet it is telling that the end of the lai, when Eliduc and his beloved are older, Eliduc builds a church, founds an order and enters it, while his second wife leaves her marriage to join Guildelüec in the convent. Marie concludes that "Each one strove to love God in good faith and they came to a good end thanks to God, the true divine" (Marie de France 1999: 126). Human love has been redirected toward love of God, and whereas the lai began with a married couple and was then complicated by an adulterous triangle, it ends with the pairing of two women. As Marie notes early in her narrative, it is the two women who are actually the central characters: "From these two the lay of *Guildelüec and Guilliadun* takes its name. It was first called *Eliduc*, but now the name has been changed, because the adventure upon which the lay is based concerns the ladies" (Marie de France 1999: 111).

The implication of this tale for an understanding of twelfth-century values regarding women's emotion is that women's capacity to feel on behalf of others both removes them from the affairs of the world and endows them with significant moral and ethical standing (Gaunt 2006: 138–67, esp. 150–5). The notion that women are especially likely to be praised for their compassion is related to the recent work by Sarah McNamer, who has argued that by the thirteenth century, images of a fragile and vulnerable Christ had come to dominate textual and pictorial representations of the Passion and that "to perform compassion—in the private drama of the heart that these texts stage—is to feel like a woman, in particular medieval iterations of that identity" (McNamer 2010: 3, see also 5–10). McNamer argues not only that the feminization of compassion is not ubiquitous (contrasting the gendering of compassion in medieval Christian thought with Ifaluk, Tibetan Buddhist, and Greek attitudes toward the emotion), but also calls for an analysis of this feeling that puts theological discourse into the larger context of a history of emotion.

The reorientation of worldly affection between spouses to the love of God recounted in Marie's story leads to another factor in understanding affective relationships in the medieval family. No matter how strong one's affection for spouse or child, the loyalty and love owed to God took precedence. Augustine's statement in his treatise on marriage (*De bono coniugali*) that "the coming of Christ is not served by the begetting of children" permeated the thinking of writers for centuries afterward (Stafford 2001: 260). In her instruction manual of 843 for her son William, Dhuoda wrote that love and loyalty to God should come before that of family (Stone 2012: 206–7). Crusading documents in the following centuries echo the view that familial bonds are to be subsumed to relationships with God. Sermons and literary texts portrayed wives as an impediment to crusading because their husbands might be drawn to stay at home either out of love or a sense of obligation to their spouse. In a thirteenth-century sermon by Gilbert de Tournai, a crusader asked that his children be brought to him before he departed so that his anguish in leaving them would enable him to "count for more with God" (Maier 2000: 203).[1] Clerical writers often wrote of the obedience that children owed to their parents and took an active role in attempting to shape familial relations. They instructed children to honor their parents, but this instruction was accompanied by reminders that loyalty to God must come before loyalty to parents (McLaughlin 2010: 111).

However, the relative importance of mortal affective ties and obligations could vary from one Christian community to the next. For example, Pope Gregory may have downplayed the hierarchy of celestial over human bonds because the political structures of the Merovingian world were such that fragile familial ties needed to be emphasized to preserve political harmony (Rosenwein 2006: 129). Religious discourse likely influenced familial relations, but clerical writers of the eleventh and twelfth centuries actually drew heavily on familial relations in the construction of their ideal portrait of the Church. For example, whereas even non-Catholics today are accustomed to addressing members of the clergy as "father," this was not such an easy move in the eleventh and early twelfth centuries where it was still a political statement to use such a title for a spiritual leader: "It was precisely because images of fathers carried such a powerful rhetorical and emotional charge that they were able to shape discussions of 'right order' within the Church and within Christian society during the central Middle Ages" (McLaughlin 2010: 187). To understand the emotions between individuals, then, we need to observe the various interrelationships between Church and state, between the private and the public, and the other social structures and values that inform attitudes toward the family.

An individual's social standing and the way she is able to navigate political relationships is a powerful shaping force for emotion. If medieval texts often characterized women as being more emotional, or less in control of their emotions, one might suggest that this comes as much from women's reduced autonomy in domestic and public affairs as it does from any dominant views of women's innate inferiority. A noblewoman with property and political power could in some measure enjoy the respect accorded to men. The feelings of a wife for her husband or a father for his son would depend, too, on how that family member reflected traits that were valued in that particular social system. In Icelandic sagas, for example, such traits as courage, pride in family, generosity, independence, and an ability to navigate the social scene were valued: "When a father or son perceives these features in the other, the emotional connection is a positive one; and saga authors draw our attention to it by describing cooperative, affectionate relations" (Itnyre 1996: 191). Changes in social status, such as inheritance, political ties with other powerful individuals or families, and shifts in social values, all inflect interpersonal relationships and shape how individuals feel toward members of their domestic community.

LOVE AND PASSION, FRIENDSHIP AND MARRIAGE

To ascertain what emotions existed between spouses or might lead to the formation of a marriage, we must investigate the intersection of the many factors discussed above: beliefs relating to Christians' obligation to orient their emotional universe toward God, political and social relations shaping domestic relations, and social values that were dominant in contemporary discourses. The contemporary narrative dominant in the West of the individual who seeks out the ideal life partner, falls in love, and then celebrates this emotional attachment in the culminating act of marriage runs up against two powerful social forces in the medieval period: the use of marriage to cement ties between families or political entities, and clerical discourses on love human and divine. Whether subordinated to the wish of one's family or the requirements of a religion that expected absolute devotion, emotional attachments to another human being, no matter how deeply felt, were not considered to be a domain for merely private or individual determination.

The long-lasting medieval debate on consent in marriage testifies to the interplay between clerical and secular frameworks subordinating the individual to communal concerns (McLaughlin 2010: 25). Anti-marriage tracts encouraged young women and men to pursue celibacy by portraying the married state as both a life of subjugation of one spouse to the other and a worldly encumbrance distracting the Christian from higher spiritual union with God. Such writings also served to keep property in the hands of the Church as the lack of spouses or children made it more likely that lands or goods would be bequeathed to monasteries and convents rather than passed on to family members (Livingston 2012: 22). However, with the growth of patrilineal inheritance in this period in which only the eldest son would inherit, monasteries provided an option for younger sons who had no lands or property of their own with which to build a family; celibacy thus served to preserve the patrimonies of families as well as of the Church (McLaughlin 2010: 32).

"Passionate love" is a term we sometimes use to distinguish this form of love from other kinds of emotional attachments, yet our contemporary hierarchy, which accords more emotional power to a life partner as opposed to someone with whom we are "just friends," was not operative in this way in the medieval period. Friendships were often described with language that we would view as highly passionate. Thus Alcuin can speak to a fellow cleric of love penetrating his breast with its flame, and poets write of the kisses and embraces from their male friends for which they long. While a modern reader might view such accounts as evidence of homosexual desire, for the elite male audiences of such texts, it was evidence of "ennobling love," based on the love of virtue in another person, which elevates both the lover and the object of his devotion. A carefully cultivated and refined form of feeling, ennobling love was a mark of social distinction that functioned to enhance reputation (Jaeger 1999: 13–17).[2] In heroic literature from the Middle Ages, men going into war march resolutely to their death with little visible sign of emotion, yet shed tears when confronting displays of friendship and loyalty by their companions (Classen 2012). Friendship between women, however, was less often portrayed, with one scholar contrasting the "verbose" discourse on male friendship with the relative silence regarding friendship and love between women (Lochrie 2003: 70).[3] This can be attributed, in part, to the fact that the authors of most of the written records were men, and to the lesser value accorded to the affairs of women. A range of didactic and literary texts point rather to the anxiety created when women gathered together, gossiping about men, or leading other women to immoral behavior, an anxiety linked to beliefs about women's weakness and greater susceptibility to carnal desires. However, we do find evidence of attachments in a variety of sources. Female religious communities, as suggested in Marie de France's tale above, likely functioned as places where women could live together as sisters, sharing affection (Lochrie 2003: 83–4). Some clerical writers raised concerns about friendship both in male and religious houses, as any love between individuals could distract the Christian from complete devotion to God (Jaeger 1999: 50). But views of monastic friendships varied widely across the Middle Ages, and the affections between individuals ("brotherly or sisterly love") could often be said to exemplify, rather than threaten, love for God.

Passionate love also bespeaks one of the central cultural preoccupations of the medieval period relating to love. Sexual desire, viewed in some cultures as a normal and natural feature of relationships between spouses, was most often viewed as sinful, a passion that the Christian must continually master and control. Augustine, in the fourth century, explained that the sinfulness of sexual desire resulted from the Fall, a punishment (along with the pains of childbirth) for human disobedience and disloyalty to God (McLaughlin 2010: 221–2). While clerical writers might argue over the value of marriage in channeling sexual desire, there was little dispute that sexual feelings were to be suppressed rather than celebrated. The implications of this are significant, as the physical desire accompanying passionate relationships could engender the experience of shame rather than deepen feelings of love. As Jerome, one of the most widely disseminated authors and the author most hostile to marriage expressed it: "The wise man loves his wife with judgment not with affection. Let not the impulse of pleasure reign in him, nor the proclivity toward intercourse. Nothing is more foul than to love a wife as an adulteress" (Baldwin 1994: 120). Jerome's statement not only characterizes sexual desire as shameful, but also suggests that love itself is suspect, and we might wonder whether the emotion of love was recognized or valued as part of the bond between spouses. While it is true that clerical writers ranked celibacy and chastity over marriage, and exalted divine love over human love, their views of what constituted legal marriage were informed by the presence of emotional attachments that bound spouses. The presence of true affection (*maritalis affectio*) defined the difference between concubinage (what we might call cohabitation) and marriage. While it began as a term to define intent to engage in a marriage, *maritalis affectio* gradually took on an emotional tone similar to "affection" or "love" and was meant to indicate not simply consent to be legally joined and to cohabit, but a commitment to care for one's spouse (McNamer 2010: 47–9).

Even clerical discourse on celestial rather than human unions can be said to be imitating, rather than repudiating, beliefs about attachments between spouses. Early church writers like Fortunatus and Gregory liken love for Christ to a wife's passionate love for a spouse, thus transposing an emotion already seen as positive to a higher plane (Rosenwein 2006: 118–19). Women putatively fleeing marriage and human husbands sought to demonstrate an emotional attachment that made them not only symbolically but legally married to Christ, and "marriage to Christ was understood to have an exceptional emotional intimacy at its core. This is what is yearned for, hoped for, promised" (McNamer 2010: 42). Conventional wisdom would have us see the bride of Christ as seeking a superior emotional state that is unavailable in human relationships, but it may be more accurate to see this state as a mirroring or replication of both the emotional and legal qualities defining human marriage.

Because so many sources on medieval marriage come to us from documents written by the clergy, it is not surprising that the accumulated evidence regarding love between spouses appears relatively indifferent to such emotional attachments. Megan McLaughlin has argued that the increasingly emotional language clerical reformers used to talk about the plight of the Church in the eleventh and twelfth centuries was accompanied by a relative absence of attention given to the experiences of actual husbands and, particularly, wives:

> Honor—scorn—mockery—longing—anger—shame: such highly charged words electrify reform rhetoric during the central Middle Ages. Writers like Humbert, Geoffrey of Vendôme, Ranger of Lucca, and Placidus of Nonantola present their demands for ecclesiastical reform with legal precedents attached, but above all with heartfelt pleas for the relief of the suffering Bride. The sympathy they fail—for whatever reason—to express for ordinary wives, they pour out for the *Sponsa Christi*.
>
> —McLaughlin 2010: 87

Other sources of information available to us come from personal letters (relatively sparse in this period), historical records relating personal relationships that led to issues of public concern, and literary texts. Emotion in medieval literature is the subject of a different chapter in this volume (Chapter Six), but there are two brief points worth considering here. First, written texts, literary or otherwise, are not so much evidence of how medieval people felt, as descriptive of values and norms relating to emotions and their expression. Rosenwein, speaking of a celebratory poem written in 566 by Fortunatus on the occasion of the marriage between King Sigibert and Brunhild, asks:

> Did Sigibert really love Brunhild? It is impossible to know ... Certainly we can be sure that Sigibert liked to hear that he loved his bride, that he was glad to have those assembled at his wedding imagine that he did, and that Fortunatus's poem evoked an emotional scenario pleasing to all. His epithalamium tells us about the image of married love prized at Sigibert's court. That is information enough for the historian. Indeed, it is more valuable than knowing whether Sigibert loved Brunhild.
>
> —Rosenwein 2006: 120

The account of Fortunatus's poem, which describes Cupid's arrows of love inflaming both the king and his bride, suggests the degree to which passionate love between husband and wife could be extolled even by an author who composed poems celebrating virginity, and one could argue that church writers borrowed from the passionate language of human relationships in their account of divine love (Rosenwein 2006: 119).

Literary texts of the medieval period were interconnected with religious discourse, and while there may be significant differences in orientation of these two (toward heaven or toward human society), it is difficult to separate one from the other. This is what limits the most recent and ambitious attempt to analyze the emotion of love in the medieval period. In *The Making of Romantic Love*, William M. Reddy argues that the set of regulations regarding sexual desire and sexual acts from the Gregorian Reform of 1050–1200, the culmination of a centuries-old tradition of viewing desire as a kind of appetite and equating it with sin, created the conditions for the invention of courtly love (or *fin'amors*), which functioned as an escape or refuge from the unrealistic and harsh view of human relationships promulgated in reform writings. Even to use the term "love," argues Reddy, is to be hopelessly entangled in a dualistic worldview that opposes desire and lust (a bodily appetite) with love (a purely spiritual emotion that cannot be sullied by bodily attachments). He therefore invents the term "longing for association." Reddy helpfully demonstrates the force and omnipresence of the equation between sexual feelings and sin in the medieval West by contrasting writings about love from this context with Heian Japan and twelfth-century India (Bengal and Orissa) where this dichotomy does not operate. He therefore argues that the dualism in the Christian West led to a "shadow religion," with "a heroic ethic of courage, self-denial, self-discipline, and devotion to the beloved every bit as demanding and rewarding as the spiritual career of Christian asceticism" (Reddy 2012: 167).[4]

Reddy is certainly correct to highlight the parallels between clerical and secular discourses and the qualities of self-denial and heroism associated with love, whether human or divine. But the considerable variety of articulations of love in both courtly and clerical contexts, and the fact that the same author could provide remarkably different accounts of passionate love, suggest less a cause-and-effect relationship than an interplay of debates about the nature of longing and ethical standing that operate in a variety of discourse and genres throughout the period. Simon Gaunt, in his study of love and death in medieval literature has, like Reddy, been struck by the quasi-religious flavor of courtly love literature, asking: "What is the import of the use of Christian imagery in erotic contexts, and what is its affective value? What did fictional scenarios in which lovers abased themselves before their ladies and worshipped them as quasi-deities mean to medieval readers and listeners?" (Gaunt 2006: 7). Like Reddy, Gaunt sees a tension between the courtly and the clerical, and views courtly literature as "an ethical system that parallels and mimics religion, incorporating religious elements, but remaining nonetheless sharply distinct," yet his reading accounts more thoroughly for the interplay of religious and secular vocabulary, the irony and self-awareness of much medieval literature, and the multivalence of literary language (209). Rather than seeing courtly love as a refuge from oppressive clerical discourse, his study suggests the way in which the discourse of courtly love itself can be viewed as a symptom of deeper questions about the forces that drive human actions and the psychically and emotionally fraught process of becoming an ethical subject.

It is difficult to know the extent to which everyday people in the Middle Ages found religious ideals about love and sexuality oppressive, and we can do little more than speculate about whether the spectrum of feelings medieval husbands and wives experienced for each other corresponds to the same kind of "love" felt in other times and places. There is less doubt, however, that an important emotion standard of the period was that a wife should subsume her own emotional disposition to the desires of her husband. Jerome, the father of the anti-marriage tradition, remarked in *Against Jovinianus* (1.47):

> Men marry, indeed, so as to get a manager for the house, to solace weariness, to banish solitude; but a faithful slave is a far better manager, more submissive to the master, more observant of his ways, than a wife who thinks she proves herself mistress if she acts in opposition to her husband, that is, if she does what pleases her, not what she is commanded.
>
> —Jerome 1893: 383

By the thirteenth century, conduct manuals and literary texts were painting the model wife as a woman who demonstrates her love for her husband through her complete submission to his wishes. In the first romance by Chrétien de Troyes, *Erec and Enide* (*c.*1180), the heroine proves to her husband that she loves him by obeying everything he asks of her. Yet her deep grief when she believes her husband to be slain endows her with a depth of feeling and internal complexity that demonstrate her character. The love-equals-obedience motif also had public consequences. In the late thirteenth-century German narrative *The Ladies' Tournament*, a group of women live apart, desiring to establish public honor equivalent to men's by creating their own jousting tournament. The men, learning of this female community, worry that if women can joust just as men, this must mean that men might have to do the housework, a threat to the natural order of the whole community; ultimately, the women must learn that loving men faithfully is what constitutes honor for them, and they are safely married off, dissolving their female community (Westphal-Wihl 1994). Ambition, the desire for honor, is defined as a domestic, rather than a public emotion for women. However, although the wife's ambition was generally confined to the home or family, her ability to use her persuasive abilities to shape the emotional disposition of her husband could ultimately lead to better public behavior by her husband; through her persuasive powers, she could "soften the heart" of her husband if he was neglecting his duties (Farmer 1986). She must not express her own anger to her husband, even if his behavior toward her was unjustified, but rather patiently endure and use her skills pragmatically to steer him back on the right path. In describing the trials of his mother in living with the quick temper of his father, Augustine noted in his *Confessions* (9.9.19), "She knew that an angry husband should not be opposed, not merely by anything she did, but even by a word" (Augustine 1991: 168). While the unhappy wife motif of much literature suggests the emotional suffering of actual wives forced into marriages by their families, or forced to endure a less than ideal husband, the model of the wife as a positive force of social change likely functioned for many women as a means of imagining their own emotional autonomy.[5]

PARENTS AND CHILDREN

Did medieval parents love their children? For many decades, historians of the family viewed the Middle Ages as lacking a concept of childhood—it was assumed that caring bonds between parents and their children would be lessened by high infant mortality rates and large families where attentions were divided among numerous children, and that such weaker emotional bonds would lead to the exploitation or abuse of children. Recent scholarship has revised this bleak family portrait, pointing out both the limited use of actual medieval evidence by the studies and the presentist narrative of modern progress informing them (Hanawalt 2002). The evidence for bonds of affection in the early medieval period can be more difficult to ascertain because there are fewer written accounts available, but historians have been resourceful. Rosenwein has examined the language of tombstones in Germany from 350 to 750, highlighting emotion words like "sweet" and "dear" used by spouses, children, and parents to express their fondness for family members (Rosenwein 2006: 68). Sally Crawford has examined not only legal codes and narratives of the Anglo-Saxon period, but also burial mounds where mothers are buried cradling their children (see Figure 7.2), and visual images of women holding the hands of older children (Crawford 1999: 10–11, 115). The letters, poems, and saints lives we do have use emotion words that indicate feelings we would regard as affection and love, particularly in accounts of grieving parents. In the late ninth century, King Alfred asked: "What sight is more intolerable than the death of a child before its father's eyes?" (Crawford 1999: 117). The late tenth- or early eleventh-century book of miracles of Saint Foy describes a woman who, faced with her dying son and "overcome by immense grief," begs God, "Do not deprive me of the sweetness of my son, whom I love in the depths of

FIGURE 7.2: Mother buried cradling a child. Grave 81 (Grave 1006 in the original excavation notes) from the cemetery at Butler's Field, Lechlade, Gloucestershire, excavated in 1985. © Oxford Archaeology.

my heart more than all my desire to live" (McLaughlin 2010: 102). References to fathers and sons in Icelandic sagas demonstrate that fathers were expected to be nurturing and supportive of their sons, and numerous fathers grieve deeply when their sons die (Itnyre 1996: 174). Children, too, grieved deeply for their parents; even Augustine speaks of his "life torn to pieces" upon the death of his mother, and how he wept for his loss (Cooper 2011: 19–20).

The recurrent images of grieving parents and children clearly contradict earlier beliefs about cold and unloving parents and abused children. But these views might be partly attributable to two central beliefs about family structures in the Middle Ages described above: the subordination of human affairs to the spiritual world, and the hierarchical view of human society. In her discussion of funerary epitaphs in Vienne, for example, Rosenwein considers one epitaph that reads: "Let her children cease to be troubled by tears and lamentation [*lacrimis planctusque*]. It is not right to groan [*gemere*] about that which ought to be celebrated." The emotions of grief are recognized, argues Rosenwein, yet "redirected from worldly things to celestial, and death was transformed from a sad to a happy event" (Rosenwein 2006: 75–6). Rosenwein also provides the example of Gregory the Great's story of Saint Felicity whose seven sons were condemned to death for refusing to sacrifice to the emperor. Whereas most mothers fear the death of their children, says Gregory, Felicity was no ordinary woman, for she feared for their souls, that they might live beyond her but lose their path to God. While this makes of her an extraordinary, even unnatural mother, Gregory noted that she nonetheless felt pain. It was precisely in overcoming the pain of losing her sons that her extraordinary love made her heroic rather than inhuman (Rosenwein 2006: 93).[6] The practice of oblation, offering up one's children to live in a monastic community, may seem to us a heartless act of abandoning children, yet in the Middle Ages it could signify parental concern for their children's well-being (Crawford 1999: 122–38).

Parents' love for their children, therefore, must consistently be oriented toward their eternal salvation, and their most important role was to train them to love God and live a moral and a well-ordered life on earth. Just as husbands were to govern their wives, so parents should ensure the obedience of their children. Early Christian writers like John Chrysostom argued that a father should be "stern and unyielding" with his son, but "gracious and kind" and reward him when he was obedient. This reflected a well-ordered universe, for "Even so God rules the world with fear of Hell and the promise of His Kingdom. So must we too rule our children" (John Chrysostom 1951: 113). In the Carolingian period, moralists worried that excessive parental love that expressed itself in indulgence would harm children by leading them into sin or immoral behavior or create political instability; by contrast, discipline, including corporal discipline, was viewed as fundamentally related to a parent's love for a child (Stone 2012: 206–8). Parents wrote "lay mirrors" or handbooks on conduct to counsel their children. In her handbook of 843, the Frankish noblewoman Dhuoda devoted a chapter to obedience owed to fathers, telling her son William that he "should fear, love, and be faithful" to his father (Stone 2012: 206–7). Her tone of instruction is mingled with words that convey her depth of love for her son. Separated from him, and fearing his imminent death due to the political turmoil of the time, she notes, "my firstborn son—you will have other teachers to present you with works of fuller and richer usefulness, but not anyone like me, your mother, whose heart burns on your behalf" (Dhuoda 1991: 13). Thus, while a stern teacher to her son, Dhuoda also displays here the love that guides her efforts.

The assumption that parents would display their love by disciplining their children applied regardless of gender, but accounts of emotional relationships between mothers, fathers, daughters, and sons have a gendered dimension. Broadly speaking, mothers were associated more with nurturing and fathers with disciplining. Archaeological evidence for Anglo-Saxon England suggests that mothers were the primary caregivers, although fathers, too, appear to have been actively engaged and emotionally invested in the rearing of children (Crawford 1999: 117). In the Carolingian period, fathers were given more advice on the rearing of sons than of daughters, and the advice typically centered on preserving chastity and fostering female modesty (Stone 2012: 208). In the central Middle Ages, while both fathers and mothers weep for ill or deceased children, it is the grief of mothers that is most usually emphasized, and images of grieving women were used to critique military campaigns, famine, or other sources of social decay (McLaughlin 2010: 93). As head of the house, a father was more often than not associated with discipline, and his authority was more likely to be viewed as unproblematic and definitive. A mother would likely be invested with a more authoritative role if she were a widow or governed the house in the absence of her husband. McLaughlin notes, "If some clerical writers attributed to mothers the potential to command and discipline their households, motherhood was more often associated in our sources with love, affection, and nurturing" (2010: 101; see also Garver 2009: 8). Yet a mother's role as nurturer often made her a powerful force for moral instruction. Prominent Christian thinkers such as Augustine and Bernard of Clairvaux wrote of the powerful moralizing influence their mothers had in their spiritual development and displayed their own devotion to their mothers in the vocabulary they used in their writing (Cooper 2011; McGuire 2011). In both clerical and lay communities, women were entrusted with ensuring virtuous households and were also viewed as potential agents of moral reform (Garver 2009: 122–69).

Likewise, the expectation of filial obedience applied more heavily to daughters than to sons. Unlike daughters, who more often stayed at home with their mothers as they grew up, sons were drawn into the world of men and separated from their mothers. A son's disobedience could even be depicted positively if it were seen as a sign of him developing his autonomy and progressing into adulthood. It may also be that, among households with significant property, inheritance laws had an effect on the way children identified with their parents. The most severe penalty for a son's disobedience was disinheritance, which may well have "raised the emotional and social temperature of the relationship between fathers and their sons" (McLaughlin 2010: 92, 165). Finally, children's more unruly emotions and disobedience could be endorsed when oriented to celestial rather than social ends. For girls, this was most often visible in accounts of daughters refusing to marry so that they could remain brides of Christ. A girl's anger toward her parents, which would otherwise be harshly condemned, could, in the account of a virgin martyr, be seen as proof of her sanctity (Peyroux 1998).

CONCLUSION

The study of emotions in the medieval family is still in its infancy. The interest in affective relationships between friends, spouses, parents, and children has gained increased currency and there is growing recognition that the love, anger, shame, grief, and pride occurring in private relationships are worthy topics of the scholar's attention. Few studies, however, have engaged in the kind of sustained analysis of emotion vocabularies and relationships between social structures and their influence on emotion standards that we need to understand fully the role emotions played in the cultural norms in various times and places across medieval Europe. Scholarship on emotion in medieval domestic communities has a long period of growing up ahead of it.

CHAPTER EIGHT

In Public: Collectivities and Polities

JEHANGIR YEZDI MALEGAM

Of the "affective life of the heroic," William Ian Miller says, "Much of the expression of emotion is mediated by the knowledge that it is presented to a public" (Miller 1990: 108). This statement conveys the importance of public expression to the history of emotions, but it does not tell the whole story. An emotional life is by definition public: it cannot be examined outside social, political, and cultural contexts that give it meaning and impact (Solomon 1984). Feelings—the subjective corollary to emotions—are shaped and ontologically validated by the regimes, conventions, subterfuges, and surrogacies in which they participate. These in turn are products of language, ritual, politics, and theatre, specific to a given society, time, and place.

Emoting is simultaneously imaginative, embodied, and social: the inhabitation of a generalized "self" that accepts conventional, that is publicly accepted, labels—happy, angry, sad—as referents to consistent categories of experience (Terada 1999). Arguably, then, a feeling cannot become conscious enough for emotional purposes without the social and cultural tools that put it to work—transform, subdue, articulate, and modify it (Reddy 2001). Emotional display provides vocabulary, strategy, and personhood for all members in an interaction, not just the person expressing their feelings. The history of emotions "in public" therefore engages a capacious category. As Stephanie Trigg puts it in an issue of *Exemplaria* dedicated to new approaches in the history of emotions, " 'emotion' is not only the response or expression of the individual romantic subject but can also refer to collective feelings and passions. This seems to be emerging as one of the distinctive contributions of emotion studies in medieval and early modern culture" (Trigg 2014: 5).

Medieval sources prompt us to include under "emotions" a range of actions, perception, events, articulations, and, importantly, reception. While describing changes in common understanding and collaborative management of these emotions between 350 and 1300, this chapter attempts the following questions: how did emotions function politically throughout the Middle Ages? How did management of feeling, its reception, and articulation, organize persons and groups? What cultural work was done by the (real or perceived) transformation of emotional states in public? Anthropological in their general interest, these questions also allow us to use expressions, representations, and discussions of emotion as pathways into medieval social and political systems.

PERIODIZATION OF EMOTIONAL STYLES AND PRACTICES OF FEELING

For historians, recovery of feeling is not an option (Ahmed 2001: 352). What we recover is the ambit of emotional activity, which is to say, how members of past societies represented, educated, privileged, enhanced, subdued, and organized feeling; how they recognized feelings in certain situations as relevant enough to record; how they misunderstood or disambiguated others. By understanding how emotionalism has been put to work in different circumstances and within changing social and political systems, it is possible to construct a history, not of emotions, but through emotions.

History through emotions requires periodization, which in turn requires the construction of a diachronic framework. Among such frameworks, the most problematic overly privilege affect, the precognitive, generalizable aspect of feeling. They trace changes in impulse and the relationship between impulse and action through time with the assumption that feeling can be boiled down to a set of neurochemical pathways involving the limbic system of the brain: so-called "rage circuits" and the like that neuro-historians such as Stephen Pinker suggest evolved over time to enable new forms of emotional control (Pinker 2011; see also Hanlon 2013). This model of historical change involves too many assumptions for our purpose and reduces culture to a "brake," "sublimation," or, at best, a teaching tool, rather than an integral component of feeling (G. M. White 1993; Leys 2011).

A more useful approach is taken by historians like William M. Reddy and Barbara Rosenwein, who rely on cognitive models of emotion in which higher-order intellectual processes and lower-order sensations are in constant communication, mutually modulating, enhancing, or suppressing each other (Reddy 2001, 2008b: 87–92; Rosenwein 2002, 2006). These cognitive models align effectively with anthropological and sociological examinations of how emotions produce and are in turn produced by social groups and political demands. In her studies of grieving and shame among the Ilongot people of the Philippines, the ethnographer Michele Rosaldo developed a pioneering model of emotions, in which the self—long privileged as the site of feeling—is a collaborative process, not determined either by culture or biology, but cultivated through social resources, needs, and demands at a local level (Rosaldo 1984). The sociologist Arlie Russell Hochschild, meanwhile, developed a theory of emotional management, studying how female Pan American Airways flight attendants "transduced" feeling, artificially cultivating their own cheerfulness in order to produce it in customers and thus achieving alienation from feelings constitutive of the self (Hochschild 1983).

Thanks to this emphasis on management and social production of self, historians like Reddy could posit "emotional regimes" and "forms of life," that is to say, political, intellectual, and social structures whose change over time related to changes in the way historical subjects were asked to feel, thought it necessary to feel, and, by extension, might actually have felt (Reddy 2008a). Importantly, the focus of change was in structures that could be historicized and in which change over time could be perceived.

Accordingly, I offer here a rough periodization of emotional styles and emotional management between 350 and 1300. However, in order to do justice to emotions as activities and practices of feeling, it is necessary also to overlay this periodization with an examination of specific communal sites that demonstrate what I call "templates" for emoting and for cycling between emotions. I will discuss Christian community, social processes of feuding, the politics of kingship and sovereignty, and, toward the end of our period, new imaginings of urban society. Only through a close examination of these sites can we elucidate the dynamic relationship between feeling, community, and polity.

THE PRODUCTION OF CHRISTIAN COMMUNITY, 350–1300

The *corpus Christianorum*, the Church conceived of as the sum of its members and the body of Christ, was the most capacious "public" imaginary of the Middle Ages in Western Europe (Lubac 2009). To understand the role of emotion in the formulation and maintenance of this collectivity, it is important to remember that the world was constituted in its political and social attributes through emotion, in this case, God's anger (Gregory the Great 1985: 25.16.34, 1260). All subsequent history was the narrative of attempts to regain God's favor, culminating in surrender to his mercy through passages of fear, faith, and love. Importantly, for this body to thrive, these passages of feeling had to take place constantly, with the different components educating and disciplining each other (Malegam 2013: 195–9).

Love in several different forms provided the core of the community, but entry required a transition to love through other emotions and retention within the community demanded that passages from love to fear not be a one-time change. To achieve a properly balanced and directed combination of love and fear (*amor et timor*), Christians looked for guidance. In their first three hundred years, when Christians remained vulnerable to persecution by Roman imperial authority, their guides were martyrs, confessors, deacons, and bishops. In the wake of large-scale Christianization after the imperial edict of toleration in 313 CE, these guides were joined, even surpassed, by emperors like Constantine and Theodosius. Christian leaders conveyed God's anger and mercy to differing degrees and under different circumstances. Martyrs in the gladiatorial arena announced that the injuries they endured would be commensurate with God's wrath against their persecutors. Bishops chastised and terrified sinners, imagining themselves as physicians administering harsh but essential treatment (Cyprian of Carthage 1972: 14.228, 16.230).

The overarching framework for these acts of feeling was the redemption of those who had sinned either before entering the Christian fold or subsequently. Until the fourth century, penance took pride of place as a mode of entry into the Christian encampment since it privileged remorse and grief at one's prior belonging in a world enraptured by Satan. The penitential process was a combination of what we might consider public and private but it was always communal: a community leader reproved the novitiate who declared sorrow and remorse before acceptance into the *pax et communio* of the religion (Swann 1980: 37–42).

This act of renunciation—letting go of past desires, obligations, and concerns and effectively inverting them—constituted conversion in the early Church. As emotional disciplining, it produced a *militia Christi* that stood in opposition to the temporal military forces of pagan imperial Rome. The *militia Christi* suffered in the present while fighting a future war, constitutive of the might of God's wrath to come. It required one to loathe a previous existence, to surrender to the new, and to yearn for the destruction of persecutors prior to the arrival of the heavenly kingdom. The initial penitential act asked the community to evaluate and accept the extent to which a new member had undergone a transformation of being. It hinged on a change in the very sense of shame itself: from *pudor*—the classical sense of self-possession that mediated one's social standing—to *pudicitia*, a sense of modesty, even self-loathing akin to what Adam and Eve felt when they realized they were naked. This *pudicitia* was the first step to despising all that the world presented to raise up one's sense of self, such as finery and aggrandizement, made most explicit in the Roman spectacles of triumphs and games (Malegam 2013: 81–6).

When a renunciate lapsed, however, their subsequent shame and remorse no longer allowed them to reenter the community, at least not for the most demanding leaders. For the rigorists, the lapsed and apostate must enter the community of the spirit only through martyrdom, which required a different emotive process—a sundering of spirit and flesh on earth to the point that the body itself became irrelevant (Swann 1980: 59). Pain and fear no longer had the same meaning: there only remained pride; the martyr had already left his or her body before that body was disposed of. While such a process was entirely located within the single body of the martyr, it simultaneously enabled membership in the eternal community. It also allowed people of different status to consider themselves equals, such as the Carthaginian slave women Felicitas who around 200 CE insisted on her right to die in the gladiatorial arena alongside her mistress and several other catechumens (Musurillo 1972: 15, 122).

As imperial persecution of Christians ceded to imperial patronage after 300 CE, new emotional registers emphasized communal boundaries. Fear and faith in the face of state power was replaced by horror of a pagan or Jewish "other." In Palestine and Egypt where several religious and ethnic groups shared elements of Roman civilization, ascetic militants cultivated horror by attacking shared temples, homes, and even towns, sites of boundary crossing between Christians, Jews, and pagans. As Thomas Sizgorich has argued, horror served a mimetic function, educating potential boundary-crossers about the alterity of non-Christian sects (Sizgorich 2009: 127–43).

Christians also drew positive inspiration from ascetics like St. Antony who set up a Christian hermitage in the Sinai desert a little before 300 CE. Ascetic men and women put their bodies through extreme rigors simultaneously to isolate themselves from community and to establish a kind of leadership by virtue of being alien and outsiders. However, these ascetics opened themselves up to accusations of unhelpful pride, pride which destroyed the fabric of community by elevating individuals (sometime literally in the case of the stylites, hermits who stood on pillars) above the rest of their fellow Christians. Reactions varied. In the first half of the fourth century, a group of Anatolian ascetics realized they also needed a communal element to provide emotional support as they underwent their rigors: their loosely connected hermitages or *coenobia* were a precursor of the monastery. Then around 380, Augustine completely reconceived the relationship between emotional change and Christian membership. The paradigmatic ascetic, the monk, had earned this name from *monos*, meaning "one." Augustine reinterpreted *monos* as "one" in the sense of a collective: many feeling as one (Leyser 2000: 11).

In Augustine's writings, cognitive and cosmological change are coextensive. The new dispensation brought about by the Incarnation has reordered history, and the criterion of Christian membership is to perceive past and present through the lens of Christian time. Breaking with earlier traditions of scriptural exegesis, Augustine argued that the Old Testament was not allegory, but history that extended into the present as typology to be read and recognized by those who had cultivated discretion. How is one to do this? Influenced by Neoplatonism, Augustine recalibrated the relationship between reason and emotion, describing them as equally important to meaningful engagement with the world.

The Bishop of Hippo asserted that the intellect had its own pleasures (Augustine 1990: 26.4, 261). Sensation and perception—key components of feeling—depended on the correct balance of reason and carnality. Correct perception of the world's temptations and chastisements became the means for the senses to discipline the self. Thus horror was no longer directed at outsiders, but inwardly to reorder a person's sensory faculties and enable their integration into a blessed community. All physical discipline, including coercion and asceticism, was only valid as a mode of educating persons in how to feel anew and how to engage with the world in concert with others (Asad 1993: 153–9; Leyser 2000: 10–11).

For Augustine, feeling was a cognitive operation, an activity that simultaneously engaged bodily senses, and, in the ideal scenario, the rational faculties. Reason interpreted sensation correctly, while carnality—another aspect of the soul—produced confusion and misdirection, so that things that were inherently wicked appeared pleasing. Whichever quality prevailed determined perception and taste. The implications for membership in the Christian polity were extreme. True conversion was not possible unless the feelings of fear and love that prompted it were clear; otherwise a person would have been brought to the altar effectively against their will, unable to experience divine mercy through the "pleasures of the intellect." Even dying in the service of the Church did not count as martyrdom if this death were undertaken for anything other than a love of righteousness: those who courted martyrdom out of hostility or self-aggrandizement could not count themselves as members of the spiritual Church.

Emotional confusion had its most detrimental impact on the sacraments: worshippers who could not experience true love of the Church were unable to benefit from the Eucharist (Malegam 2013: 135–8). Their inability to respond correctly to sacred signs prevented them from living as part of the community of Christ's body. The emotional emphasis of church membership took on a new dimension under Augustine. The sacraments became a proving ground for proper emotional engagement and community became first and foremost a matter of good will.

The change in "emotional regimes" becomes clear if we compare third-century notions of penance, which privileged reproof and sorrow, with articulations of the process in the fifth century. Echoes of the Augustinian emphasis on emotive states appear across the Mediterranean in 450, in Pope Leo the Great's description of the difference between the penitential attitudes of St. Peter and Judas Iscariot. As Kevin Uhalde explains Leo's distinction, both Peter and Judas felt grief, fear, and revulsion at their betrayal of Christ, but only Peter translated these feelings into faith and hope. He therefore benefited from the sacrament of penance and was able to rejoin the community. Meanwhile Judas gave in to despair and committed suicide (see Figures 8.1 and 8.2) (Uhalde 2005; Murray 2000: 323–68). Thus, by the fifth century, in parts of the Christian world influenced by Augustinian theology, horror of others no longer policed the outer limits of the Church. Instead, the sacraments and their ministers constituted the outlines, and horror was only useful as a trigger to faith, hope, and love.

By 500, the Roman empire in the West had dissipated, its political and ideological traces picked up by barbarian polities such as the Ostrogoths and Lombards in northern Italy, and the more enduring Franks who ranged across what today comprises France, the Low Countries, and western Germany. The post-Roman political system consisted of face-to-face interactions, fluctuating friendships, elaborate and injurious complaint, and constant performance. Accordingly, Christianity changed as well, and this included the construction and representation of sacraments such as penance. Feelings

FIGURE 8.1: Peter looking remorseful. Carved alabaster column from the tabernacle of the high altar, St Mark's Basilica, Venice. © Erich Lessing / lessingimages.com.

emerged in exemplary redemptive situations, invariably public, but their display allowed a certain degree of ambiguity, debate, and evaluation, which furthered political and intercommunal bonds. The famous public penances of the Frankish emperor Louis the Pious, son of Charlemagne, contributed greatly to his political capital, partly because they embodied an emotional regime of regular reproof and amelioration, but also because they provided an occasion for *others* to feel and to reflect feeling off a central character (de Jong 2009).

In the centuries between 300 and 1100, one commonly accessible public manifestation of extreme feeling was exorcism, in which demons departed in fury brought about

FIGURE 8.2: Suicide of Judas. Carved alabaster column from the tabernacle of the high altar, St Mark's Basilica, Venice. © Erich Lessing/lessingimages.com.

by the presence of the sacred. Most descriptions of exorcism from the early and central Middle Ages follow a sequence between silence and excessive speech: a mute congregant might suddenly start spewing obscenities before a relic or in church or a lying priest might suddenly find his tongue locked up. The ability to reverse or quiet such fury and to instill fear in demons marked out the numinous power of many a saint including the great eleventh-century reformer Pope Leo IX. Leo's *vita*, begun around 1053 by a monk from his old diocese of Toul (in modern Lorraine), largely ignores the complexity of papal reforms in Rome in favor of descriptions of Leo's exorcistic miracles among lay and clerical defilers of churches. Effectively, church reform and restoration are conveyed through the transformation of emotional states (Krause 2007: 2.10, 194).

The furious exchanges of exorcism also provided an accessible trope for descriptions of conversion—not necessarily conversion from other religions to Christianity, but a sort of conversion anew of persons who had lapsed through contact with pagans or other sorts of bad friendships. Remote areas in the Low Countries, Saxony, and Denmark continued to have pagan populations into the eleventh and twelfth centuries. Parts of Poland, such as Pomerania and Wendland, and the greater Baltic remained largely pagan into the thirteenth century. In 1060, antagonists in Flemish towns give every sign of having been exorcised as the relic of a seventh-century missionary, St. Ursmar, was brought before them; at one point a diabolical dog manifested itself when Ursmar's handlers were creating a circle of persons joined in peace, love, and forgiveness (Malegam 2008). Around 1125, in the Pomeranian town of Stettin, the missionary bishop Otto of Bamberg provoked a confrontation with a local big man, Domislav, who had once been a Christian. Faced with his anger, Otto adopted an accepted mode for confessors, miming the feelings expected of a penitent. Domislav followed Otto's lead, and ran a gamut from rage to fear, remorse, and love. His wife and companions went through similar transitions, while witnessing the event, even as they remarked on it and expressed uncertainty as to who was feeling what (Herbord of Michelsberg 1856: 2.26–27, 791–2; Malegam 2013: 219, 2016). Such total, communal events—we may call them public—were essential for the collective transformations that enabled membership in a community, or even for the formation of a community anew, essentially two sides of the same coin. Descriptions of this kind of exorcism suggest that in some regions, conversion to Christianity was a long-term process that required several layers of inscription and confrontation.

Between 1050 and 1300 in France, Italy, and the Holy Roman Empire, cultural movements of the high Middle Ages produced new redemptive templates. Starting in the late tenth century, monasteries and episcopal patrons in Lorraine and southern France had begun undertaking a self-conscious process of institutional reform. In many ways this early reform resembled developments in other parts of Western Europe, a general restoration after a period of raiding and settlement by Scandinavian and Muslim forces. However, along with the reordering of property, these new reformers made changes to the liturgical round and administration. They reorganized relationships between churches and the armed landlords around them, producing networks that came to be known as the Cluniac and Gorzian reform. In the Auvergne region, reformers organized councils between local bishops and lay lords that became the Peace of God movement. While charters from these councils are relatively matter-of-fact, accounts from the first half of the eleventh century describe great collective emotion and devotion, calls for peace and submission to the authority of bishops.

By the end of the eleventh century, devotional imperatives had begun to shape monastic reform. In Burgundy, an order of monks originating at Cîteaux and its sister monasteries reconfigured the monastic daily round to devote more time to the contemplation of God. They predicated the boundaries of their order on *caritas*, the highest form of love (Newman 1996). The disciplinary ideals formulated by Augustine persisted in the new order, but were reconfigured to place a greater emphasis on discretion, taste, and judgment. The most influential Cistercian leader of the early twelfth century understood discretion to be an "ordering" of love (Bernard of Clairvaux 1885: 49, 1018B).

In England, Bernard's Cistercian contemporary, Abbot Aelred of Rievaulx, wrote a treatise on love: the basic love of self ascends to love of neighbors and finally to love of God, miming the division of history between the time before the Law, the Law, and the age of Grace. For all his interest in love, however, Aelred pays considerable attention to feelings that we do not today associate with that emotion: fear, horror, even abhorrence. These were the stimuli for a self-centered mind to examine itself truly, a prerequisite for realizing the divinely bestowed potential for love (Aelred of Rievaulx 1971: 2.8.20–21, 75). Thus a single emotion was not enough to bring someone into the reformed community. It was the transformative process that enabled them to enter, driven by superficially negative feelings that accompanied the first correct perception of truth.

Even as these redemptive practices were reorganizing the institutional Church through the management of feeling in the high Middle Ages, sectarian groups were navigating their own path to an affective connection with divinity. Characterized, not to say caricatured, as extreme behaviors of fasting and self-flagellation, affective piety of the high and late Middle Ages nonetheless exhibited a convergence of cognitive and sensory faculties. Witness the testimony of Angela of Foligno in late thirteenth-century Italy who insisted that her confessor not record the joy she felt at a mystical encounter with Christ. Observe her process of emotional modulation and her conception of how articulation and recollection reorganize feeling. Angela noted how memory distorted sensation: she would never lose or doubt the feeling, but she might doubt its recollection. She also acknowledged "great distress" that because of this she could not describe the encounter to someone else. At the same time, Angela welcomed this distress because she was not ready to experience the fullness of divine pleasure (Angela di Foligno 1996: 154–5).

Caroline Walker Bynum insists upon this confluence of the cognitive and perceptual, meaning and affect, in her masterly study of the food practices of religious women between the twelfth and fifteenth centuries (Bynum 1986). The affective schemas of these mystics could also extend to a whole range of persons eager to participate in piety but not considered remarkable or threatening enough to record. For this larger group of men and women we can only reconstruct the affective component of piety through what William Miller calls "surrogate senses" (Miller 1993a: 66, 1993b: 94). But we can perceive clerical insistence on intense, lucid feeling reflected in the emotive *aspirations* of the laity. Moreover, as I suggest below, the influence was mutual. Lay emotional practice provided templates for clerical understandings of community formation through the transformation, management, and navigation of feeling.

FEUDING PROCESSES OF THE LAY ELITE IN WESTERN EUROPE, 500–1300

An image of the irrational medieval warrior continues to fascinate students of the Middle Ages. It parallels the now discarded narrative of a dramatic demise of classical culture in the West, epitomized by the cruelty and lack of restraint of Rome's barbarian successors. The first king of the Franks, Clovis, allegedly lamented the demise of his relatives only because he was left with no one to kill.

Our sources have contributed to this image: in his *Deeds of the Franks*, written in the late 500s, the senator-bishop Gregory of Tours took care to distinguish himself and his fellow Gallo-Romans from the Frankish-speaking retinue of Clovis and his descendants, and he did so by presenting them as quick to anger, quick to move from anger to action, and yet paradoxically emotionless in their killing. The gruesome homicides of which he writes most likely did take place, but this bifurcated image of emotional and emotionless only makes sense when we realize that Gregory is presenting the Franks as bereft of rational faculties; their emotion or lack thereof is not the marker of difference.

During the late tenth century, after a period of Viking and Saracen raids in Western Europe, a change in memory-making and documentary culture enhanced this image of the unstable warrior (Geary 1994b; Hummer 2013; Innes 2013). In the west Frankish kingdoms, where political authority was localized and ad hoc judicial instruments were the norm, monastic chronicles and in-house hagiographies celebrated an abbey's founder, patron, or recent administrator who defended the monasteries against marauding outsiders. The narratives of victimization elided past Viking incursions with more recent land disputes with lay neighbors who were presented as violent unreasonable bullies.

For monks and laymen alike, the mode of asserting claims was confrontational, enabling a range of emotional display (Patzold 2000). As a form of complaint, monks mocked the relics of their saints by kicking dust over them and surrounding them with thorns. They sometimes adopted postures of extreme penitence and deep grief, and at other times cursed (Little 1993; Geary 1994a). Like the horror-inducing ascetics of Late Antiquity that Sizgorich describes, these medieval monks were miming past and present persecution. At the same time, through mimesis and inversion, they were raising the stakes, depicting their neighbors' actions as insults to God and his saints.

Eleventh-century emotional politics also featured in lay feuds. From around 1030, a document called the *Conventum* of Hugh of Lusignan records every painful detail of a patron–client relationship in southwest France, including repeated betrayals and episodes of anger and grief. William of Poitou and Aquitaine denied Hugh a fief, a castle, and an advantageous marriage, but in each case Hugh would grant him a new accord, one of several *conventi*. Despite a peaceful resolution, turbulent emotions permeate the document, most likely because strong feelings played a part in the original claims and remained a resource for future negotiations of the bond. These feelings were retained for posterity to safeguard the alliance and to extend, if need be, the claims of Hugh's family or William's (Hugh of Lusignan 1969; Beech 1966; Barthélemy 1995).

Often recorded in these accounts of emotional exchange are self-imposed ceremonies of humiliation, likely to gain sympathy or impress others with their sincere desire for concord. As with the public penances of the same period, these were highly visible, semantically charged events meant to provoke comment from a social group, and additionally to mime and therefore reinscribe the shame of the person undergoing them. They include the *harmiscara*, crawling on one's knees while wearing or carrying a saddle, which William of Poitou offered. The *harmiscara* has generic similarities to humiliations such as riding backward or riding a camel. In Chrétien de Troyes' *The Knight of the Cart*, Lancelot undergoes the humiliation of a prisoner, horseless, riding in a cart driven by a dwarf. One of the female characters in the *Romance of Lancelot du Lac* agrees to ride a horse without a tail (see Figure 8.3). Litigants could use these ceremonies to induce fellow-feeling from an audience. In the early twelfth-century epic *Raoul de Cambrai*, the titular character subverts a public negotiation by offering the *harmiscara* and gains support from his peer group when his adversary refuses to let him undertake it (Kay 1992: 87, lines 110–12). Even without the actual ceremony, shame has been read and registered to political effect.

FIGURE 8.3: Penance on a tailless horse, *Romance of Lancelot du Lac*, Oxford, Bodleian Library, MS Rawl. Q. b. 6, fol. 194ᵛ (detail), *c*.1320–30. © The Bodleian Libraries, The University of Oxford.

Performative anger or remorse should not be confused with impulsiveness. Recent scholarship on the politics of lay emotionalism reveals a considered approach to expressions of feeling that goes beyond mere performance. Literary sources from twelfth- and thirteenth-century France show great sensitivity among peer groups to the appropriateness or legitimacy of a warrior's emotions at any juncture of an interpersonal engagement; the group expressed its disapproval verbally, but often approved simply through a correspondence of feelings, be they anger or joy; we might assume the same for audiences. Raoul de Cambrai gathers allies by flying into a rage and his companions show support through their own. This rage is not automatic: Raoul's uncle must goad him

(Kay 1992: 40–2, lines 32–3). At the same time, when Raoul's behavior overbalances into immoderate and misdirected actions, members of his circle are ready to scold: "*trop ies demesurez!*" (You are being excessive) (Kay 1992: 80, line 62). This pattern of goading and restraint by a social group is also evident in Scandinavian sagas from the thirteenth century which share oral traditions with these French *chansons* (Miller 1990: 213–14). In all these literary genres, an initial angry act precipitates a series of actions and feelings that contribute to a final accord.

Anger allowed the "renegotiation" of aristocratic relationships: it did not end them (Barton 1998). Additionally, by providing an occasion to comment on and ascribe feeling, anger worked similarly to the public penances discussed earlier. It should not surprise, then, that medieval accounts of religious conversion often borrow imagery from both conflict resolution and the penitential. In the 1120s in Pomerania, the aforementioned missionary Otto of Bamberg returned a man to the faith by *first* provoking him to anger and *then* taking on the tearful role of both penitent and confessor during their confrontation (Herbord of Michelsberg 1856: 2.26–27).

The model of anger presented here runs counter to that proposed by Daniel Smail who emphasizes its precognitive aspects, seeing it as a trigger to hasty, vengeful action. According to Smail, a more successful politics lies in the concealment of such emotions, not an option for fierce warriors like Raoul whose countenance displays the ebb and flow of angry blood (Smail 2005). However, consigning anger to the precognitive ignores the delays and wrangling that attended most passages between anger and fighting. To describe warfare *a priori* as vengeance is to make an artificial link between anger and conflict and assign it a single cause, without taking into account the multiple interlacing social identities and political relationships that might have contributed. It is to take largely at face value texts that are dialogic, polyphonous, and engaged in conveyance of right or wrong through representation of emotions (White 1996).

Lay and clerical modes of reconciliation employed the same semiotic system even if semantics varied. Even practices of conflict settlement that the Church disavowed (like the ordeal or jousting) took from a shared system of making truth, via the advocacy of a saint. Seemingly bizarre shaming ceremonies, like the *harmiscara*, share an important structural quality with penances. Humiliation is imposed mimetically and then read and evaluated by a collective. The publicity of the shame produces a site for constantly styling the event and for collectively interpreting, remembering, and reinscribing the feelings that were in play. Does this mean we cannot understand emotions as anything more than political or textual strategies tagged to particular circumstances? No, because if so, we could not make sense of an extensive clerical and lay culture of managing feeling. This culture is manifested in art as well as text. We have images of anger committing suicide, associated (like Judas) with despair (McNamara and Ruys 2014). According to Lester K. Little, monastic curses are pointedly described as bereft of anger (Little 1998; Hyams 1998).

It would be easy then to assume that clergy simply disapproved of anger and sought to reduce it among themselves and the laity through "emotional regimes." However, among clerical and lay authors criticism of a seemingly "negative" emotion does not concern the emotion per se but rather its role in a larger social performance. Angry occasions are also occasions for tempering, advice, parlay, and friendship; grief and pity are aspects of reconciliation as well as occasions for severing ties. Their presentation in lay entertainment and documentary culture is ultimately as occasions for response from audiences whose participation is seamless with the actors. The narratives also target the reactions of future readers who thus become witnesses in their own right through their own acts of feeling.

THE EMOTIONAL TEMPLATE OF RULERSHIP, 750–1300

The anthropologist Max Gluckman suggested that the kind of conciliation systems described above were most effective in societies with shallow social gradations where rival villages or kin-groups often had family members from the other side embedded through marriage who had a stake in assuring mutual rather than one-sided resolution (Gluckman 1955). However, shallow hierarchies often mean *more* hierarchies, suggesting that minor differences of status, and markers of status like the display of emotions, have greater sociopolitical consequence than otherwise. It also means that more persons determine the meaning and outcome of an emotional exchange. Every emotional event provided an occasion for someone to test his or her political and social standing among potential allies.

There emerged nonetheless in Central and Western Europe between 750 and 1300 certain figures who relied on more than intersubjective ritual for the maintenance of their authority: the Carolingian, Ottonian, Salian, and Staufer emperors and the Angevin and Capetian monarchs. In this system, what emotional mechanisms might the sovereign use to be exceptional? Remember that a king had multiple identities. As a lord, his emotions functioned differently, enabling the construction or dismantling of patronage networks similar to those discussed above. *Chanson* and *romance*, never very favorable to royal hegemony, often portray the king—even one as eminent as Charlemagne—as just another lord, and they do so through presentations of his anger.

In his capacity as the representative of God's wrath, however, the ruler employed different templates of anger. Emperors might blind their subjects as just denial of divine luminescence, but mere kings who blinded were exhibiting vengeful anger (Bührer-Thierry 1998). Biographers of the German king-emperor Frederic Barbarossa styled his anger as *indignatio*. Meanwhile, on his behalf, courtiers were allowed to exhibit the more problematic *ira*, an emotion that often pairs with *furor* or madness (Malegam 2013: 271).

Such "outsourcing" of anger forces us to pay closer attention to the social and cultural regimes that constructed the ruler himself. If, as I suggest, clergy and laity concentrated more on emotional modulation and discernment than on any single feeling per se, we must imagine royal anger as an emotion controlled like all other emotions by the collective. J. E. A. Jolliffe suggests that the unpredictable anger of thirteenth-century English monarchs only enhanced their subjects' awe (Jolliffe 1955: 98–100). Nonetheless, these kings remained subject to clerical restraint and the reproof of their counselors. Among his inner circle, then, a king must balance relatively unchanging expectations with the modulations demanded by political circumstance.

According to Gerd Althoff, Christian kings had been known for wrath since Late Antiquity, but in the age of Charlemagne, an emotional regime equated the king's anger and other negative emotions with injustice—the antithesis of right governance. By the twelfth century, another change had taken place: the king's anger was admonitory, it highlighted the injustice of *others*. Royal anger thus served changing modes of communication between ruler and subject, forming the basis of complaint in one century, but a few centuries later, a demonstration of his willingness to take right action.

FIGURE 8.4: Gestures and emotions in council, Bayeux Tapestry, eleventh century. Musée de la Tapisserie, Bayeux, France. © Erich Lessing/lessingimages.com.

For Althoff, within a medieval political system, such emotions were cultural codes, having no significance beyond the gestures that expressed them: "Many of the mannerisms of medieval communication, which may appear to us as overemotionalized, were bound up with this demonstrative function" (Althoff 1998: 74). However, such codes can be deliberately misunderstood or reinvented for contrary communication (Buc 2001). Medieval observers realized that the memory of a ceremony's emotional impact shaped its success: had observers expressed joy, consternation, or just apathy? (Malegam 2011). Accordingly, the extent to which an emotion was "culturally" appropriate (that is, the right move in the game) depended on the willingness of witnesses and chroniclers to grant the emotion authority or legitimacy.

What Althoff sees as strictures on anger may not then be about anger per se but part of a broader royal culture of *admonitio* managed effectively by some kings but not by others. *Admonitio* translates as a public form of correction. Carolingian liturgists and chroniclers understood it as a collective duty for clergy and laity based in collective accountability to God. It was a reciprocal system, the absence of which was termed *negligentia*. A king elevated himself by his willingness to atone, patterned on the remorse shown by the biblical King David. Louis the Pious adopted this version of the Davidic model during his penance at Attigny in 822, and importantly it was recognized as such by members of his court (de Jong 2009: 112–22).

His emotional display made the king in some senses a supplicant to his audience. Relations between king and subject involved a great deal of reciprocity rather than dominance, so a demonstration of anger was only one move—an opening gambit—that left the angry king vulnerable, often by design. Medieval kings invariably relied on extension and push back, asserting themselves through presence, largess, and acquisition of resources. Periodic and seemingly haphazard recourse to emotional display was of a piece with this staccato politics, which relied on referendum and acclamation (Orning 2008a, 2008b).

The public nature of anger made it a political claim and raised the stakes for a ruler who was effectively counting heads among his counselors. Politically unsuccessful kings, like England's John Lackland, could be accused of overdone or inappropriate anger. Such censure devalued the specific injury done the king, and by extension signaled a transfer of support to his antagonist (White 2007). The unpopular John and his successor Henry III had little to gain from such public referendum. Paul Hyams detects a "squeezing out" of royal anger by the early 1200s. Read another way, such an emotional regime might have been self-inflicted, John and Henry dispensing with a politics of anger weighted against them (Hyams 1998).

EMOTIONAL LIFE OF URBAN COMMUNITIES, 1050–1300

I began this chapter with a discussion of religious community. An examination of the part played by emotionalism in the construction of urban community takes us to the end of the period under examination. With our chronological boundary at 1300, a discussion of emotions among the urban middle classes might appear premature. Nevertheless, since the first communes emerged at the end of the eleventh century and several religious sects gestated in an urban environment during the next 250 years, there are at least two distinct categories of emotional life that apply: feeling as a marker of collective identity, and as means of organizing space and time.

By the middle of the eleventh century, new cities began to emerge in northern Europe and older, smaller, Roman-era towns began to expand and specialize in trade and production. In Italy, the civic identity of diocesan towns began to harden and communes emerged as cities went to war. Flanders saw a rapid transformation of small settlements like Lille (literally, "the island") (Verhulst 1999). New markets powered much of this urban development, but legal and clerical schools also played a role, attracting scholars from various parts of Europe. The cities nurtured new social groups—intellectuals, merchants, craftsmen—and with these new social identities came new attitudes toward the scriptures and religious life. Taking scriptural imprecations to poverty literally, many charismatic leaders such as Francis of Assisi in Italy and Peter Waldo in France formed sects of laymen who abandoned their positions and wandered from town to town, preaching and offering townspeople the opportunity to practice charity. Others, like Norbert of Xanten, created communities of regular canons who lived collectively under a rule, but in important cities like Laon, near Paris (Little 1978).

The towns thus became centers of a lay devotion that is often termed "affective piety": laypersons with means, social standing, and a modicum of learning devoted themselves to Christ primarily through an emotional connection. They had synesthetic experiences: revelatory visions of the Crucifixion gave mystics like Catherine of Siena physical pain, and the sight of saints or the Savior often activated other senses such as smell and taste. Such sensory experience highlighted the humanity of Christ and his suffering; they paralleled an increased interest in the Host as the body of Christ. Rich patrons created new civic ceremonies around the Host, such as the Corpus Christi procession in the Low Countries. Jewish citizens, who were increasingly being excluded from society, found themselves implicated in this emotional event. Many Christians feared that "the Jews" looked on the passing Host "invidiously," that is to say with the wrong feelings in play, and attacks on Jewish communities often accompanied Host processions (Rubin 1991). Such attitudes and fears demonstrate how intertwined were understandings of perception and feeling, and how for these urban communities, emotion meant acting as much as being acted upon.

As a space for broadly accessible action and performance, the town became the site for the collective display of social identity through public acts of feeling such as grief. Strictures on displays and intensity of grief during occasions of mourning date from early Christianity. While they tell us about how people registered and managed grief, they also reveal how a society imagined itself through the display and management of grieving. Emotion organizes: as Arlie Hochschild notes, in mid-twentieth-century middle-class America, women were often given the task of setting an emotional "tone" for an event (Hochschild 1983: 164–70). Similarly, civic regulation of public displays of grief made apparent divisions of gender and status in medieval Europe.

These circumscriptions varied with time and place. In fourth-century Byzantium, women were counseled against indecorous or "irrational" grief, while in thirteenth-century Italian communes like Orvieto, sumptuary legislation restricted grief displays to women only. The reasons given for restricting grief also tell how practices of emoting were understood. No distinction seems to have been made in early Christian statutes between display and affect in the grieving process. When fourth-century Byzantines decried the "unreason" of excessive grief, they were not implying that the emotion was, so to speak, "precognitive." According to Henry Maguire, by lack of reason they meant lack of faith. John Chrysostom said excess tears suggested a permanent rather than a temporary goodbye, inappropriate when considering that mourner and departed would be reunited at the final resurrection (Maguire 2012). Moral enhancement through behavioral correction suggests that early Christians understood that practice could modulate feeling. As with notions of modesty and shame, early Christian codes around grief were conceived not in a vacuum, but built against extant modes of behavior seen to shape feeling itself. Thus social conventions—levels of mourning that signaled a long or short separation—made manifest the spiritual state that such display conveyed. All these concerns ultimately collaborated in the construction of gender: read as more susceptible to grief, female mourners had their grief organized further into that appropriate for a wife, mother, etc.

If we understand grieving as an embodied act of feeling, then meaning, awareness, sensation, bodily position, gesture, and movement are connected and influence each other. The more bodies involved, the greater the resonance that made public mourning an especially charged site for a society to see itself and transform its "socioemotional reality" (White 1990). Accordingly, Carol Lansing argues that under the influence of Stoicism, late medieval strictures on grieving in the commune of Orvieto crafted a particular image of the social body, differentiated and ennobled by self-restraint (Lansing 2008).

Restraint implies the possibility of an intervention between feeling and expression as distinct practices. It does not reeducate feeling, only blocks it. Concerns about self-restraint thus signal the appearance of an imagined "self" with distinct categories for reason and emotion, private and public. Men and women alike experienced grief in medieval Orvieto, but by the late thirteenth century, they had begun to compartmentalize it in newly conceived inner and outer landscapes.

FIGURE 8.5: An extravagant female mourner. Polyptych with scenes from the life of Christ, the life of the Virgin, and saints, workshop of Ferrer Bassa, Spain, c.1345–50. © The Pierpont Morgan Library, New York. AZ071. Bequest of J. P. Morgan, Jr.

CONCLUSION

The study of emotions confronts the same methodological problems that have dogged performance history. Of archival sources for performance, Carol Symes notes, "the text is the vestigial remains of enactments that were either being disciplined by the imposition of an official template or translated into a new medium" (Symes 2011: 37). As with performance, the key elements of an emotional event necessarily remain silent and any attempt to recover them relies on surrogates for present, not past, feeling. Respectful agnosticism may be a more conscientious option.

This does not leave us with nothing: changing templates for feeling are important resources for cultural historians of the Middle Ages. We cannot grasp the significance of early Christian conversion without understanding the social implications of transforming *pudor*. Without a nuanced understanding of the role played by anger in processes of redemption and reconciliation, we are unable to associate it "reasonably" with feelings like pity, joy, and love. Furthermore, for scholars of emotion in the Middle Ages, historical changes in the organization of feeling may provide the key to an ontological mystery in Western cultural schemas: how did communal acts of feeling generate a private, autonomous self?

NOTES ON CONTRIBUTORS

Daniel Anlezark is Associate Professor in the English Department at The University of Sydney, Australia, where he teaches Old and Middle English language and literature. He has previously taught at Trinity College Dublin and Durham University. He has published widely on a range of early medieval texts, and especially on Old English biblical poetry and religious literature, with an interest in the relationship between literature and society. His books include *Water and Fire: The Myth of the Flood in Anglo-Saxon England* (2006), editions of Old English biblical poetry, and most recently a study of the life and legend of Alfred the Great. He currently holds an Australian Research Council Future Fellowship, and is a Fellow of the Australian Academy of the Humanities.

Nicole Archambeau is an Assistant Professor of History at Colorado State University, USA, working at the intersection of religion and learned medicine. She has published with the *Bulletin of the History of Medicine* and the *Journal of the Social History of Medicine*. Her current book project explores a community in Provence coping with the difficulties of plague, war, and confession.

Katherine M. Boivin is Assistant Professor of Art History at Bard College, USA, where she has taught since 2013. Her research focuses on the spatiality of medieval artistic programs, examining in particular dynamic interactions among architecture, figurative art, and liturgical practice. She is the recipient of numerous grants and awards, including an NEH Summer Stipend Award, an ICMA / Kress Research Grant, a Fulbright Research Fellowship, and a DAAD Research Grant. Her articles have appeared in *The Art Bulletin* and the British Archaeological Association's volume on Norwich. She received her PhD from Columbia University in 2013 and lectures regularly at the Cloisters Museum in New York. In 2017, she co-organized the international conference *Riemenschneider in Situ*, which was sponsored by the Samuel H. Kress Foundation and the Deutsche Forschungsgemeinschaft (DFG).

Sarah Brazil holds a doctorate from the University of Geneva, Switzerland, where she currently holds the position of Senior Research and Teaching Assistant in medieval English literature. Her forthcoming monograph, entitled *The Corporeality of Clothing in Medieval Literature: Cognition, Kinesis, and the Sacred*, will be published in the series Early Drama, Art and Music (MIP, Kalamazoo), and is a revised version of her doctoral thesis. Sarah is currently pursuing a postdoctoral project funded by the Swiss National Science Foundation, which is hosted by the University of Edinburgh and the Institute for the Advanced Studies of the Humanities, where she aims to develop a critical approach to the presence of humor within early English religious drama.

Jehangir Yezdi Malegam is Associate Professor of History at Duke University in Durham, USA. He studies areas of intersection between clergy and laity in the central Middle Ages. His book *The Sleep of Behemoth: Disputing Peace and Violence in Medieval Europe*,

1000–1200 (2013) placed attempts to define true peace on earth at the center of several cultural and intellectual changes of the twelfth century. More recently, he has devoted himself to the study of aesthetic regimes (especially emotion, sound, and color) that express how medieval clerics and religious negotiated the material demands of their sojourn in the world. He lives in North Carolina with his wife, twin children, and a large orange cat.

Constant J. Mews gained his BA and MA from the University of Auckland, New Zealand, and his PhD from Oxford University. He is Professor within the School of Philosophical, Historical and International Studies at Monash University, Australia, where he is also Director of the Centre for Religious Studies. He has published widely on medieval thought, ethics, and religious culture, with particular reference to the writings of Abelard, Heloise, Hildegard of Bingen, and their contemporaries, including *Abelard and Heloise* (2005) and *The Lost Love Letters of Heloise and Abelard: Perceptions of Dialogue in Twelfth-Century France* (2nd edn, 2008). His research interests cover medieval religious and intellectual culture, and the interface between various religious and ethical traditions.

Clare Monagle received her doctorate from The Johns Hopkins University in 2007. She is currently Associate Professor in the Department of Modern History, Politics and International Relations at Macquarie University, Australia. Clare has published widely in the fields of medieval intellectual history, as well as in the history of political and theoretical medievalism in the twentieth century. In 2017, she published *The Scholastic Project*, with Medieval Institute Publications, as well as an article titled "The Politics of Extra / Ordinary Time: Encyclical Thinking" in *Cogent Arts and Humanities*.

Lisa Perfetti is Associate Dean for Faculty Development and Professor of French and English at Whitman College in Walla Walla, Washington, USA. Her scholarly work focuses primarily on gender in medieval literature with an emphasis on comic texts. Her publications include *Women and Laughter in Medieval Comic Literature* (2003) and an edited collection of essays, *The Representation of Women's Emotions in Medieval and Early Modern Culture* (2005). After teaching French language and literature for fifteen years at Muhlenberg College in Pennsylvania, she now works primarily in administration, supporting faculty in their growth as teachers and scholars and overseeing policies and practices for the academic program.

Juanita Feros Ruys (The University of Sydney, Australia) is an intellectual historian of the Middle Ages. She is the author of *The Repentant Abelard* (2014) and *Demons in the Middle Ages* (2017). She is currently co-editing a volume on medieval and early modern emotions terminology (*Before Emotion*, Routledge) and curating a special issue of the journal *Emotions: History, Culture, Society* on the long history of disempathy (December 2018). She also works on the intersections between medieval demonology and the colonial European experience of the Australian landscape, and is the producer of the documentary *The Devil's Country* on this subject. She is currently completing a monograph on the first-person life writings, including demonic temptations, of the medieval monk Otloh of St. Emmeram.

Carol J. Williams is an Honorary Associate Investigator (AI 2012) with the ARC Centre of Excellence for the History of Emotions, 1100–1800, Australia. She is an Adjunct Research Fellow of the Centre for Medieval and Renaissance Studies of Monash University,

Australia. She is one of the collaborating editors and translators of the *Ars Musice* of Johannes de Grocheio (2011) and the *Tractatus de tonis* of Guy of Saint-Denis (2017). Solo publications include the essay "Modes and Manipulation: Music, the State, and Emotion" in *Ordering Emotions in Europe, 1100–1800* (ed. Susan Broomhall, 2015), and more recently, "The Tonary as Analytic Guidebook for the Performance of Chant" in *Music Performance and Analysis* (ed. Jonathan Paget et al., 2017).

NOTES

Chapter 1

1. Although the term "emotion" is problematic for this time period, I will use it to fit the standard usage of this series. For more on the emergence of the term "emotion," see Richards 2005.
2. Caelius Aurelianus did not agree with Boethius's idea, but instead believed that music "congests the head," making emotional distress worse: see Caelius Aurelianus 1950: 557.
3. This Galenic text was not available in Latin until the late fourteenth century: see McVaugh 1997. The ideas of humility and control of emotion, however, were common in Stoic texts that influenced late antique medicine.
4. Pessaries are soluble medicines inserted into the vagina; erysiplas is a bacterial rash.
5. Haly Abbas is the westernized name of ʿAlī ibn al-ʿAbbās al-Majusi, who taught and worked in Baghdad in the tenth century.
6. The texts in the *Articella* included Hippocrates' *Aphorisms* and *Prognostics*, a Galenic text referred to as the *Tegni*, a modified version of Hunayn ibn Ishaq's introduction to Galenic medicine called the *Isagoge*, and short texts on the pulse and urine analysis. For the *Articella* (or *ars medicinae*) at the University of Paris, see O'Boyle 1998.
7. Although I will present the *Pantegni* rather simply, it has a complex history: see Burnett and Jacquart 1994.
8. The history of the practical portion of this text is particularly complex: see Green 1994.
9. Avicenna is the westernized name of Husain ibn Abdullah ibn ʿAlī ibn Sina, considered one of the greatest Arabic-speaking philosophers and physicians, who wrote in the eleventh century.
10. This was a highly contentious part of the process and medieval scholars did not always clearly agree: see Harvey 1975: 16–17 and Wolfson 1935: 69–117.
11. This is different from natural philosophical approaches that agreed with Aristotle that the heart and its vital spirit (which controlled the passions) were the most important to the body: see Harvey 1975: 23–5.
12. For a detailed analysis of the changes that translators introduced to the *Pantegni*'s presentation of the three spirits, see Burnett 1994.
13. Some physicians argued that the eyes sent out rays to see things, but by the fourteenth century most physicians did not believe this: see Siraisi 1981: 204–5.
14. The number of ventricles and faculties could differ: see McVaugh 2005.
15. Alderotti and his students drew heavily on the ideas of Avicenna, who was both a physician and a philosopher: see Siraisi 1981: 210–16.

Chapter 2

1. The critical edition of *The Dream of the Rood* is Swanton 1987; all translations in this chapter are my own.

2. There are many manuscripts witnessing variant textual traditions. The most recent edition is Millett 2005–6. On the date and provenance, see Dobson 1976 and Millett 1992. On anchoritism as a movement in England, see Clay 1914.
3. Gregory the Great's commentary was influential in the West: see Gregory the Great 1963. On the tension between the allegorical and literal in the application of the Song of Songs to the spiritual lives of women, see Robertson 1990: 41–3.
4. All citations from the *Ancrene Wisse* in this chapter are from the translation by H. White 1993.
5. See, for example, "The Lady in the Wood," in Sisam and Sisam 1973: 115–17.

Chapter 3

1. On singing as a means of focusing the congregation's attention see Ambrose 1913: 7.25, 144; on drowning out background noise, see Ambrose 1919: 1.9, 7; also Basil of Caesarea 2004: 207.3–4, 242.
2. Backman 1952: 28–30 notes the ambiguity of whether these texts refer to actual dance.
3. A melisma is an extended melody sung on a single syllable.
4. Barrett 2013: 2. 234–42 identifies thirty-three neumed manuscripts from this period relating their decline in the twelfth century to shifting educational taste.
5. On the evolution of tonaries, manuals that identify chants according to their mode, see Huglo 1971.
6. The names of the Dorian, Phrygian, Lydian, and Mixolydian modes are taken from the names of ancient Greek tribes and were used by some theorists. Others, including Guido, preferred to use the Greek numbering system, as in the terms "*protus*," "*deuterus*," "*tritus*," and "*tetrardus*."
7. The passage reproduces passages from Beleth 1976: 117a, 117d, 120a, pp. 219, 223; and Honorius Augustudonensis 1885: 139, PL 172. 587CD.
8. Translated in Thorndike 1944: 29; see also Pseudo-Boethius 1976: 99. That students still had to grasp the essentials of *musica* is evident from Lafleur 1988.
9. William (or Thomas) also sent a copy to Albert the Great in Cologne, who produced a short commentary on the *Politics* sometime before 1267, but this did not have wide influence. On the diffusion of the *Politics* see Jeffreys 2009.
10. For a translation of the lyric, see Rosenberg and Tischler 1981: 339–40; for the melody, see Tischler 1997: no. 1184, 13. 1.
11. The Latin text is also available through the *Thesaurus Musicarum Latinarum*, at http://www.chmtl.indiana.edu/tml/. For a study and translation of these questions, see Dyer 2016; we are indebted to the author for sharing an advance copy of this work. See also Jeffreys 2011.

Chapter 4

1. I do not use the term "audience" here as it is problematic in relation to a liturgical performance where all present participate in what is being enacted.
2. I have altered the translation altered here: "*Noli, virgo Rachel . . . fletus retinere dolorum. / Si quae tristaris, exulta quae lacrimaris. / Namque tui nati vivunt super astra beati*" (Bevington 1975: 70).
3. "*Tunc Herodes, quasi corruptus, arrepto gladio, paret seipsum occidere; sed prohibeatur tandem a suis et pacificetur, dicens: Incendium meum ruina restinguam!*" (Bevington 1975: 68).

4. "*O filia . . . non confundor, non contristor, sed valedico tibi exultando et osculor os oculosque prae gaudio lacrimando*" (Hrotsvit 1970: 367).

Chapter 5

1. An early example of Christ on the Cross shown in stoic triumph is found on a panel of the Passion Casket (*c.*420), now in the British Museum in London. By contrast, an example (*c.*1304) from the end of our period showing the extreme suffering of Christ on the Cross is found in the church of St. Maria im Kapitol in Cologne. On the changing types of crucifix, see Haussherr 1963; Lutz 2004.
2. Garnier distinguishes this gesture from the formally similar "*orans*" gesture, where both arms are raised with palms facing upward to indicate prayer (Garnier 1982: 223).
3. Augustine does claim, however, that "the pair lived in a partnership of unalloyed felicity; their love for God and for each other was undisturbed. This love was the source of immense gladness, since the beloved object was always at hand for their enjoyment." He thus differentiates between the divine, blissful love of God and earthly emotions associated with evil and sin: Augustine 1972: 567.
4. The Cathedral of Autun has an unusual orientation, with the apse in the south, the principal nave entrance in the north and the transept running from east to west: see Bleeke 2012: 20. On the sculpture of the Cathedral of Autun, see also Seidel 1999.

Chapter 6

This essay is an output of the Australian Research Council Centre of Excellence for the History of Emotions (project number CE110001011).

1. Because Latin has grammatical gender and many of the abstract terms for emotions, vices, and virtues are in the feminine gender, these are anthropomorphized in the *Psychomachia* as female persons.
2. All references to this text are to Prudentius 1949.
3. All references to this text are to Augustine 1961.
4. All references to this text are to Boethius 1969.
5. Because Charlemagne was known in Latin as Carolus Magnus, the term "Carolingian" is the adjective associated with his rule and legacy.
6. All references to this text are to Swanton 1978.
7. While we might think of parental love as a sign of affective capacity, in the medieval period it was dismissed as natural to all beasts, worthy of no merit. In the *Roman de la Rose*, discussed at the end of this chapter, the figure of Reason says this explicitly (Dahlberg 1983: 116).
8. All references to the Anglo-Saxon text are to Krapp 1931; translation by Oldrieve 2010.
9. All references to this text are to Finnegan 1977.
10. All references to the three poems from the Exeter manuscript are to Klinck 1992.
11. Beguines were women who gathered together voluntarily to live holy and communal lives but without professing a monastic Rule and without official Church oversight. For this reason, the Church remained uneasy about Beguines and constantly attempted to draw (or coerce) them back within official structures. During the Middle Ages, a number of Beguines were punished with imprisonment or exile, and some even executed, for continuing to live, worship, and write outside of the Church.
12. All references to this text are to the online translation of van den Dungen 2016.

Chapter 7

1. Whereas in 1095 Pope Urban II had urged clergy to counsel men leaving for the Crusades to get permission from their wives, in 1209 Innocent III declared that husbands could go without such permission; see Brundage 1969: 77, and for other sermons that represent a wife as impediment to crusading, see Maier 2000: 121 and 133.
2. For Jaeger's distinction between homosexuality and passionate friendship between men, see Jaeger 1999: 13–17. Although beyond the scope of this chapter, numerous books have investigated a range of texts where same-sex desire and love is expressed, and while homosexuals as a category did not exist, this is not to say that men and women did not experience deeply felt attachments among members of the same sex. To this, we could add a wide body of scholarship pointing to malleable views of gender in the medieval period that complicate a simple male/female binary.
3. Lochrie also refers to condemnations of sex between women as early as the seventh century, although this was less frequent than references to sexual acts between men; see Lochrie 2003: 77–8.
4. Reddy's argument about courtly love could be seen as an extension of Jaeger's claim that "The cult of high, ennobling, spiritual love was at least in part a response to clerical fear and mistrust of passionate love and human sexuality" (Jaeger 1999: 164).
5. The distinction between emotional autonomy and economic economy is suggested by Sally Livingston's analysis of female authors who critique marriage as an institution that makes women the property of men. One example is Heloise, who even as abbess, claims provocatively in her letters to Abelard that she would rather be a whore or lover than a wife, which "redefines the conjugal debt as based not on marriage, but on consent freely given and unencumbered by external forces. He 'owes' her because she has selflessly given him her love" (Livingston 2012: 41). Thus, although it is true that Heloise's letters defy conventional Christian morality, her critique is oriented more toward defending the selfless, yet free, giving of her affections—which runs counter to both secular and clerical notions of the legal obligations of spouses—than they are a defense of sexual passion per se, as Reddy would see it (Reddy 2012: 99).
6. It is important to note that Rosenwein contrasts this show of motherly affection with the tendency in the Neustrian court of the early seventh century to portray mothers' love as exaggerated and petty, a reflection of the ascetic traditions of the male elite rulers of the period and perhaps a response to the previous rule dominated by Queen Brunhild. This distinction is yet another illustration of how we should not overlook significant differences in how emotion standards are expressed in specific communities within the large geographical and chronological span of the Middle Ages.

REFERENCES

PRIMARY

Aelred of Rievaulx (1885), *Speculum Charitatis, Patrologia Latina*, ed. J.-P. Migne, 195. 520–620.

Aelred of Rievaulx (1971), *De speculo caritatis*, in *Opera omnia I: Opera ascetica*, ed. A. Hoste and C. H. Talbot, CCCM 1, 3–161, Turnhout: Brepols.

Aelred of Rievaulx (1990), *The Mirror of Charity*, trans. Elizabeth Connor, Kalamazoo, MI: Cistercian Publications.

Aldhelm of Malmesbury (2001), *Prosa de uirginitate*, ed. Scott Gwara and Rudolf Ehwald, CCSL 124A, Turnhout: Brepols.

Ambrose (1913), *Expositio Psalmi CXVIII*, ed. M. Petschenig, CSEL 62, Vienna: Tempsky.

Ambrose (1919), *Explanatio psalmorum XII*, ed. M. Petschenig, CSEL 64, Vienna: Tempsky.

Angela di Foligno (1996), *Liber de vere fidelium experientia*, trans. and excerpt. in *Visions and Longings: Medieval Women Mystics*, ed. Monica Furlong, 148–56, Boston, MA: Shambhala Publications.

Aristotle (1952), *Rhetoric*, trans. W. Rhys Roberts, in Robert Maynard Hutchins (ed.), Great Books of the Western World, Vol. 9, *The Works of Aristotle, II*, 593–675, Chicago: University of Chicago Press.

Augustine (1885), *De musica*, Patrologia Latina, ed. J.-P. Migne, 32. 1081–1194.

Augustine (1955), Sancti Aurelii Augustini, *De ciuitate Dei*, ed. B. Dombart and A. Kalb, CCSL 47–48, Turnhout: Brepols.

Augustine (1956), *Enarrationes in Psalmos LI–C*, ed. E. Dekkers and J. Fraipont, CCSL 39, Turnhout: Brepols.

Augustine (1961), Saint Augustine, *Confessions*, trans. R. S. Pine-Coffin, London: Penguin.

Augustine (1972), *City of God*, trans. Henry Bettenson, London: Penguin Books.

Augustine (1981), *Confessionum libri XIII*, ed. L. Verheijen, CCSL 27, Turnhout: Brepols.

Augustine (1990), *In Iohannis evangelium tractatus CXXIV*, ed. R. Willems, 2nd edn., CCSL 36, Turnhout: Brepols.

Augustine (1991), *The Confessions*, trans. Henry Chadwick, Oxford: Oxford University Press.

Augustine (2014), *Confessions*, ed. and trans. Carolyn J.-B. Hammond, 2 vols., Loeb Classical Library, Cambridge, MA: Harvard University Press.

Babinsky, Ellen, trans. (1993), Marguerite Porete, *The Mirror of Simple Souls*, New York: Paulist Press.

Basil of Caesarea (2004), "Letters," in Everett Ferguson, *Inheriting Wisdom: Readings for Today from Ancient Christian Writers*, Peabody, MA: Hendrickson Publishers.

Beleth, John (1976), *Summa de ecclesiasticis officiis*, ed. H. Douteil, CCCM 41 and 41A, Turnhout: Brepols.

Benedict of Nursia (1975), *The Rule of St. Benedict*, ed. and trans. Anthony C. Meisel and M. L. del Mastro, New York: Doubleday.

Bernard of Clairvaux (1885), *Sermones in Cantica Canticorum*, Patrologia Latina, ed. J.-P. Migne, 183.

Bernard of Clairvaux (1957–77), *Sancti Bernardi Opera*, ed. J. Leclercq and H. M. Rochais, 8 vols., Rome: Editiones Cistercienses.

Bernard of Clairvaux (1959), *On Loving God, and Selections from Sermons*, trans. Hugh Martin, London: SCM Press.

Bernard of Clairvaux (1971–80), *On the Song of Songs*, trans. Kilian Walsh and Irene M. Edmonds, 4 vols., Kalamazoo, MI: Cistercian Publications.

Bevington, David, ed. and trans. (1975), *Medieval Drama*, Boston, MA: Houghton Mifflin.

Boethius (1957), *Philosophiae consolatio*, ed. L. Bieler, CCSL 94, Turnhout: Brepols.

Boethius (1969), *The Consolation of Philosophy*, trans. V. E. Watts, Harmondsworth: Penguin.

Boethius (1989), Anicius Manlius Severinus Boethius, *Fundamentals of Music* [*De institutione musica*], trans. Calvin M. Bower, ed. Claude V. Palisca, New Haven: Yale University Press.

Caelius Aurelianus (1950), Caelius Aurelianus, *On Acute Diseases and on Chronic Diseases*, ed. and trans. I. E. Drabkin, Chicago: University of Chicago Press.

Calcidius (2011), *Commentaire au Timée de Platon*, ed. and trans. Béatrice Bakhouche, 2 vols., Paris: J. Vrin.

Cassian, John (1886), *Iohannis Cassiani Conlationes XXIIII*, ed. Michael Petschenig, Vienna: C. Gerold.

Chrysostom, John (1862), *Homilia contra ludos et theatra*, Patrologia Graeca, ed. J.-P. Migne, 56.263–70.

Chrysostom, John (1951), *On Vainglory and How Parents Should Educate their Children*, trans. M. L. W. Laistner, in M. L. W. Laistner, *Christianity and Pagan Culture in the Later Roman Empire*, 85–122, Ithaca, NY: Cornell University Press (reprint 1978).

Cicero (1915), *De finibus bonorum et malorum*, ed. T. Schiche, Leipzig: Teubner.

Cicero (1945), Cicero, *Tusculan Disputations*, trans. J. E. King, Loeb Classical Library, Cambridge, MA: Harvard University Press.

Cicero (2002), *Cicero on the Emotions: Tusculan Disputations 3 and 4*, trans. Margaret Graver, Chicago: University of Chicago Press.

Cyprian of Carthage (1972), *De lapsis*, in Cyprianus, *Opera I: Ad Quirinum; Ad Fortunatum; De lapsis; De ecclesiae catholicae unitate*, ed. R. Weber and M. Bévenot, CCSL 3, 221–42, Turnhout: Brepols.

Dahlberg, Charles, trans. (1983), *The Romance of the Rose by Guillaume de Lorris and Jean de Meun*, Hanover and London: University Press of New England.

Denifle, Heinrich and Emile Châtelain, eds. (1964), *Chartularium Universitatis Parisiensis*, 4 vols., Paris, 1889–97; reprint Brussels: Culture et Civilisation.

Dhuoda (1991), Dhuoda, *Handbook for William: A Carolingian Woman's Counsel for Her Son*, trans. Carol Neel, Lincoln: University of Nebraska Press.

Dhuoda (1998), Dhuoda, *Handbook for her Warrior Son; Liber Manualis*, ed. and trans. Marcelle Thiébaux, Cambridge: Cambridge University Press.

Dioscorides (2005), Pedanius Dioscorides of Anazarbus, *De materia medica*, trans. Lily Y. Beck, Hildesheim: Georg Olms.

Dronke, Peter, ed. (1968), *Medieval Latin and the Rise of European Love-Lyric*, 2nd edn., Oxford: Clarendon Press.

Dronke, Peter, ed. (1994), *Nine Medieval Latin Plays*, Cambridge: Cambridge University Press.

Durandus (1995–2000), *Rationale divinorum officiorum*, ed. A. Davril, T. M. Thibodeau, and B. G. Guyot, 3 vols., CCCM 140–140B, Turnhout: Brepols.

Edwards, Cyril, trans. (2006), Wolfram von Eschenbach, *Parzival and Titurel*, Oxford: Oxford University Press.

Evagrius Ponticus (1971), *Évagre de Pontique, Traité pratique ou le moine*, ed. and trans. Antoine Guillaumont and Claire Guillaumont, 2 vols., SC 170–71, Paris: Éditions du Cerf.

Finnegan, Robert Emmett, ed. (1977), *Christ and Satan: A Critical Edition*, Waterloo, Ont.: Wilfrid Laurier University Press.

Galen (1980), *On the Doctrines of Hippocrates and Plato*, vol. 2, ed. and trans. Phillip de Lacy, Berlin: Akademie.

Godman, Peter (1985), *Poetry of the Carolingian Renaissance*, London: Duckworth.

Gregory of Tours (1974), *The History of the Franks*, trans. Lewis Thorpe, London: Penguin.

Gregory the Great (1963), Gregorius Magnus, *Expositiones in Canticum canticorum; In librum primum Regum*, ed. P.-P. Verbraken, CCSL 144, Turnhout: Brepols.

Gregory the Great (1985), Gregorius Magnus, *Moralia in Iob. Libri XXIII-XXXV*, ed. M. Adriaen, CCSL 143B, Turnhout: Brepols.

Gregory the Great (2004), *The Letters of Gregory the Great*, trans. J. R. C. Martyn, Toronto: Pontifical Institute for Mediaeval Studies, 2004.

Grocheio, Johannes de (2011), *Ars musice*, ed. and trans. Constant J. Mews, John N. Crossley, Catherine Jeffreys, Leigh McKinnon, and Carol J. Williams, Kalamazoo, MI: Medieval Institute Publications.

Guido of Arezzo (1978), *Micrologus*, trans. Warren Babb, ed. Claude V. Palisca, in *Hucbald, Guido, and John on Music: Three Medieval Treatises*, 57–83, New Haven, CT: Yale University Press.

Guy of Saint-Denis (2017), *Tractatus de tonis*, ed. and trans. Constant J. Mews, Carol J. Williams, John N. Crossley, and Catherine Jeffreys, Kalamazoo, MI: Medieval Institute Publications.

Hart, Columba, trans. (1980), *Hadewijch: The Complete Works*, Mahwah, NJ: Paulist Press.

Hatto, A. T., trans. (1967), Gottfried von Strassburg, *Tristan*, With the surviving fragments of the *Tristan* of Thomas, London: Penguin.

Herbord of Michelsberg (1856), *Vita Ottonis episcopi Babenbergensis*, ed. R. Köpke, MGH SS 12, Hannover: Hahn.

Hildegard of Bingen (1994), *The Letters of Hildegard of Bingen*, trans. Joseph L. Baird and Radd K. Ehrman, Vol. 1, Oxford: Oxford University Press.

Honorius Augustudonensis (1885), *Gemma animae*, Patrologia Latina, ed. J.-P. Migne, 172. 541–738.

Hrotsvit of Gandersheim (1923), *The Plays of Roswitha*, trans. Christopher St. John, London: Chatto and Windus.

Hrotsvit of Gandersheim (1970), *Hrotsvithae Opera*, ed. H. Homeyer, Munich: Schöningh.

Hugh of Lusignan (1969), *Conventum*, in Jane Martindale, "Conventum inter Guillelmum Aquitanorum comitem et Hugonum Chiliarchum," *English Historical Review*, 74: 528–48.

Isidore of Seville (2006), *The Etymologies of Isidore of Seville*, ed. and trans. Stephen A. Barney, W. J. Lewis, J. A. Beach, and Oliver Berghof, with Muriel Hall, Cambridge: Cambridge University Press.

Jerome (1893): St Jerome, *Letters and Select Works*, trans. W. H. Fremantle, A Select Library of Nicene and Post-Nicene Fathers of the Christian Church, Ser. 2, Vol. 6, Oxford: Parker.

John of Salisbury (1993), *Policraticus*, ed. K. S. B. Keats-Rohan, CCCM 118, Turnhout: Brepols.

Kay, Sarah, ed. and trans. (1992), *Raoul de Cambrai*, Oxford: Clarendon Press.

Kibler, William W., trans. (1991), Chrétien de Troyes, *Arthurian Romances* [*Erec and Enide* trans. Carleton W. Carroll], London: Penguin.

Klinck, Anne L., ed. (1992), *The Old English Elegies: A Critical Edition and Genre Study*, Montreal: McGill-Queen's University Press.

Krapp, George Philip, ed. (1931), *The Junius Manuscript*, New York: Columbia University Press.
Krause, Hans-George, ed., with Detlev Jasper and Veronika Lukas (2007), *Die Touler Vita Leos IX* [*Vita Leonis IX papae*], Hanover: Hahn.
Lafleur, Claude, ed. (1988), *Quatre introductions à la philosophie au XIIIe siècle*, Montréal-Paris: Institut d'études médiévales-Vrin.
Lucian (2008), *On Dancing*, in Edith Hall and Rosie Wyles (eds.), *New Directions in Ancient Pantomime*, 378–419, Oxford: Oxford University Press.
Marie de France (1999), *The Lais of Marie de France*, trans. Glyn S. Burgess and Keith Busby, 2nd edn., London: Penguin.
Mews, Constant J. (2008), *The Lost Love Letters of Heloise and Abelard: Perceptions of Dialogue in Twelfth-Century France*, 2nd edn., New York: Palgrave Macmillan.
Meyer, Christian, ed. (2003), "Le tonaire cistercien et sa tradition" [*Tonale Sancti Bernardi*], *Revue de Musicologie*, 89: 57–92.
Millett, Bella, ed. (2005), Ancrene Wisse: *A Corrected Edition of the Text in Cambridge, Corpus Christi College, MS 402, with Variants from Other Manuscript*, 2 vols., Early English Text Society 325, 326, Oxford: Oxford University Press.
Musurillo, Herbert, ed. and trans. (1972), *Passio Sanctarum Perpetuae et Felicitatis* in *Acts of the Christian Martyrs*, 106–31, Oxford: Clarendon Press.
Newman, Barbara (2016), *Making Love in the Twelfth Century:* Letters of Two Lovers *in Context*, Philadelphia: University of Pennsylvania Press.
Niceta of Remesiana (1905), *Niceta of Remesiana, His Life and Works*, ed. A. E. Burn, Cambridge: Cambridge University Press.
Oldrieve, Susan (2010), "Genesis B: Introduction and Translation," Baldwin Wallace College, The Department of English. Available online: http://homepages.bw.edu/~uncover/oldrievegenesisb.htm (accessed 14 June 2018).
Plato (1888), *The Timaeus of Plato*, ed. and trans. R. D. Archer-Hind, London: Macmillan.
Prudentius (1949), *Psychomachia*, in *Prudentius*, Volume 1, ed. Jeffrey Henderson, trans. H. J. Thomson, Loeb Classical Library, 274–341, Cambridge, MA: Harvard University Press.
Pseudo-Boethius (1976), *De disciplina scolarium*, ed. Olga Weijers, Leiden: Brill.
Rosenberg, Samuel N. and Hans Tischler (1981), *Chanter m'estuet: Songs of the Trouvères*, London: Faber Music.
Russell, Norman, trans. (1981), *The Lives of the Desert Fathers*, Kalamazoo, MI: Cistercian Publications.
Shepherd, Geoffrey, ed. (1959), *Ancrene Wisse: Parts Six and Seven*, London: Nelson.
Sicard of Cremona (2008), *Mitrale*, ed. G. Sarbak and L. Weinrich, CCCM 228, Turnhout: Brepols.
Sisam, Celia and Kenneth Sisam, eds. (1973), *The Oxford Book of Medieval English Verse*, Oxford: Oxford University Press.
Swanton, Michael, ed. and trans. (1978), *Beowulf*, Manchester: Manchester University Press.
Swanton, Michael, ed. (1987), *The Dream of the Rood*, Exeter: University of Exeter Press.
Thorndike, Lynne (1944), *University Records and Life in the Middle Ages*, New York: Columbia University Press.
Tischler, Hans (1997), *Trouvère Lyrics with Melodies: Complete Comparative Edition. Tropatorum septemtrionalum poemata cum suis melodiis: opera omnia*, 15 vols., American Institute of Musicology, Neuhausen: Hänssler-Verlag.
van den Dungen, Wim, trans. (2016), Beatrice of Nazareth, *On Seven Ways of Holy Love*, Antwerp: Taurus Press. Available at: http://www.sofiatopia.org/equiaeon/7ways.htm (accessed 14 June 2018).

Ward, Benedicta, trans. (1984), *The Sayings of the Desert Fathers: The Alphabetical Collection*, revised edn., Kalamazoo, MI: Cistercian Publications.
White, Caroline, trans. (1998), *Early Christian Lives*, London: Penguin.
White, Hugh, trans. (1993), *Ancrene Wisse: Guide for Anchoresses*, Harmondsworth: Penguin.
Zum Brunn, Emilie and Georgette Epiney-Burgard (1989), *Women Mystics in Medieval Europe*, New York: Paragon House.

SECONDARY

Ahmed, Sara (2001), "The Organisation of Hate," *Law and Critique*, 12(3): 345–65.
Althoff, Gerd (1998), "*Ira Regis*: Prolegomena to a History of Royal Anger," in Barbara Rosenwein (ed.), *Anger's Past: The Social Uses of an Emotion in the Middle Ages*, 59–74, Ithaca, NY: Cornell University Press.
Amundsen, Darrel (1971), "Visigothic Medical Legislation," *Bulletin of the History of Medicine*, 45(6): 553–69.
Anderson, Warren (2001), "Hymn," in Stanley Sadie and John Tyrell (eds.), *New Grove Dictionary of Music and Musicians*, 29 vols., 2nd edn., 12.17–22, London: Macmillan.
Arano, Luisa Cogliati (1976), *The Medieval Health Handbook: Tacuinum Sanitatis*, New York: George Braziller.
Archambeau, Nicole (2011), "Healing Options During the Plague: Survivor Stories from a Fourteenth-Century Canonization Inquest," *Bulletin of the History of Medicine*, 85(4): 531–59.
Asad, Talal (1993), "On Discipline and Humility in Medieval Christian Monasticism," in Asad, *Genealogies of Religion: Discipline and Reasons of Power in Christianity and Islam*, 125–67, Baltimore, MD: Johns Hopkins University Press.
Atkinson, Charles M. (1988), "On the Interpretation of *Modi, quos abusive tonos dicimus*," in Patrick J. Gallacher and Helen Damico (eds.), *Hermeneutics and Medieval Culture*, 147–62, Albany: State University of New York.
Augoustakis, Antony (2013), "Hrotsvit of Gandersheim Christianizes Terence," in Antony Augoustakis and Ariana Traill (eds.), *A Companion to Terence*, 397–409, Chichester: Wiley-Blackwell.
Backman, E. Louis (1952), *Religious Dances in the Christian Church and in Popular Medicine*, London: George Allen & Unwin.
Baldwin, John W. (1994), *The Language of Sex: Five Voices from Northern France Around 1200*, Chicago: University of Chicago Press.
Barasch, Moshe (1976), *Gestures of Despair in Medieval and Early Renaissance Art*, New York: New York University Press.
Barasch, Moshe (1987), *Giotto and the Language of Gesture*, Cambridge: Cambridge University Press.
Barnes, T. D. (1996), "Christians and the Theater," in William J. Slater (ed.), *Roman Theater and Society, E. Togo Salmon Papers I*, 161–180, Ann Arbor: University of Michigan Press.
Barrett, Sam (2013), *The Melodic Tradition of Boethius'* De consolatione philosophiae *in the Middle Ages*, 2 vols., Kassell: Bärenreiter.
Barthélemy, Dominique (1995), "Du nouveau sur le *Conventum Hugonis?*," *Bibliothèque de l'école des chartes*, 153(2): 483–95.
Barton, Richard (1998), " 'Zealous Anger' and the Renegotiation of Aristocratic Relationships in Eleventh- and Twelfth-Century France," in Barbara Rosenwein (ed.), *Anger's Past: The Social Uses of an Emotion in the Middle Ages*, 153–70, Ithaca, NY: Cornell University Press.

Beech, George (1966), "A Feudal Document of Early Eleventh-Century Poitou," in Pierre Gallais and Yves-Jean Riou (eds.), *Mélanges offerts à René Crozet: à l'occasion de son 70 anniversaire, par ses amis, ses collèques, ses élèves*, 2 vols., 1.203–13, Poitiers: Société d'études médiévales.

Belting, Hans (1990), *The Image and Its Public in the Middle Ages: Form and Function of Early Paintings of the Passion*, trans. Mark Bartusis and Raymond Meyer, New Rochelle, NY: A. D. Caratzas.

Belting, Hans (1994), *Likeness and Presence: A History of the Image Before the Era of Art*, trans. Edmund Jephcott, Chicago: University of Chicago Press.

Bleeke, Marian (2012), "The Eve Fragment from Autun and the Emotionalism of Pilgrimage," in Elina Gertsman (ed.), *Crying in the Middle Ages: Tears of History*, 16–34, New York: Routledge.

Bond, Gerald A. (1995), *The Loving Subject: Desire, Eloquence, and Power in Romanesque France*, Philadelphia: University of Pennsylvania Press.

Boquet, Damien and Piroska Nagy (2015), *Sensible Moyen Âge: Une histoire des émotions dans l'Occident médiéval*, Paris: Éditions du Seuil.

Bower, Calvin (2001), "Boethius," in Stanley Sadie and John Tyrell (eds.), *New Grove Dictionary of Music and Musicians*, 29 vols., 2nd edn., 3.784–6, London: Macmillan.

Boynton, Susan (2004), "From the Lament of Rachel to the Lament of Mary: A Transformation in the History of Drama and Spirituality," in Nils Holger Petersen, Claus Clüver, and Nicolas Bell (eds.), *Signs of Change: Transformations of Christian Traditions and their Representation in the Arts, 1000–2000*, 319–40, Amsterdam: Rodopi.

Brazil, Sarah Jane, "Covering and Discovering the Body in Medieval Theology, Literature and Drama," Doctoral diss., University of Geneva, 2015.

Brennan, Brian (1988), "Augustine's *De Musica*," *Vigiliae Christianae*, 42(3): 267–81.

Brown, Peter (1971), *The World of Late Antiquity*, London: Thames & Hudson.

Brundage, James A. (1969), *Medieval Canon Law and the Crusader*, Madison: University of Wisconsin Press.

Buc, Philippe (2001), *The Dangers of Ritual: Between Early Medieval Texts and Social Scientific Theory*, Princeton, NJ: Princeton University Press.

Bührer-Thierry, Geneviève (1998), " 'Just Anger' or 'Vengeful Anger'? The Punishment of Blinding in the Early Medieval West," in Barbara Rosenwein (ed.), *Anger's Past: The Social Uses of an Emotion in the Middle Ages*, 75–91, Ithaca, NY: Cornell University Press.

Burlin, Robert B. (1968), "The Ruthwell Cross, 'The Dream of the Rood' and the Vita Contemplativa," *Studies in Philology*, 65: 23–43.

Burnett, Charles (1994), "The Chapter on the Spirits in the *Pantegni* of Constantine the African," in Charles Burnett and Danielle Jacquart (eds.), *Constantine the African and 'Alī ibn Al-'Abbās Al-Maǧūsī, The Pantegni and Related Texts*, 99–120, Leiden: Brill.

Burnett, Charles and Danielle Jacquart, eds. (1994), *Constantine the African and 'Alī ibn Al-'Abbās Al-Maǧūsī, The Pantegni and Related Texts*, Leiden: Brill.

Büttner, F. O. (1983), *Imitatio Pietatis: Motive der christlichen Iknographie als Modelle zur Verähnlichung*, Berlin: G. Mann.

Bylebyl, Jerome (1971), "Galen on the Non-Natural Causes of Variation in the Pulse," *Bulletin of the History of Medicine*, 45(5): 482–85.

Bynum, Caroline Walker (1986), *Holy Feast and Holy Fast: The Religious Significance of Food to Medieval Women*, Berkeley: University of California Press.

Cameron, Malcolm (1993), *Anglo-Saxon Medicine*, Cambridge: Cambridge University Press.

Carli, Enzo (1986), *Giovanni Pisano: Il Pulpito di Pistoia*, Milan: G. Mondadori & Associati.

Carroll, Michael P. (1986), *The Cult of the Virgin Mary: Psychological Origins*, Princeton, NJ: Princeton University Press.

Carruthers, Mary (2013), *The Experience of Beauty in the Middle Ages*, Oxford: Oxford University Press.

Casiday, Augustine (2013), *Reconstructing the Theology of Evagrius Ponticus: Beyond Heresy*, Cambridge: Cambridge University Press.

Chaguinian, Christophe (2015), "Origine institutionnelle et géographique du Jeu d'Adam: quelques hypothèses," *Le Moyen Âge: Revue d'histoire et de philologie*, 121(2): 361–82.

Chamberlain, David S. (1970), "Philosophy of Music in the *Consolatio* of Boethius," *Speculum*, 45(1): 80–97.

Christe, Yves (1999), *Jugements derniers*, Saint-Léger-Vauban: Zodiaque.

Classen, Albrecht (2012), "Crying in Public and in Private: Tears and Crying in Medieval German Literature," in Elina Gertsman (ed.), *Crying in the Middle Ages: Tears of History*, 230–48, New York: Routledge.

Clay, Rotha Mary (1914), *The Hermits and Anchorites of England*, London: Methuen.

Clayton, Mary (1990), *The Cult of the Virgin Mary in Anglo-Saxon England*, Cambridge: Cambridge University Press.

Cohen-Hanegbi, Naama (2017), *Caring for the Living Soul: Emotions, Medicine and Penance in the Late Medieval Mediterranean*, Leiden: Brill.

Colish, Marcia L. (1990a), *The Stoic Tradition from Antiquity to the Early Middle Ages. 1: Stoicism in Classical Latin Literature*, Leiden: Brill.

Colish, Marcia L. (1990b), *The Stoic Tradition from Antiquity to the Early Middle Ages. 2: Stoicism in Christian Latin Thought Through the Sixth Century*, Leiden: Brill.

Collins, Minta (2000), *Medieval Herbals: The Illustrative Traditions*, Toronto: University of Toronto Press.

Cooper, Kate (2011), "Augustine and Monica," in Conrad Leyser and Lesley Smith (eds.), *Motherhood, Religion, and Society in Medieval Europe, 400–1400: Essays Presented to Henrietta Leyser*, 7–20, Farnham: Ashgate.

Crawford, Sally (1999), *Childhood in Anglo-Saxon England*, Stroud: Sutton.

Davis, Leo Donald (1983), *The First Seven Ecumenical Councils (325–787): Their History and Theology*, Collegeville, MN: Liturgical Press.

de Jong, Mayke (2009), *The Penitential State: Authority and Atonement in the Age of Louis the Pious, 814–840*: Cambridge: Cambridge University Press.

Decker, John R. (2008), "Engendering Contrition, Wounding the Soul: Geertgen tot Sint Jans' *Man of Sorrows*," *Artibus et Historiae*, 29(57): 59–73.

Demaitre, Luke E. (2013), *Medieval Medicine: The Art of Healing from Head to Toe*, Santa Barbara, CA: Praeger.

Diller, Hans-Jürgen (1992), *The Middle English Mystery Play: A Study in Dramatic Speech and Form*, trans. Frances Wessels, Cambridge: Cambridge University Press.

Dobson, E. J. (1976), *The Origins of* Ancrene Wisse, Oxford: Clarendon Press.

Dox, Donnalee (2004), *The Idea of the Theater in Latin Christian Thought: Augustine to the Fourteenth Century*, Ann Arbor: University of Michigan Press.

Duffin, Jacalyn (2005), *Lovers and Livers: Disease Concepts in History*, Toronto: University of Toronto Press.

Duran-Reynals, M. L. and C.-E. A. Winslow (1949), "Regiment de preservacio a epidimia o pestilencia e mortaldats. Epistola de Maestre Jacme d'Agramont als honrats e discrets seynnors pahers e conseyll de la Ciutat de leyda, 1348," *Bulletin of the History of Medicine*, 23: 57–89.

Dyer, Joe (2016), "Music, the Passions, and Virtue in Two Quodlibetal Questions of the Philosopher Pierre d'Auvergne," *Philomusica On-line*, 15(2): 1–54.

Elias, Norbert (2000), *The Civilizing Process: Sociogenetic and Psychogenetic Investigations*, rev. edn., Oxford: Blackwell.

Farmer, Sharon (1986), "Persuasive Voices: Clerical Images of Medieval Wives," *Speculum*, 61(3): 517–43.

Fassler, Margot E. (2010), *The Virgin of Chartres: Making History Through Liturgy and the Arts*, New Haven, CT: Yale University Press.

Fishhof, Gil (2013), "The Frescoes of Berzé-la-Ville: The Beatitude of the Blessed Saint Hugh and the Concept of Happiness in the Middle Ages," in Ronit Milano and William L. Barcham (eds.), *Happiness or Its Absence in Art*, 27–44, Cambridge: Cambridge Scholars Publishing.

Fleming, John V. (1966), " 'The Dream of the Rood' and Anglo-Saxon Monasticism," *Traditio*, 22: 43–72.

Foka, Anna (2015), "Gender Subversion and the Early Christian East: Reconstructing the Byzantine Comic Mime," in Anna Foka and Jonas Liliequist (eds.), *Laughter, Humor, and the (Un)Making of Gender: Historical and Cultural Perspectives*, 65–84, New York: Palgrave.

Forsyth, Ilene H. (1972), *The Throne of Wisdom: Wood Sculptures of the Madonna in Romanesque France*, Princeton, NJ: Princeton University Press.

Garcia-Ballester, Luis (1988), "Soul and Body: Disease of the Soul and Disease of the Body in Galen's Medical Thought," in Paolo Manuli and Mario Vegetti (eds.), *Atti del terzo colloquio Galenico internazionale (Pavia: 10–12 Settembre 1986)*, 117–52, Naples: Bibliopolis.

Garcia-Ballester, Luis (1992), "Changes in the *Regimina sanitatis*: The Role of the Jewish Physicians," in Sheila Campbell, Bert Hall, and David Klausner (eds.), *Health, Disease, and Healing in Medieval Culture*, 119–31, New York: St. Martin's Press.

Garnier, François (1982), *Le Langage de l'image au Moyen Âge: 1. Signification et symbolique*, Paris: Le Léopard d'Or.

Garver, Valerie L. (2009), *Women and Aristocratic Culture in the Carolingian World*, Ithaca, NY: Cornell University Press.

Gaunt, Simon (2006), *Love and Death in Medieval French and Occitan Courtly Literature: Martyrs to Love*, Oxford: Oxford University Press.

Geary, Patrick J. (1994a), *Living with the Dead in the Middle Ages*, Ithaca, NY: Cornell University Press.

Geary, Patrick J. (1994b), *Phantoms of Remembrance: Memory and Oblivion at the End of the First Millennium*, Princeton, NJ: Princeton University Press.

Georgianna, Linda (1981), *The Solitary Self: Individuality in the Ancrene Wisse*, Cambridge, MA: Harvard University Press.

Gertsman, Elina, ed. (2012), *Crying in the Middle Ages: Tears of History*, New York: Routledge.

Gil Sotres, Pedro (1994), "Modelo teórico y observación clínica: Las pasiones del alma en la psicología médica medieval," in *Comprendre et maîtriser la nature au Moyen Âge. Mélanges d'histoire des sciences offert à Guy Beaujouan*, 181–204, Geneva: Librairie Droz.

Gil Sotres, Pedro (1998), "The Regimens of Health," in Mirko D. Grmek (ed.), Antony Shugaar (trans.), *Western Medical Thought from Antiquity to the Middle Ages*, 291–318, Cambridge, MA: Harvard University Press.

Giralt, Sebastià (2002), "The *Consilia* Attributed to Arnau De Vilanova," *Early Science and Medicine*, 7(4): 311–56.

Gluckman, Max (1955), "The Peace in the Feud," *Past and Present*, 8(1): 1–14.

Gourevitch, Danielle (1998), "The Paths of Knowledge: Medicine in the Roman World," in Mirko D. Grmek (ed.), Antony Shugaar (trans.), *Western Medical Thought from Antiquity to the Middle Ages*, 104–38, Cambridge, MA: Harvard University Press.

Grasso, Anthony R. (1991), "Theology and Structure in 'The Dream of the Rood,' " *Religion and Literature*, 23(2): 23–38.

Grattan, John and Charles Singer (1971), *Anglo-Saxon Magic and Medicine*, Oxford: Oxford University Press.

Grayson, Janet (1974), *Structure and Imagery in* Ancrene Wisse, Hanover, NH: University Press of New England.

Green, Monica (1994), "The Re-creation of *Pantegni Practica* Book VIII," in Charles Burnett and Danielle Jacquart (eds.), *Constantine the African and ʿAlī ibn Al-ʿAbbās Al-Maǧūsī, The Pantegni and Related Texts*, 121–60, Leiden: Brill.

Hall, Edith (2008), "Introduction: Pantomime, a Lost Chord of Ancient Culture," in Edith Hall and Rosie Wyles (eds.), *New Directions in Ancient Pantomime*, 1–40, Oxford: Oxford University Press.

Hanawalt, Barbara A. (2002), "Medievalists and the Study of Childhood," *Speculum*, 77(2): 440–60.

Hanlon, Gregory (2013), "The Decline of Violence in the West: From Cultural to Post-Cultural History," *English Historical Review*, 128(531): 367–400.

Harvey, Ruth (1975), *The Inward Wits: Psychological Theory in the Middle Ages and Renaissance*, London: The Warburg Institute.

Haussherr, Reiner (1963), "Der Tote Christus am Kreuz: Zur Ikonographie des Gerokreuzes," Doctoral diss., Rheinischen Friedrich-Wilhelms-Universität, Bonn.

Hentschel, Frank (2000), "Der verjagte Dämon: Mittelalterliche Gedanken zur Wirkung der Musik aus der Zeit um 1300, mit einer Edition der Quaestiones 16 und 17 aus Quodlibet VI des Petrus d'Auvergne," in Jan A. Aertsen and Andreas Speer (eds.), *Geistesleben im 13. Jahrhundert*, 395–421, Berlin: De Gruyter.

Hochschild, Arlie Russell (1983), *The Managed Heart: Commercialization of Human Feeling*, Berkeley: University of California Press.

Horden, Peregrine (2000), "Commentary on Part II, with a Note on the Early Middle Ages," in Peregrine Horden (ed.), *Music as Medicine: The History of Music Therapy Since Antiquity*, Aldershot: Ashgate.

Horden, Peregrine (2007), "A Non-Natural Environment: Medicine without Doctors and the Medieval European Hospital," in Barbara Bowers (ed.), *The Medieval Hospital and Medical Practice*, 133–45, Aldershot: Ashgate.

Horden, Peregrine (2011), "What's Wrong with Early Medieval Medicine?," *Social History of Medicine*, 24(1): 5–25.

Huglo, Michel (1971), *Les tonaires: inventaire, analyse, comparaison*, Paris: Société française de musicologie.

Hummer, Hans (2013), "The Production and Preservation of Documents in Francia: The Evidence of Cartularies," in Warren C. Brown, Marios Costambeys, Matthew Innes, and Adam J. Kosto (eds.), *Documentary Culture and the Laity in the Early Middle Ages*, 189–230, Cambridge: Cambridge University Press.

Hyams, Paul R. (1998), "What Did Henry III of England Think in Bed and in French About Kingship and Anger?," in Barbara Rosenwein (ed.), *Anger's Past: The Social Uses of an Emotion in the Middle Ages*, 92–124, Ithaca, NY: Cornell University Press.

Ingham, Patricia Clare (2003), "From Kinship to Kingship: Mourning, Gender, and Anglo-Saxon Community," in Jennifer C. Vaught and Lynne Dickson Bruckner (eds.), *Grief and Gender, 700–1700*, 17–32, New York: Palgrave.

Innes, Matthew (2013), "On the Material Culture of Legal Documents: Charters and Their Preservation in the Cluny Archive, Ninth to Eleventh Centuries," in Warren C. Brown,

Marios Costambeys, Matthew Innes, and Adam J. Kosto (eds.), *Documentary Culture and the Laity in the Early Middle Ages*, 283–320, Cambridge: Cambridge University Press.

Inwood, Brad (1993), "Seneca and Psychological Dualism," in Jacques Brunschwig and Martha C. Nussbaum (eds.), *Passions and Perceptions: Studies in Hellenistic Philosophy of Mind. Proceedings of the Fifth Symposium Hellenisticum*, 150–83, Cambridge: Cambridge University Press.

Itnyre, Cathy Jorgensen (1996), "The Emotional Universe of Medieval Icelandic Fathers and Sons," in Cathy Jorgensen Itnyre (ed.), *Medieval Family Roles: A Book of Essays*, 173–96, New York: Garland.

Jacobus, Laura (1999), "Motherhood and Massacre: The Massacre of the Innocents in Late-Medieval Art and Drama," in Mark Levene and Penny Roberts (eds.), *The Massacre in History*, 39–54, New York: Berghahn Books.

Jaeger, C. Stephen (1999), *Ennobling Love: In Search of a Lost Sensibility*, Philadelphia: University of Pennsylvania Press.

Jarcho, Saul (1970), "Galen's Six Non-Naturals," *Bulletin of the History of Medicine*, 44(4): 372–77.

Jeffreys, Catherine (2009), "Some Early References to Aristotle's *Politics* in Parisian Writings About Music," in Jason Stoessel (ed.), *Identity and Locality in Early European Music*, 83–106, London: Ashgate.

Jeffreys, Catherine (2011), "The Exchange of Ideas about Music in Paris *c.*1270–1304: Guy of Saint-Denis, Johannes de Grocheio, and Peter of Auvergne," in C. J. Mews and J. N. Crossley (eds.), *Communities of Learning: Networks and the Shaping of Intellectual Identity in Europe, 1100–1500*, 151–75, Turnhout: Brepols.

Jolliffe, J. E. A. (1955), *Angevin Kingship*, London: Adam and Charles Black.

Jung, Jacqueline (2000), "Beyond the Barrier: The Unifying Role of the Choir Screen in Gothic Churches," *The Art Bulletin*, 82(4): 622–57.

Jung, Jacqueline (2012), *The Gothic Screen: Space, Sculpture, and Community in the Cathedrals of France and Germany, ca.1200–1400*, Cambridge: Cambridge University Press.

Juslin, Patrik N. and John A. Sloboda, eds. (2010), *Handbook of Music and Emotion: Theory, Research, Applications*, Oxford: Oxford University Press.

Kieckhefer, Richard (1989), *Magic in the Middle Ages*, Cambridge: Cambridge University Press.

Kieckhefer, Richard (1994), "The Specific Rationality of Medieval Magic," *American Historical Review*, 99(3): 813–36.

Knuuttila, Simo (2004), *Emotions in Ancient and Medieval Philosophy*, Oxford: Oxford University Press.

Konstan, David (2006), *The Emotions of the Ancient Greeks: Studies in Aristotle and Classical Literature*, Toronto: University of Toronto Press.

Krueger, Paul, ed. (1906), *Corpus iuris civilis, Vol. 2: Codex Justinianus*. Berlin: Apud Weidmannos.

Lansing, Carol (2008), *Passion and Order: Restraint of Grief in the Medieval Italian Communes*, Ithaca, NY: Cornell University Press.

Largier, Niklaus (2008), "Medieval Mysticism," in John Corrigan (ed.), *The Oxford Handbook of Religion and Emotion*, 364–79, Oxford: Oxford University Press.

Leach, Elizabeth Eva (2009), "Music and Masculinity in the Middle Ages," in Ian Biddle and Kirsten Gibson (eds.), *Masculinity and Western Musical Practice*, 21–40, Farnham: Ashgate.

Leys, Ruth (2011), "The Turn to Affect: A Critique," *Critical Inquiry*, 37(3): 434–72.

Leyser, Conrad (2000), *Authority and Asceticism from Augustine to Gregory the Great*, Oxford: Clarendon Press.

Lightbourne, Ruth (1991), "The Question of Instruments and Dance in Hildegard of Bingen's Twelfth-Century Music Drama *Ordo Virtutum*," *Parergon*, 9(2): 45–65.

Lindberg, David (1992), *The Beginnings of Western Science: The European Scientific Tradition in Philosophical, Religious, and Institutional Context, Prehistory to AD 1450*, Chicago: University of Chicago Press.

Little, Lester K. (1978), *Religious Poverty and the Profit Economy in Medieval Europe*, Ithaca, NY: Cornell University Press.

Little, Lester K. (1993), *Benedictine Maledictions: Liturgical Cursing in Romanesque France*, Ithaca, NY: Cornell University Press.

Little, Lester K. (1998), "Anger in Monastic Curses," in Barbara Rosenwein (ed.), *Anger's Past: The Social Uses of an Emotion in the Middle Ages*, 9–35, Ithaca, NY: Cornell University Press.

Livingston, Sally A. (2012), *Marriage, Property, and Women's Narratives*, New York: Palgrave Macmillan.

Lochrie, Karma (2003), "Between Women," in Carolyn Dinshaw and David Wallace (eds.), *The Cambridge Companion to Medieval Women's Writing*, 70–88, Cambridge: Cambridge University Press.

Lubac, Henri de (2009), *Corpus mysticum: l'eucharistie et l'Église au Moyen Âge—Étude historique*, Paris: Cerf.

Lutz, Gerhard (2004), *Das Bild des Gekreuzigten im Wandel: Die sächsischen und westfälischen Kruzifixe der ersten Hälfte des 13. Jahrhunderts*, Petersberg: Michael Imhof.

Maguire, Henry (1977), "The Depiction of Sorrow in Middle Byzantine Art," *Dumbarton Oaks Papers*, 31: 123–74.

Maguire, Henry (2012), "Women Mourners in Byzantine Art, Literature, and Society," in Elina Gertsman (ed.), *Crying in the Middle Ages: Tears of History*, 3–15, New York: Routledge.

Maier, Christoph T. (2000), *Crusade Propaganda and Ideology: Model Sermons for the Preaching of the Cross*, Cambridge: Cambridge University Press.

Maître, Claire (1995), *La réforme cistercienne du plain-chant: étude d'un traité théorique*, 108–233, Brecht: Cîteaux, Comentarii Cistercienses.

Malegam, Jehangir Yezdi (2008), "No Peace for the Wicked: Conflicting Visions of Peacemaking in an Eleventh-Century Monastic Narrative," *Viator*, 39(1): 23–49.

Malegam, Jehangir Yezdi (2011), "Love Between Peace and Violence: Not a Crisis but a Critique of Fidelity After 1000," *Quaestiones Medii Aevi Novae*, 16: 321–36.

Malegam, Jehangir Yezdi (2013), *The Sleep of Behemoth: Disputing Peace and Violence in Medieval Europe, 1000–1200*, Ithaca, NY: Cornell University Press.

Malegam, Jehangir Yezdi (2016), "Evangelic Provocation: Location of Anger in Medieval Conversion Narratives," *Literature Compass*, 13(6): 372–88.

Martyn, John R. C. (2004), "Gregory the Great: On Organ Lessons and on Equipping Monasteries," *Medievalia et humanistica*, 30: 107–13.

Maunder, Chris, ed. (2008), *Origins of the Cult of the Virgin Mary*, London: Burns & Oates.

McCormick, Michael (2001), *Origins of the European Economy: Communications and Commerce, AD 300–900*, Cambridge: Cambridge University Press.

McGuire, Brian Patrick (2011), "In Search of the Good Mother: Twelfth-Century Celibacy and Affectivity," in Conrad Leyser and Lesley Smith (eds.), *Motherhood, Religion, and Society in Medieval Europe, 400–1400: Essays Presented to Henrietta Leyser*, 85–102, Farnham: Ashgate.

McLaughlin, Megan (2010), *Sex, Gender, and Episcopal Authority in an Age of Reform, 1000–1122*, Cambridge: Cambridge University Press.

McMillin, Linda A. (2013), "The Audience of Hrotsvit," in Phyllis R. Brown and Stephen L. Wailes (eds.), *A Companion to Hrotsvit of Gandersheim (fl. 960): Contextual and Interpretive Approaches*, 311–28, Leiden: Brill.

McNamara, Rebecca F. and Juanita Feros Ruys (2014), "Unlocking the Silences of the Self-Murdered: Textual Approaches to Suicidal Emotions in the Middle Ages," *Exemplaria*, 26(1): 58–80.

McNamer, Sarah (2010), *Affective Meditation and the Invention of Medieval Compassion*, Philadelphia: University of Pennsylvania Press.

McVaugh, Michael (1966), " "*Apud Antiquos* And Medieval Pharmacology," *Medizinhistorisches Journal*, 1: 16–23.

McVaugh, Michael (1997), "Armengaud Blaise as a Translator of Galen," in Edith Sylla and Michael McVaugh (eds.), *Texts and Contexts in Ancient and Medieval Science*, 115–33, Leiden: Brill.

McVaugh, Michael (2005), "Arnau de Vilanova and the Pathology of Cognition," in Graziella Federici Vescovini, Valeria Sorge and Carlo Vinti (eds.), *Corpo e anima, sensi interni e intelletto dai secoli XIII-XIV ai post-cartesiani e spinoziani*, 119–38, Turnhout: Brepols.

Mews, Constant J. (2009), "Liturgists and Dance in the Twelfth Century: The Witness of John Beleth and Sicard of Cremona," *Church History*, 78(3): 512–48.

Mews, Constant J. (2011), "Gregory the Great, the Rule of Benedict and Roman Liturgy: The Evolution of a Legend," *Journal of Medieval History*, 37(2): 125–44.

Mews, Constant J., John N. Crossley, and Carol Williams (2014), "Guy of St. Denis on the Tones: Thinking about Chant for Saint-Denis c. 1300," *Journal of Plainsong and Medieval Music*, 23(2): 151–76.

Mews, Constant J., Catherine Jeffreys, Leigh McKinnon, Carol Williams, and John N. Crossley (2008), "Guy of Saint-Denis and the Compilation of Texts about Music in London, British Library, Harl. MS. 281," *Electronic British Library Journal*, art. 6: 1–34, http://www.bl.uk/eblj/2008articles/article6.html.

Meyer, Mati (2013), "Constructing Emotions and Weaving Meaning in Byzantine Art," in Ronit Milano and William L. Barcham (eds.), *Happiness or Its Absence in Art*, 9–26, Cambridge: Cambridge Scholars Publishing.

Miller, William I. (1990), *Bloodtaking and Peacemaking: Feud, Law, and Society in Saga Iceland*, Chicago: University of Chicago Press.

Miller, William I. (1993a), "Getting a Fix on Violence," in Miller, *Humiliation and Other Essays on Honor, Social Discomfort, and Violence*, 53–92, Ithaca, NY: Cornell University Press.

Miller, William I. (1993b), "Emotions, Honor and the Affective Life of the Heroic," in Miller, *Humiliation and Other Essays on Honor, Social Discomfort, and Violence*, 93–130, Ithaca, NY: Cornell University Press.

Millett, Bella (1992), "The Origins of the *Ancrene Wisse*: New Answers, New Questions," *Medium Ævum*, 61: 206–28.

Moore, R. I. (2007), *The Formation of a Persecuting Society: Authority and Deviance in Western Europe 950–1250*, 2nd edn., Oxford: Blackwell.

Morris, Colin (1972), *The Discovery of the Individual, 1050–1200*, New York: Harper & Row.

Mullally, Robert (2011), *The Carole: A Study of a Medieval Dance*, Farnham: Ashgate.

Murray, Alexander (2000), *Suicide in the Middle Ages, Vol. II: The Curse on Self-Murder*: Oxford: Oxford University Press.

Nagy, Piroska (2000), *Le don des larmes au Moyen Âge: Un instrument spirituel en quête d'institution (Ve-XIIIe siècle)*, Paris: Albin Michel.

Newman, Martha (1996), *The Boundaries of Charity: Cistercian Culture and Ecclesiastical Reform, 1098–1180*, Stanford, CA: Stanford University Press.

Niebyl, Peter H. (1971), "The Non-Naturals," *Bulletin of the History of Medicine*, 45(5): 486–92.

Nussbaum, Martha C. (2001), *Upheavals of Thought: The Intelligence of Emotions*, Cambridge: Cambridge University Press.

Nutton, Vivian (2013), *Ancient Medicine*, 2nd edn., New York: Routledge.

Ó Carragáin, Éamonn (2005), *Ritual and the Rood: Liturgical Images and the Old English Poems of the Dream of the Rood Tradition*, London: British Library; Toronto: University of Toronto Press.

O'Boyle, Cornelius (1998), *The Art of Medicine: Medical Teaching at the University of Paris, 1250–1400*, Leiden: Brill.

Orning, Hans Jacob (2008a), *Unpredictability and Presence: Norwegian Kingship in the High Middle Ages*, trans. Alan Crozier, Leiden: Brill.

Orning, Hans Jacob (2008b), "The Interplay Between Law, Sin and Honor in Conflicts Between Magnates and Kings in Thirteenth Century Norway," in Per Andersen, Mia Münster-Swendsen, and Helle Vogt (eds.), *Law and Power in the Middle Ages: Proceedings of the Fourth Carlsberg Academy Conference on Medieval Legal History 2007*, 27–42, Copenhagen: DJØF.

Ottosson, Per-Gunnar (1984), *Scholastic Medicine and Philosophy: A Study of Commentaries on Galen's Tegni (ca. 1300–1450)*, Naples: Bibliopolis.

Palisca, Claude V. and Dolores Pesce (2001), "Guido of Arezzo," in Stanley Sadie and John Tyrell (eds.), *New Grove Dictionary of Music and Musicians*, 29 vols., 2nd edn., 10.522–6, London: Macmillan.

Patzold, Steffen (2000), *Konflikte im Kloster: Studien zu Auseinandersetzungen in monastischen Gemeinschaften des ottonische-salischen Reichs*, Husum: Matthiesen.

Perfetti, Lisa, ed. (2005), *The Representation of Women's Emotions in Medieval and Early Modern Culture*, Gainesville: University Press of Florida.

Pétré, Hélène (1948), *Caritas: Étude sur le vocabulaire latin de la charité chrétienne*, Louvain: Spicilegium Sacrum Lovaniense.

Peyroux, Catherine (1998), "Gertrude's *Furor*: Reading Anger in an Early Medieval Saint's Life," in Barbara Rosenwein (ed.), *Anger's Past: The Social Uses of an Emotion in the Middle Ages*, 36–58, Ithaca, NY: Cornell University Press.

Pinker, Steven (2011), *The Better Angels of Our Nature: The Decline of Violence in History and Its Causes*, London: Allen Lane.

Plamper, Jan (2010), "The History of Emotions: An Interview with William Reddy, Barbara Rosenwein, and Peter Stearns," *History and Theory*, 49(2): 237–65.

Rankin, S. (1990), "Liturgical Drama," in Richard L. Crocker and David Hiley (eds.), *The New Oxford History of Music: The Early Middle Ages to 1300*, 2nd edn., 310–56, Oxford: Oxford University Press.

Rasmussen, Ann Marie (1997), *Mothers and Daughters in Medieval German Literature*, Syracuse, NY: Syracuse University Press.

Rather, J. L. (1968), "The 'Six Things Non-Natural': A Note on the Origins and Fate of a Doctrine and Phrase," *Clio Medica*, 3: 337–47.

Rawcliffe, Carole (2010), "The Concept of Health in Late Medieval Society," in Simonetta Cavaciocchi (ed.), *Le interazioni fra economia e ambiente biologico nell'Europa preindustriale secc. XIII–XVIII*, 321–38, Florence: Firenza University Press.

Reddy, William M. (1997), "Against Constructionism: The Historical Ethnography of Emotions," *Current Anthropology*, 38(3): 327–51.

Reddy, William M. (2001), *The Navigation of Feeling: A Framework for the History of Emotions*, Cambridge: Cambridge University Press.

Reddy, William M. (2008a), "The Anti-Empire of General de Boigne: Sentimentalism, Love and Cultural Difference in the Eighteenth Century," *Historical Reflections*, 34(1): 4–25.

Reddy, William M. (2008b), "Emotional Styles and Modern Forms of Life," in Nicole C. Karafyllis and Gotlind Ulshöfer (eds.), *Sexualized Brains: Scientific Modeling of Emotional Intelligence from a Cultural Perspective*, 81–100, Cambridge, MA: MIT.

Reddy, William M. (2012), *The Making of Romantic Love: Longing and Sexuality in Europe, South Asia, and Japan, 900–1200 CE*, Chicago: University of Chicago Press.

Richards, Graham (2005), "Emotions into Words—or Words into Emotions?," in Penelope Gouk and Helen Hills (eds.), *Representing Emotions: New Connections in the Histories of Art, Music and Medicine*, 49–68, Aldershot: Ashgate.

Robertson, Elizabeth (1990), *Early English Devotional Prose and the Female Audience*, Knoxville: University of Tennessee Press.

Rocca, Julius (2012), "From Doubt to Certainty: Aspects of the Conceptualization and Interpretation of Galen's Natural Pneuma," in Manfred Horstmanshoff, Helen King, and Claus Zittel (eds.), *Blood, Sweat and Tears: The Changing Concepts of Physiology from Antiquity into Early Modern Europe*, 629–59, Leiden: Brill.

Rosaldo, Michelle Z. (1984), "Toward an Anthropology of Self and Feeling," in Richard A. Shweder and Robert A. LeVine (eds.), *Culture Theory: Essays on Mind, Self and Emotion*, 137–57, Cambridge: Cambridge University Press.

Rosenwein, Barbara H. (2002), "Worrying About Emotions in History," *American Historical Review*, 107(3): 821–45.

Rosenwein, Barbara H. (2006), *Emotional Communities in the Early Middle Ages*, Ithaca, NY: Cornell University Press.

Rosenwein, Barbara H. (2010), "Problems and Methods in the History of Emotions," *Passions in Context*, 1: 3–5.

Rubin, Miri (1991), *Corpus Christi: The Eucharist in Late Medieval Culture*, Cambridge: Cambridge University Press.

Rubin, Miri (2009), *Emotion and Devotion: The Meaning of Mary in Medieval Religious Cultures*, New York: Central European University Press.

Sauerländer, Willibald (2006), "The Fate of the Face in Medieval Art," in Charles T. Little (ed.), *Set in Stone: The Face in Medieval Sculpture*, 2–17, New York: The Metropolitan Museum of Art.

Seidel, Linda (1999), *Legends in Limestone: Lazarus, Gislebertus, and the Cathedral of Autun*, Chicago: University of Chicago Press.

Siraisi, Nancy G. (1981), *Taddeo Alderotti and His Pupils: Two Generations of Italian Medical Learning*, Princeton, NJ: Princeton University Press.

Siraisi, Nancy G. (1990), *Medieval and Early Renaissance Medicine: An Introduction to Knowledge and Practice*, Chicago: University of Chicago Press.

Sizgorich, Thomas (2009), *Violence and Belief in Late Antiquity: Militant Devotion in Christianity and Islam*, Philadelphia: University of Pennsylvania Press.

Smail, Daniel L. (2005), "Emotions and Somatic Gestures in Medieval Narratives: The Case of Raoul de Cambrai," *Zeitschrift für Literaturwissenschaft und Linguistik*, 138: 34–48.

Solomon, Robert C. (1984), "Getting Angry: The Jamesian Theory of Emotion in Anthropology," in Richard A. Shweder and Robert A. LeVine (eds.), *Culture Theory: Essays on Mind, Self and Emotion*, 238–54, Cambridge: Cambridge University Press.

Sorabji, Richard (2000), *Emotion and Peace of Mind: From Stoic Agitation to Christian Temptation*, Oxford: Oxford University Press.

Staden, Heinrich von (2000), "Body, Soul, and Nerves: Epicurus, Herophilus, Erasistratus, the Stoics, and Galen," in John Wright and Paul Potter (eds.), *Psyche and Soma: Physicians and Metaphysicians on the Mind–Body Problem from Antiquity to Enlightenment*, 79–116, Oxford: Clarendon Press.

Stafford, Pauline (2001), "Review Article: Parents and Children in the Early Middle Ages," *Early Medieval Europe*, 10(2): 257–71.

Stahl, William Harris (1962), *Roman Science: Origins, Development, and Influence to the Later Middle Ages*, Madison: University of Wisconsin Press.

Steinhoff, Judith (2012), "Weeping Women: Social Roles and Images in Fourteenth-Century Tuscany," in Elina Gertsman (ed.), *Crying in the Middle Ages: Tears of History*, 35–52, New York: Routledge.

Stevens, John (1986), *Words and Music in the Middle Ages: Song, Narrative, Dance and Drama, 1050–1350*, Cambridge: Cambridge University Press, 1986.

Sticca, Sandro (1987), "The *Planctus Mariae* in the Medieval European Theater: Theology and Drama," in Albert H. Tricomi (ed.), *Early Drama to 1600* (ACTA vol. 13), 49–62, Binghamton, NY: SUNY Binghamton, Center for Medieval and Early Renaissance Studies.

Stock, Brian (1983), *The Implications of Literacy: Written Language and Models of Interpretation in the Eleventh and Twelfth Centuries*, Princeton, NJ: Princeton University Press.

Stone, Rachel (2012), *Morality and Masculinity in the Carolingian Empire*, Cambridge: Cambridge University Press.

Swann, William (1980), "The Relationship Between Penance, Reconciliation with the Church, and Admission to the Eucharist in the Letters and the *De Lapsis* of Cyprian of Carthage," Doctoral diss., Catholic University of America, Washington, DC.

Symes, Carol (2011), "The Medieval Archive and the History of the Theatre: Assessing the Written and Unwritten Evidence for Premodern Performance," *Theatre Survey*, 52(1): 29–58.

Tallon, Andrew (2008), "Christianity," in John Corrigan (ed.), *The Oxford Handbook of Religion and Emotion*, 111–24, Oxford: Oxford University Press.

Temkin, Owsei (1973), *Galenism: Rise and Decline of a Medical Philosophy*, Ithaca, NY: Cornell University Press.

Terada, Rei (1999), "Imaginary Seductions: Derrida and Emotion Theory," *Comparative Literature*, 51(3): 193–216.

Thijssen, J. M. M. H. (1998), *Censure and Heresy at the University of Paris, 1200–1400*, Philadelphia: University of Pennsylvania Press.

Thijssen, J. M. M. H. (2000), "Late Medieval Natural Philosophy: Some Recent Trends in Scholarship," *Recherches de Théologie et Philosophie Médiévales*, 67(1): 158–90.

Touwaide, Alain (1998), "Therapeutic Strategies: Drugs," in Mirko D. Grmek (ed.), Antony Shugaar (trans.), *Western Medical Thought from Antiquity to the Middle Ages*, 259–72, Cambridge, MA: Harvard University Press.

Triandis, Harry C. (1994), "Major Cultural Syndromes and Emotion," in Shinobu Kitayama and Hazel Rose Markus (eds.), *Emotion and Culture: Empirical Studies of Mutual Influence*, 285–306, Washington, DC: American Psychological Association.

Trigg, Stephanie (2014), "Introduction: Emotional Histories—Beyond the Personalization of the Past and the Abstraction of Affect Theory," *Exemplaria*, 26(1): 3–15.

Uhalde, Kevin (2005), "Pope Leo I on Power and Failure," *Catholic Historical Review*, 95(4): 671–88.

Uibert-Schede, Ute (1960), "Das Andachtsbild des Kreuztragenden Christus in der deutschen Kunst: Von den Anfängen bis zum Beginn des 16. Jahrhunderts. Eine ikonographische Untersuchung," Doctoral diss., Ludwig-Maximilians-Universität, Munich.

Vegetti, Mario (1995), *La medicina in Platone*, Venice: Cardo.

Verhulst, Adriaan (1999), *The Rise of Cities in North-West Europe*, Cambridge: Cambridge University Press.

Viano, Cristina (2003), "Competitive Emotions and *Thumos* in Aristotle's *Rhetoric*," in David Konstan and N. Keith Rutter (eds.), *Envy, Spite and Jealousy: The Rivalrous Emotions in Ancient Greece*, 85–97, Edinburgh: Edinburgh University Press.

Vince, R. W. (1984), *Ancient and Medieval Theatre: A Historiographical Handbook*, Westport, CT: Greenwood Press.

Voigts, Linda (1979), "Anglo-Saxon Plant Remedies and the Anglo-Saxons," *Isis*, 70(2): 250–68.

Wack, Mary Frances (1990), *Lovesickness in the Middle Ages: The Viaticum and Its Commentaries*, Philadelphia: University of Pennsylvania Press.

Waddell, Chrysogonus (1985), "The Pre-Cistercian Background of Cîteaux and the Cistercian Liturgy," in E. Rozanne Elder (ed.), *Goad and Nail: Studies in Medieval Cistercian History*, 109–32, Kalamazoo, MI: Cistercian Publications.

Wailes, Stephen L. (2013), "Hrotsvit's Plays," in Phyllis R. Brown and Stephen L. Wailes (eds.), *A Companion to Hrotsvit of Gandersheim (fl. 960): Contextual and Interpretive Approaches*, 121–48, Leiden: Brill.

Webb, Ruth (2008), *Demons and Dancers: Performance in Late Antiquity*, Cambridge, MA: Harvard University Press.

Weilandt, Gerhard (2007), *Die Sebalduskirche in Nürnberg: Bild und Gesellschaft im Zeitalter der Gotik und Renaissance*, Petersberg: Michael Imhof.

Weiss, Zeev (2004), "Games and Spectacles in Ancient Gaza: Performances for the Masses Held in Buildings Now Lost," in Brouria Bitton-Ashkelony and Aryeh Kofsky (eds.), *Christian Gaza in Late Antiquity*, 23–41, Leiden: Brill.

Weitzmann, Kurt, ed. (1979), *Age of Spirituality: Late Antique and Early Christian Art, Third to Seventh Century. Catalogue of the Exhibition at the Metropolitan Museum of Art, November 19, 1977, Through February 12, 1978*, New York: Metropolitan Museum of Art.

Wenzel, Siegfried (1960), *The Sin of Sloth: Acedia in Medieval Thought and Literature*, Chapel Hill: University of North Carolina Press.

Westphal-Wihl, Sarah (1994), "The Ladies' Tournament: Marriage, Sex, and Honor in Thirteenth-Century Germany," in Judith M. Bennett, Elizabeth A. Clark, Jean F. O'Barr, B. Anne Vilen and Sarah Westphal-Wihl (eds.), *Sisters and Workers in the Middle Ages*, 162–89, Chicago: University of Chicago Press.

Wetzel, James (2008), "Augustine," in John Corrigan (ed.), *The Oxford Handbook of Religion and Emotion*, 349–63, Oxford: Oxford University Press.

White, Geoffrey M. (1990), "Moral Discourse and the Rhetoric of Emotions," in Catherine A. Lutz and Lila Abu-Lughod (eds.), *Language and the Politics of Emotion: Studies in Emotion and Social Interaction*, 46–68, Cambridge: Cambridge University Press.

White, Geoffrey M. (1993), "Emotions Inside Out: The Anthropology of Affect," in Michael Lewis and Jeannette M. Haviland (eds.), *Handbook of Emotions*, 29–39, New York: Guilford Press.

White, Stephen D. (1996), "Clotilde's Revenge: Politics, Kinship and Ideology in the Merovingian Blood Feud," in Samuel K. Cohn, Jr. and Steven A. Epstein (eds.), *Portraits of Medieval and Renaissance Living: Essays in Memory of David Herlihy*, 107–30, Ann Arbor: University of Michigan Press.

White, Stephen D. (2007), "Alternative Constructions of Treason in the Angevin Political World: *Traïson* in the *History of William Marshal*," *e-Spania*, 4: 2–27.

Wilson, Katharina M. (1988), *Hrotsvit of Gandersheim: The Ethics of Authorial Stance*, Leiden: Brill.

Wolfson, Harry (1935), "The Internal Senses in Latin, Arabic, and Hebrew Philosophic Texts," *Harvard Theological Review*, 28(2): 69–117.

Woolf, Rosemary (1986), "Doctrinal Influences on *The Dream of the Rood*," *Medium Ævum*, 27 (1958), 137–53; reprinted in Woolf, *Art and Doctrine: Essays on Medieval Literature*, ed. Heather O'Donoghue, 29–48, London: Hambledon Press.

Zampelli, Michael A. (2013), "The Necessity of Hrotsvit: Evangelizing Theatre," in Phyllis R. Brown and Stephen L. Wailes (eds.), *A Companion to Hrotsvit of Gandersheim (fl. 960): Contextual and Interpretive Approaches*, 147–200, Leiden: Brill.

Ziegler, Joanna E. (1992), *Sculpture of Compassion: The Pietà and the Beguines in the Southern Low Countries, c.1300–c.1600*, Brussels: Brepols.

Ziolkowski, Jan (2010), "Laments for Lost Children: Latin Traditions," in Jane Tolmie and M. J. Toswell (eds.), *Laments for the Lost in Medieval Literature*, 81–108, Turnhout: Brepols.

INDEX

Italic numbers are used for illustrations.

Abelard and Heloise 15, 111
accidens anima (accidents of the soul) 24–5, 28, 30
acrostics 108
Adam 13, 57, *80*, 81, 89–90, *91*–2
admonitio (public correction) 146
Aelred of Rievaulx 14–15, 74, 141
affection 124, 126
affective piety 15, 141, 147
affectus (disposition of the mind) 42
Agramont, Jacme d' 30
Alderotti, Taddeo 28
Alfred, king 129
allegorical texts 42, 45–7, 107, 113–15, 118
   See also *Psychomachia*
Althoff, Gerd 145–6
Ambrose 50
amor (love) 35
anchoresses 41–7
Ancrene Wisse (*Guide for Anchoresses*) 41–7
Angela of Foligno 141
anger 6, 33, 73, 75–6, *75*, 86, 108–9, 143–7
Anglo-Saxon
   literature 38–40, 108–10
   medical texts 19–20, 22
Anima (character) 79–80
animals, used in medicine 20–1
anthropological studies of emotions 134
antique inheritance of religion and spirituality 32–7
aphrodisiacs 20, 22
Apuleius 22
Aquinas 16, 60, 62
archaeological evidence for emotions 129, *130*
Aristotle 15–16, 28, 33, 49, 60, 61–2
Arthurian romances 114–16
Articella 22
asceticism 32, 34–5, 35–6, 37, 44, 45, 136
Augustine of Hippo
   Confessions 103–5
   drama, hostility to 11, 68–9, 76
   on emotions 37, 88–9
   influence of 9, *10*, 11, 37
   on love 35
   on marriage 124, 129
   on reason and emotion 136–7
   on sexual desire 126
   on singing and music 50–2
   on sorrow and grief 104–5, 130
Avicenna 23

Bald's *Leechbook* 19
Barasch, Moshe 84
Barnes, T. D. 66
Baudri, Abbot of Bourgueil 110
Beatrice of Nazareth 113
Beguines 112–13
Beleth, John 58
Benedict of Nursia 20
Benedictine Rule 71
Beowulf 108
Bernard of Clairvaux 42, 45, 57, 111–12, 140
bestiaries 20–1
Bleeke, Marian 93
Boethius 19, 52–3, 55, 105–6, *106*
Boquet, Damien 74
brain 25, 27, *27*, 28
Brown, Peter 8
Bynum, Caroline Walker 141

Caelius Aurelianus 18–19, 155 n.2
caritas (love) 35
Carmina Burana 111
Carolingian Renaissance 84, 88, 107–8
Carruthers, Mary 93
Cassian, John 37
Cassiodorus 18
celibacy 125
chant 53, 55, 57, 62–3
character traits and music 55–6
childhood 13–14, 129–32
Choricius of Gaza 69–70

Chrétien de Troyes 114–15, 116–17, 128, 142
Christ and Satan 108, 109
Christ, humanity of 38, 39–40
Christian community 135–41
Christian conversion 11, 12, 135, 137, 140
Christianity, spread of 8, 10–11, 33–4
Christ's Passion 15
Chrysostom, John 50, 69, 131, 148
Cicero 33, 50
Cistercians 14–15, 57, 140
cities and towns 147–8
Clangam filii 107
Codex Egberti 86–7, *87*
cogitationes malaei (evil thoughts) 35
cognitive models of emotion 134
communion, receiving of 43, 137
compassion 11, 68, 123
complaint by monks 142
complexio of the body 23–4, 25, 28
Confessions (Augustine) 103–5
consilia texts 29
Consolation of Philosophy (Boethius) 105–6, *106*
Constance, nun of Le Ronceray 110
Constantine the African 29
control of emotions
    in literature 102–3
    by reason 33, 118
    self-management of 13–14
    and spiritual experience 89, 120
    through medicine 20, 30
    through music 52, 55
    by women 121, 123, 124, 148
    See also display of emotions; Stoicism
Conventum (Hugh of Lusignan) 142
conversion 11, 12, 135, 137, 140
cosmic music (*musica mundana*) 52, 61
courtly love 46–7, 128
courtly romances 114–18
Crawford, Sally 129
Crusade 94, 124
crying 73, 74
    See also weeping
cults in the early Middle Ages 12

dance 49, 50, 53, 57, 58, 61, 66–8
delight 50, 53, 56, 62, 69, 107
Der Winsbecke 121
Desert Fathers of Egypt 32, 34–5, 35–6, 37, 136
desire
    enflamed by actors 69

for God 12, 38, 45, 47
of God 47
homoerotic 110–11
lack of 22
music and 11, 53
sacrifice of 123
sexual 118, 126, 127–8
despair 71, 79
Devil 12, 108–9
Dhuoda 107–8, 124, 131
Die Winsbeckin 121, *122*
diet, texts on 20
Diller, Hans-Jürgen 75
Dioscorides 20–2
directions for performers 71, 79–81, 88
discretion 136, 140
display of emotions 71, 73, 75, 83, 85, 88–9, 148, *149*
    See also control of emotions
dispositions of the mind 42
Dox, Donnalee 68, 70
drama 65–81
    emotion in liturgical drama 70–1
    grief and anger in liturgical drama 73–6
    Hrotsvit of Gandersheim and the Roman legacy 76–8
    medieval drama 70
    mime, pantomime and Christian denunciation 66–70
    performing emotion, 11th and 12th centuries 78–81
Dream of the Rood 13, 38–40
Dronke, Peter 78, 80
Durand, William 58

early Middle Ages (500–1000 CE)
    Christian community 137–40
    definition of 8
    drama 70–1, 76–8
    Dream of the Rood 38–40
    kingship and sovereignty 145–7
    lay feuds 141
    literature 107–10
    music and dance 52–5
    parents and children 129–31
    visual arts 86, *87*, 90, *91*
    world-building 12–14
education
    expansion of 14
    medical 17–18, 22, 30
    and music 53, 60
Elias, Norbert 4, 6

Eliduc (Marie de France) 123
embarrassment 77
emotion
  definitions of 49, 83, 133, 134
  study of 4, 6–7
emotional communities 6–7, 31–2
emotional regimes 7, 32, 134
ennobling love 125
Epistulae duorum amantium (Letters of Two Lovers) 111
Erec and Enide (Chrétien de Troyes) 114, 128
erotic love 42, 43, 45–7
erotic spirituality 110–13
Evagrius Ponticus 36–7
Eve 13, *80*, 81, 89–90, *91*–2, 93
Exeter manuscript 109
exile 107, 109
exorcism 12, *13*, 138–40
expressions 76, 77–8, 80–1, 84, 86, 90

facial expressions 76, 77–8, 80–1, 84, 86, 90
Fall of Adam and Eve 13, 81, 89–90, *91*–2
family, concept of 121–5
fathers and children 77, 78–9, 121, 129–32
fear 28, 77, 86, 99
feelings 3, 133–4
Felicity, saint 131
feuds of lay people 142
first movements 33, 37
Fishhof, Gil 89
Flowing Light of the Godhead (Mechthild of Magdeburg) 113
Foka, Anna 69
Fortunatus 127
four elements in the body 23–4, 62
Foy, saint 129–30
Frederic Barbarossa 145
friendships 125–6

Galen 17–18, 24, 28
games 58
Garnier, François 84, 86
Gaunt, Simon 128
Genesis B 108
gestures 74–5, 81, 83, 84, 86, 90, 93
Gil Sotres, Pedro 24
Gilbert de Tournai 124
Giotto 97, *98*
Gluckman, Max 145
Godman, Peter 107
Gottfried von Strassbourg 115
Gottschalk 107

grand chans songs and music 61
Gregory of Tours 19, 141–2
Gregory the Great, pope 37, 53, 55, 124, 131
grief
  of Augustine 104–5, 130
  depictions of 6
  felt on behalf of others 123
  gestures of 86
  in images of the Fall 90
  in images of the raising of Lazarus 93
  in liturgical drama 73–5
  of parents for children 13–14, 79, 129, 130–1
  public display of 148, *149*
  as a social state 120
  virtuousness of 89
Grocheio, Johannes de 60–1
Guido of Arezzo 55–6, *56*
Guillaume de Lorris 118
Guy of Eu 57
Guy of Saint-Denis 62

Hadewijch 112–13
Hall, Edith 68
Haly Abbas 22
handbooks of instruction 131
happiness 77–8, 106
harmiscara (act of humiliation) 142, 144
Hart, Columba 112
heart
  in Arthurian romances 114
  influence of music on 53, 57, 61
  as locus of feeling 44, 104–5, 108–9, 113
  as locus of knowing God 44
  purity of 12, 43, 45
  and vital spirit 25, *26*, 28
herbs, use of in medicine 20–2, *21*
heretics 114
Herod 73, 75–6, 86
high Middle Ages (1000–1350 CE)
  Christian conversion 140–1
  concept of family 121–5
  definition of 9
  drama 73–6, 78–83
  feeling for God and *Ancrene Wisse* 41–7
  lay feuds 142–5
  literature 110–16
  love, passion, friendship and marriage 125–9
  medical approaches to emotion 22–8
  music and dance 55–63
  parents and children 131–2

transformation of society 14–16
treatment of disordered emotions 28–30
urban communities 147–9
visual arts 83–6, 88–99
Hildegard of Bingen 57–8, 79–80, *112*
Hippocratic texts 18
historical empathy 3, 7
Hochschild, Arlie Russell 134, 148
homoerotic desire 110–11
hope 99
Horden, Peregrine 19
horror of pagan others 136, 137
Hrotsvit of Gandersheim 76–8
Hugh of Lusignan 142
humiliation ceremonies 142, *143*, 144
Hyams, Paul 147
hygiene, texts on 20
hymns 50–1, 61
  See also plainchant

Ibn Butlan, Abu al Hasan 30
Icelandic sagas 120, 124, 130
illustrated manuscripts, gestures shown in 86, *87*, 90, *91*, *98*, 99
impassivity in art 14, 89
individual, concept of 119
Isagoge 22–4
Isidore of Seville 20, 22

Jacobus, Laura 86, 88
Jean de Meun 118
Jerome 35, *36*, 126, 128
Jeu d'Adam 80–1
John, king of England 147
John of Salisbury 58, 60
Jolliffe, J. E. A. 145
joy
  in dance 58
  depiction of 89
  evoked by drama 69, 71
  and fear 77
  of love 79, 114
  of martyrs 78
  of Mary, mother of Jesus 73
  of Rachel 74–5
  in singing 51
Judas Iscariot 137, *139*
judgment of emotion in visual art 88–94
Junius XI manuscript 108–9

kingship and sovereignty 145–7
Klinck, Anne L. 109

Knight of the Cart (Chrétien de Troyes) 116–17, 142
Knight with the Lion (Chrétien de Troyes) 114

Lacnunga (*Remedies*) 20, 22
Ladies' Tournament 129
lais 123
lamentation 74, 80, 97, *98*
Lancelot and Guinevere 116–17
language of emotions 35
languages used in literature 9, 101–2
Lansing, Carol 148
Largier, Niklaus 94
lascivious modes, dangers of 52
Last Judgment 85, 89, 90, 92–3, 93–4
Late Antiquity (250–750 CE)
  Christian community 135–8
  conversion and renunciation 10–12
  definition of 8
  drama 66–70
  lay feuds 141–2
  literature 102–6
  love, passion, friendship and marriage 127–8
  medical texts 17–22
  music and dance 50–5
  religion and spirituality 32–7
Latin 9, 35, 37, 101, 102–3, 110–11
lay devotion 15, 141, 147
Lazarus, raising of 93
Leechbook (Bald) 19
Leo I, the Great, pope 137
Leo IX, pope 139–40
letters between lovers 110–11
literature 101–18
  Late Antiquity 102–6
  Carolingian Renaissance 107–8
  Anglo-Saxon 38–40, 108–10
  High Middle Ages 110–18
Little, Lester K. 144
liturgical drama 70–6
liturgical music 50, 53, 55, 57, 58, 60, 61
longing for association 128
Louis the Pious 138, 146
love
  Aelred of Rievaulx on 141
  and Christian community 135
  concepts of 31–2, 35, 42, 99
  courtly 46–7, 128
  depiction of 89
  erotic 42, 43, 45–7
  of God 42–7, 89, 111–13, 124

and insanity 19
and marriage 125, 126–7
and melancholy 29
between parents and children 79, 108, 124, 129–30, 131
between women 110–11
Love (character) 112–13, 114, 116
love letters 110–11
lovesickness, treatment of 29–30, 61
Lucian 66
lust 55, 69

Magi plays 75
magic and medicine 17
Maguire, Henry 148
mania, treatment of 19
Marie de France 123
marriage 120, 125, 126–8
martyrdom 78, 136
Mary, mother of Jesus 15, 73, 88, 94–7, 96–7, 98
Massacre of the Innocents 74, 75–6, 85–8, 87
materia medica (pharmacy), texts on 20–2
McLaughlin, Megan 127, 132
McMillin, Linda A. 77
McNamer, Sarah 123
Mechthild of Magdeburg 113
mediation of medieval culture 1, 3
medical and scientific understanding 17–30
    medical texts of Late Antiquity 17–22
    High and Late Medieval Western medicine 22–8
    treatment of disordered emotions 28–30
medical education 17–18, 22, 30
medieval, definition of 8
melancholy, treatment of 29, 30
memory and emotions 105, 141, 146
Methodic medicine 18
Miller, William Ian 120, 133
mime 66, 68–70
mimesis of emotion 94–7
Mirror of Simple Souls (Porete) 114
modes, of music 51, 52, 55, 57
modesty 77
monasteries 14, 18, 20, 71, 125, 140
mourning 73, 74, 85, 86–7
music and dance 49–63
    Ambrose and Augustine, patristic legacy of 50–2
    Aristotle, his 13th century impact 60–3
    Boethius and his legacy 52–5
    Guido of Arezzo and the renewal of chant 55–8
    liturgy, dance, and ecclesiastical caution 58–60
music, as a treatment 19, 52–3, 55, 61
mysticism 111–13

Nagy, Piroska 74
natural and nonnatural things of the body 23, 24, 28
natural philosophers 27–8
Niceta of Remesiana 50
Nicolas, saint 78–9, 79
nightmare, treatment of 18–19
Notker the Stammered of St. Gall 74, 107
Nussbaum, Martha 31–2
Nutton, Vivian 18

oblation 131
Old Testament, Song of Songs 42, 45
Ordo Rachelis 74, 86, 87–8
Ordo Virtutem (Hildegard of Bingen) 79–80
Origen of Alexandria 36–7
otherness of medieval people 4
Otto of Bamberg 140, 144

pain of emotions 33, 109
paintings 34, 79, 97, *98*
Pantegni 22–5, 26, 28
pantomime 66–8
parents and children 121, 129–32
Parzival (Wolfram von Eschenbach) 115
Passion plays 73–4
passionate love 125, 126
passiones (thoughts) of Cassian 37
passions 24, 28, 30
pathē (passions, emotions) 49–50
Patience (character) *75*, 76, 103
penitential process 135, 137, 138
penitents 94, 141
Peter of Auvergne 62
Peter, saint 137, *138*
pharmacy, texts on 20–2
Philosophy (character) 105–6, *106*
physicians 27–8
Pietà 94, 95–6, *96*
plague treatises 30
plainchant 53, 55, 57, 62–3
Planctus Mariae 73–4
Plato 32–3, 52
play in poetry 107, 108
plays 11, 70–1, 73–81

pleasure of emotions 33
poetry 101, 107–11, 112–13, 115, 118
　　See also Dream of the Rood; Psychomachia;
　　　Song of Songs
Porete, Marguerite 114
practica medical texts 29
pre-emotions 33, 37
private life 119–32
　　introduction 119–21
　　affective ties and the concept of family
　　　121–5
　　love and passion, friendship and marriage
　　　125–9
　　parents and children 129–32
Prudentius 76, 102–3, *104*
psalms, singing of 50
Psychomachia (Prudentius) 75, 76, 102–3,
　　104
public life 133–49
　　Christian community 135–41
　　feuding of the lay elite 141–5
　　kingship and sovereignty 145–7
　　periodization of emotional styles and
　　　practices of feeling 134
　　urban communities 147–8

Rachel 73, 74, 86, 87, 107
Rankin, Susan 70–1, 75
Raoul de Cambrai 142–4
reason 28, 49, 74, 106, 136–7
Reason (character) 114, 117, 118
reconciliation 144, 145
Reddy, William M. 7, 32, 127–8, 134
regimens, texts on 20, 30
Regularis Concordia 71
religion and spirituality 31–48
　　Ancrene Wisse (*Guide for Anchoresses*)
　　　41–7
　　antique inheritance 32–7
　　The Dream of the Rood 38–40
renunciation, act of 135
repentant powers of emotion 107
restraint of emotions 118, 148
Roman de la Rose (Romance of the Rose) 59,
　　117, 118
Romance of Lancelot du Lac 142, *143*
romances 114–18, 142, *143*
Rosaldo, Michele 134
Rosenwein, Barbara 6–7, 31–2, 35, 120–1,
　　127, 129, 130–1, 134
Rubin, Miri 83, 94, 96
rules to be lived by 20, 41–3

sacraments 43, 137
sadness 69, 77, 86, 88, 95
saffron, use of in medicine 21–2, *21*
Satan 12, 108–9
scientific and medical understanding 17–30
　　medical texts of Late Antiquity 17–22
　　High and Late Medieval Western medicine
　　　22–8
　　treatment of disordered emotions 28–30
sculpture 67, 90, *92–3*, 93, *94–6*, *96–7*
Seafarer 109
secular music 49, 61
seduction, of anchoresses 44
Seven Manners of Love (Beatrice of Nazareth)
　　113
sexual desire 118, 126, 127–8
sexual intercourse 19, 24, 30, 115
shame 89–90, 126, 135–6, 142
Sicard of Cremona 58
sins 20, 35, 37, 89–90, 104, 120
Sizgorich, Thomas 136
Slaughter of the Innocents 74, 75–6, 85–8, *87*
Smail, Daniel 144
sociological studies of emotions 134
Song of Songs 42, 45, 111–12
sorrow 71, 73, 79, 88, 96–7, 104, 105,
　　108–10
soul
　　affected by music 50, 51, 56, 62
　　definition of 25
　　face as mirror of 78
　　impact of music on 62
　　love of Christ for 42, 43
　　struggle of 104
　　visualization of 90
Soul (character) 79–80
sources for medieval history 4
spirits in the human body 25, *25*, 28
stained glass 90, 92
Stevens, John 73
Stoicism 11–12, 32, 33, 35, 49–50, 102, 103
Story of the Grail (Chrétien de Troyes) 115
suffering 13, 39, 94, 96
suicide 76, 103, 116
suppression of emotions 89, 120, 121, 123
Symes, Carol 149

Tacuinum Sanitatis (ibn Butlan) 30
Tallon, Andrew 93–4
Tempier, Stephen 61
Terence 76
Thomas (Angevin writer) 115–16

Thomas Aquinas 16, 60, 62
thoughts 35, 37
Throne of Wisdom 94–6, *95*
tones, musical 62
towns and cities 147–8
treatment of disordered emotions 28–30
Tres filie 78–9
Trigg, Stephanie 133
tripudia (dances by clergy) 58
tripudium (notion of joy while dancing) 58
Tristan and Isolde 115–16, *116*
Tristan (Gottfried von Strassbourg) 115
Tristan (Thomas) 115–16
troubadour songs and music 61
trouvère songs and music 61
Twelfth-Century Renaissance 110

Uhalde, Kevin 137
urban communities 147–8

vernacular languages 9
vernacular music 61
Viaticum 29
vices 32, 33, 97, 103
Vince, Ronald W. 66
Virgin Mary. *See* Mary, mother of Jesus
virtues in the human body 25, 26, 28
virtuous emotions 89
Visitatio Sepulchri 70–1
visual arts 83–99
    gestures of emotion 85–8
    judgment of emotion 88–94
    mimesis of emotion 94–7

vitium (vice) 33
vocabulary of emotions 35
Voigts, Linda 22
voluntas (will) 33
Vulgate Bible 35

Wanderer 109
warriors, instability of 141–2
Webb, Ruth 68–9
weeping 3, *3*, 73, 74, 86, 87, 114
Wife's Lament 110
will, acts of 33, 37, 89
Wilson, Katharina 76
Wolfram von Eschenbach 115
women
    acting on stage of 69
    in art 86–8, *91–2*, 93–7, *95–6*, *98*
    authors 57–8, 76–80, 107–8, 110,
        111–14, *112*
    control of emotions by 121, 123, 124
    domestic roles of 119, 124, 129,
        131–2
    friendships of 125–6
    grief, display of 148, *149*
    holy lives of 15, 126
    in love letters 110–11
wooing, of anchoresses 44
Woolf, Rosemary 38–9
word games 107, 108
Wrath (character) 76, 97, 103
wrath (emotion). *See* anger

Ziolkowski, Jan 73